Philip Larkin

Also by James Booth

NEW LARKINS FOR OLD: Critical Essays (ed.)

PHILIP LARKIN: Writer

SYLLOGE OF COINS OF THE BRITISH ISLES 48: Northern Museums

TROUBLE AT WILLOW GABLES AND OTHER FICTIONS by Philip Larkin (ed.)

WRITERS AND POLITICS IN NIGERIA

Philip Larkin

The Poet's Plight

by

James Booth

First published 2005 by
PALGRAVE MACMILLAN
Houndmills, Basingstoke, Hampshire RG21 6XS and
175 Fifth Avenue, New York, N. Y. 10010
Companies and representatives throughout the world

PALGRAVE MACMILLAN is the global academic imprint of the Palgrave Macmillan division of St. Martin's Press, LLC and of Palgrave Macmillan Ltd. Macmillan® is a registered trademark in the United States, United Kingdom and other countries. Palgrave is a registered trademark in the European Union and other countries.

ISBN-13: 978–1–4039–1834–5 hardback
ISBN-10: 1–4039–1834–1 hardback

This book is printed on paper suitable for recycling and made from fully managed and sustained forest sources.

A catalogue record for this book is available from the British Library.

Library of Congress Cataloging-in-Publication Data

Booth, James, 1945–
    Philip Larkin : the poet's plight / by James Booth.
        p. cm.
    Includes bibliographical references and index.
    ISBN 1–4039–1834–1 (cloth)
        1. Larkin, Philip—Criticism and interpretation. I. Title.

PR6023.A66Z55 2005
821'.914–dc22   2005043194

10   9   8   7   6   5   4   3   2   1
14 13 12 11 10 09 08 07 06 05

Printed and bound in Great Britain by
Antony Rowe Ltd, Chippenham and Eastbourne

Contents

Acknowledgements

My thanks are due to Angela Leighton (Hull), ever my first and best reader. Suzanne Uniacke (Hull) also provided many exact insights. Douglas Dunn (St Andrews) and Janice Rossen read the typescript and made useful suggestions.

I am also grateful to Betty Mackereth, Winifred Dawson, Jean Hartley, Father Anthony Storey, the late Maeve Brennan, and the late Monica Jones, for generously sharing with me their insights into the Larkin they knew.

Larkin's literary executors, Andrew Motion and Anthony Thwaite have been constant in their encouragement and Jeremy Crow of the Society of Authors has been helpful at every stage. My thanks are due also to Judy Burg (Hull University Archivist) and the staff of the Brynmor Jones Library, Hull.

Numerous other friends and colleagues have helped with specific points: Jonathan Sawday (Strathclyde), Antony Rowland (Salford), Diana, Duchess of Hamilton, Edna Longley (Queen's University, Belfast), John Carey (Merton, Oxford), Judith Priestman (Bodleian Library), Martine Semblat (Dijon), Danielle Pinkstein (Paris X), Elena Miraglia (Rome), Raphaël Ingelbien (Leuven), István Rácz (Debrecen), Stephen Regan (Durham), Stephen Cooper, Philip Weaver, Linda Hart, and my colleagues at the University of Hull, particularly Graham Chesters, Rowlie Wymer, Valerie Sanders, John Hoyles, John Osborne, Jane Thomas and John Howarth.

My fellow members on the Committee of the Philip Larkin Society have been most supportive, in particular Don Lee, Edwin Dawes, Carole Collinson, Jim Orwin, Belinda Hakes and Paul Walker.

I must also thank the Arts and Humanities Research Board for a Research Leave Award which made the completion of this book possible.

Abbreviations

FR Philip Larkin, *Further Requirements: Interviews, Broadcasts, Statements and Book Reviews 1952–1985*, ed Anthony Thwaite (London: Faber and Faber, pbk edn with two additional chapters, 2002).

Motion Andrew Motion, *Philip Larkin: A Writer's Life* (London: Faber and Faber, 1993).

RW Philip Larkin, *Required Writing: Miscellaneous Pieces 1955–1982* (London: Faber, 1983).

SL Philip Larkin, *Selected Letters*, ed Anthony Thwaite (London: Faber, 1992).

NOTE: Larkin's poems are cited from the 1988 *Collected Poems*, ed. Anthony Thwaite (London: Marvell Press/Faber and Faber, revised 1990). This volume is currently out of print, and the available 2003 *Collected Poems* (London: Marvell Press/Faber and Faber) omits a number of the poems which I discuss. In order to avoid confusion between the two volumes page references to Larkin's poems have been omitted throughout.

1
The Poet's Plight

> I feel that my prime responsibility is to the experience itself,
> which I am trying to keep from oblivion for its own sake.
> Why I should do this I have no idea, but I think the impulse
> to preserve lies at the bottom of all art. (*RW* 79)

Larkin writes of his vocation in terms of 'responsibility', not to a
person or an ideology, but, impersonally, to 'the experience'. He attributes no useful purpose to this impulse. The experience is valued 'for its
own sake', and he has 'no idea' why he feels the responsibility to preserve it. In writing of the poet's 'plight' I mean to foreground firstly
this mysterious obligation. The poet is 'plighted' to poetry, from the
Middle English for 'to pledge oneself'. That 'lifted, rough-tongued bell
/ (Art, if you like)' commands allegiance, and the poet has no choice
but to attend: 'It speaks; I hear' ('Reasons for Attendance'). Larkin may
make a show of 'Movement' demystification: 'The days when one
could claim to be the priest of a mystery are gone: today mystery
means either ignorance or hokum, neither fashionable qualities.'
However, within a couple of sentences his scepticism dissolves, and
the mystery of inspiration is restored:

> Yet writing a poem is still not an act of the will. The distinction
> between subjects is not an act of the will. Whatever makes a poem
> successful is not an act of the will… the poems that get written,
> even if they do not please the will, evidently please that mysterious
> something that has to be pleased.
>
> *RW* 83–4

It is characteristic of Larkin to express his intense emotional commitment to art in as unpretentious a manner as possible: in this case

1

through a series of negatives ending in a tautology. The writer is impelled to please a 'mysterious something that has to be pleased'.

Despite his contempt for the 'myth-kitty', Larkin's work frequently refracts the familiar archetypal, or stereotypical plights of 'the poet' in disguised form. In 'The Spirit Wooed' and 'Send No Money', the poet is the humble servant of the muse. In 'Latest Face' he is Pygmalion creating a perfection which he prefers to reality. In 'If, My Darling', and 'Livings II' he plays the bohemian misfit in his garret. In 'The Whitsun Weddings' and 'High Windows' he aspires to occupy the ivory tower of aesthetic detachment. In 'Love Again' he is the *poète maudit*, cut off from the normal lot of marriage and family, wondering 'why it never worked for me'. Larkin's plight as an artist, is, as he put it in an early letter, to be caught between 'art and 'life' (*SL* 116), or between the 'unreal' and the 'real' ('Guitar Piece II'). In his high-windowed flat or railway carriage he is always either on the disconsolate margin or the euphoric threshold. The plight of the poet is to be between society and isolation, between engagement and detachment, between personal and impersonal, between history and the fleeting moment.

The second meaning of plight derives by a separate etymology from the Middle English for 'manner of being, condition, state' (*OED*). The 'manner of being' of the lyric poet is a matter of existential 'conditions' or 'states', rather than of verdicts or conclusions. My second intention in writing of the poet's 'plight' is to focus on the poetry itself, rather than other elements in the poems, however interesting or important these may be. The ostensible subject of a lyric poem is frequently the least important thing about it. As Thomas Gray wrote: 'sense is nothing in poetry'.[1] Poetry concerns life as process: in Gray's phrase, 'our pleasing anxious being'.[2] It catches a mood, a tone of voice, a glimpse of transcendence. In view of its intangible, liminal condition, it is difficult to write directly about poetry. It is far easier to write about that 'something else', whether it be philosophy, politics, morality or cultural fashion, which, as A. E. Housman laments, most readers mistake for poetry, and prefer to the poetry of the passage before them.[3] Speaking on a level beyond mere personality or ideology, poetry is frequently misread by an audience which prefers something more 'relevant', more useful, or simply more topical. Larkin's work is thus used by commentators to illustrate Englishness, or the post-war mood, or middle-class masculinity. None of these elements, however, is intrinsic to his poetry.

Though Larkin belongs, like any poet, to a particular time and place, the distinctive qualities for which we value his poetry cannot be constructed or predicted from politics or cultural history. Though this book explores contexts and influences, my concern is first and foremost with Larkin's texts, his distinctive 'verbal devices' (*RW* 83). I do not aim to explain his work in terms of socio-politics, nor to determine his place within the 'development' of twentieth-century poetry. I am interested, more intimately, in his poetic condition, his own unique manner of being as a poet. Larkin ridiculed what he called the 'Ford Car' view of literature, which sees art as progressing like technology, discarding old-fashioned, inefficient elements, and adopting new, up-to-date ones. The poet's plight certainly entails the obligation to 'make it new'. Artistic fashion changes and develops, and its history is a fascinating study. But no poem contributes to the progress of poetry in the sense that a scientific or technological discovery contributes to the progress of knowledge. A true artist is always, strictly speaking, unique and incomparable. The poet's plight, as Eliot put it, is to find 'every attempt / ... a wholly new start'.[4] Fleur Adcock writes:

> there have been poets, and they have been individuals, and a few of them have influenced a few others, but on the whole there is no clear thread. This is only natural. No one pretends that poetry in general has shown one single line of development throughout the twentieth century.[5]

She is referring specifically to recent women poets, but her remarks are true enough of all poetry at all times. Larkin's statement that each poem should be 'its own sole freshly created universe' is not a mystification (*RW* 79).

Poetry is what is lost in translation; and this is not simply an issue of language. The young Larkin wrote: 'As for the vision itself, it's got something to do with sex. I don't know what and I don't particularly want to know.'[6] He refuses to interrogate or reduce 'the vision'. While at Oxford he abandoned his attempt to record his dreams, apprehensive that to translate his inspiration into Jungian psychology would kill his creativity. In a later interview he said: 'I find theorizing in the abstract no help to me as a writer. In fact it would be true to say that I make a point of not knowing what poetry is or how to read a page or about the function of myth' (*RW* 79). Once again he expresses a preference for mystery, perversely, in tones of blunt common sense. He would boast, with apparent philistinism, of his comprehensive ignorance: of religion, of science, of foreign poetry, of other English poets. Ignorance was profoundly important to him; he even wrote a poem with this title. But his is an ignorance close to religious humility. D. H. Lawrence was his early idol, and Larkin's unwillingness to seem knowledgeable, or too clever or 'literary' can frequently be attributed to a sacramental, Lawrentian desire not to explain away 'the experience. The beauty' (*RW* 68).

Larkin's plight is that of the dedicated poet, but also that of the common man. He celebrates living in his poems; but he makes his living by the toad work, in a nine-to-five job. He is always the alienated, isolated artist; but he is also scathing about the aestheticist arrogance or simple egotism which traditionally attends this pose. He is plighted to art, but in an offhand parenthesis: '(Art, if you like)'. He serves the muse, but in the form of a grotesque Dickensian personification of Time ('Send No Money'). This scepticism may seem to dampen the poetic spirit, but in fact it does the opposite, guaranteeing, as it were, his emotional intensities and sublimities. It is his distrust of the ostensibly poetical which makes Larkin, in poems like 'Absences', 'Here' and 'High Windows', the most convincing poet of transcendence since Eliot. It also ensures his popularity among readers who find much twentieth-century poetry too rarefied or 'difficult'. The most moving epiphanies in his work often take the form of mere 'realistic' observation. He said of 'The Whitsun Weddings': 'I didn't change a thing... It only needed writing down. Anybody could have done it' (*FR* 57).

Larkin's scepticism concerning the poet's role helps persuade the reader that he shares his or her unpoetic plight. He touches the reader's heart by showing his own (*FR* 30). His longer meditative poems, 'An Arundel Tomb', 'The Whitsun Weddings', 'Dockery and Son', 'Aubade', begin with an initial 'I' or 'me', but end with an inclusive 'we' or 'us'. His work has no didacticism or satire: 'To be a satirist, you have to think you know better than everyone else. I've never done that' (*RW* 73). He is, it seems, no different from his readers: 'I don't want to transcend the commonplace, I love the commonplace, I lead a very commonplace life. Everyday things are lovely to me' (*FR* 57). The pedestrianism of 'I don't want to transcend' validates the aestheticist fervour of 'Everyday things are lovely'. The poet's plight is a mysterious obligation; but it is also a common condition shared with his readers.

The delight of poetry

In a letter of July 1943, written a few weeks before his twenty-first birthday, Larkin depicted his artistic vocation as a blessing: 'The life of the artist is a continual richness and delight – perhaps of everyone, for all I know.'[7] In a later essay he championed 'The Pleasure Principle' in art. Few poems of the twentieth century express such engaging delight in being alive as 'Lines on a Young Lady's Photograph Album', 'The Whitsun Weddings', 'Here' and 'Toads Revisited'. Even his most pessimistic poems lift the spirit with surly *jouissance* ('Where has it gone, the lifetime? / Search me'),[8] or with sombre eloquence ('The sure extinction that we travel to / And shall be lost in always').[9] The sentiments are bleak, but their expression is a delight. As Larkin said: 'A good poem about failure is a success' (*RW* 74). His late elegies 'The Building', 'The Old Fools' and 'Aubade' enact an affirmative tragic catharsis. Even at his most despairing moments Larkin evokes 'the million-petalled flower / Of being here' ('The Old Fools'). Poetry turns plight into delight.

The delight of Larkin's poetry, for both writer and reader, is generated by the craft of words. In 1943, at the age of twenty, he was not quite sure of the delightfulness of life to those who lacked artistic creativity: 'of everyone, *for all I know*'. He was certain, however, of his own delight in the practice of his art. For Larkin, unlike for many writers, writing itself was an emotional, even a physical pleasure. He carefully sewed his juvenile verses into booklets, typing the title-page of the girl's-school poems, 'Sugar and Spice', with elaborate patternings of letters in two colours and stitching them between art-paper covers.[10] His letters show intimate awareness of the kind of paper he is writing on, the different colours of his ink. There is something sensuous in his use of a soft 2B pencil for the drafts of his mature poetry. To trace his revisions, day by day, in the workbooks, is to be drawn into an absorbed world of rapt creation. It was the fact that he could no longer write that most blighted his last eight years. His *oeuvre* was completed before his life, the cruellest of fates for a writer who lived so intensely through his art.

Fundamental to any poet's plight, or 'manner of being', is his or her artistic medium, language. What brings the poem, and thus the poet, into being is the compulsive wrestle with words and meanings. As T. S. Eliot says, the poet raids 'the inarticulate' with his 'shabby equipment' of words, 'always deteriorating'.[11] The plight of the poet is to be confined within the pale of words, within the *langue* or pre-established communal structure of semantics and grammar. Living, however, constantly demonstrates the inadequacy of words or leaves them behind. In the letter to James Sutton quoted earlier Larkin continued, diffidently: 'I am continually seeing things for which there are no words, no music, no colours, so perhaps art is only incidental.'[12] He projected the poet's plight in terms of mediation between ultimately ineffable experience and the expressive possibilities of language. In 'The Pleasure Principle' he wrote that poetry is 'born of the tension between what [the poet] non-verbally feels and what can be got over in common word-usage to someone who hasn't had his experience or education or travel-grant' (*RW* 82), disguising his philosophical pretensions in a bluff joke. Some of his poems, however, give fulsome expression to this sense that language mediates a non-verbal world. At the extreme the reader is left on the threshold of the ineffable. The 'unfenced existence' at the end of 'Here' is 'untalkative, out of reach'. In 'The Trees' the unfolding buds are like 'something almost being said'. At the end of 'High Windows', rather than words comes 'the thought of high windows'. And in 'Love Again' the poet loses patience with his poetic medium: 'but why put it into words?'

However, this awareness of verbal limits does not lead Larkin to break violently through the conventions of grammar and syntax as do some Modernist and post-modern poets. Whether writing in direct demotic ('They fuck you up, your mum and dad'), or high rhetoric ('Time has transfigured them'),[13] Larkin keeps to 'common word-usage'. 'Common' here, however, is a very elastic term indeed, encompassing awkward double negatives and elliptical puns which fail to yield the plain meaning which their common language promises. Casual though it sounds, the line 'Nothing, like something, happens anywhere' ('I Remember, I Remember'), opens out haunting depths of meaning. Out of context it becomes a Wittgensteinian linguistic puzzle. As frequently in Larkin's work, there is no show of poeticism, but the effect is intensely poetic. There is as much aesthetic *hubris* as pragmatism in his apparently reductive theory that to write a poem is 'to construct a verbal device that [will] preserve an experience indefinitely by reproducing it in whoever reads the poem' (*RW* 83). The underlying theme of this book is this fundamental plight of the poet: the struggle to transform the 'non-verbal' flux of experience into 'word-usage', to preserve experience in distinctive and memorable 'verbal devices', whether they be single words, phrases, poems, genres, or ultimately the entire *oeuvre*.

Idiolect

Larkin frequently lamented the exiguousness of his poetic output. It was his plight to be always waiting 'for it to come to me' (*RW* 74). In a letter to Michael Hamburger of February 1956, he commented on *The Less Deceived*: 'As a product of ten years I feel it's not much of [an] achievement, but covering a comparatively long time it does perhaps gain in variety. I expect it will take another 10 years to do another one.'[14] A stubborn undertone betrays his conviction that this slowness is essential to his art. Derek Walcott, indeed, makes a point of celebrating Larkin's 'narrowness':

> Poetry is a narrow spring, the mountain cold brook of Helicon, and it is not its narrowness that matters but the crystalline, tongue-numbing cold of its freshness, which... glitters like an unpolluted spring. Larkin is of that stream.[15]

Larkin sacrifices the voluminousness of a Ted Hughes or a Seamus Heaney for the freshness and sharp variety of his words. Less than two decades after his death, his phrases are widely quoted, even by those with only a slight knowledge of his work. Larkin has succeeded in making his words and phrases count for more than those of his contemporaries.

Speaking of his novel *A Girl in Winter*, Larkin said: 'I took great care not to use particular words too often and so on' (*FR* 32). Elsewhere he mused over the unfinished novels which followed *A Girl in Winter*: 'Looking back on them, I think they were over-sized poems. They were certainly written with intense care for detail. If one word was used on page 15 I didn't re-use it on page 115' (*FR* 24). These casual remarks illuminate what seems to have been an important turning point in Larkin's growth to artistic maturity: his development in the mid-1940s, at the time he was working on *A Girl in Winter*, of a new and deliberate verbal fastidiousness. Though he refers here specifically to prose fiction, it was in his later poetry that this care for detail and scrupulous rationing of words was to have its greatest impact. The fluent profusion, even prolixity of his teens and early twenties, seen in Trevor Tolley's collection of his *juvenilia*,[16] was replaced around 1946 by a verbal economy which imparts to the mature *oeuvre* a unity and lexical economy unique in modern poetry.

The simplest aspect of this verbal self-consciousness is a preference for certain kinds of word. The *Concordance to the Poetry of Philip Larkin*[17] records, in the 1988 *Collected Poems*, 559 different words ending in '-ing', the great majority of them present participles of verbs used as adjective or noun, and signifying ongoing action: 'being', 'living', 'dying', 'going', 'coming', 'closing', 'unclosing', 'gathering', 'unresting', 'solving'. Larkin, it is apparent, responds to life as transient process rather than as fixed entity. A similar insecurity is also audible in the sceptical negativity which qualifies even his most transcendental moments. The appearance of 'not' 150 times after 1945 (in seventy-five poems) is perhaps scarcely remarkable in itself. But his 'not' phrases are peculiarly resonant, particularly those which double the negative: 'It had not done so then, and could not now'; 'Not untrue and not unkind'; 'Not knowing how, not hearing who'; 'The good not done, the love not given', 'Not to be here, / Not to be anywhere'.[18]

Perhaps Larkin's most notorious lexical idiosyncrasy is his fondness for the negative prefix 'un-'. Excluding words where the prefix lacks a negative connotation ('uncle', 'understand', 'until' etc.), there are 157 such words in his work after 1945, of which no fewer than 105 appear only on a single occasion. They create a tone of diffidence or irony, though they often have positive implications. They are frequently highly distinctive. A single 'un-' word may instantaneously remind a reader familiar with Larkin's work of the phrase in which it occurs, and thus of the whole poem: 'All but the unmolesting meadows' ('At Grass'), 'real untidy air' ('Latest Face'), 'her unpriceable pivot' ('If, My Darling'), 'Uncontradicting solitude' ('Best Society'), 'Unvariably lovely there' ('Lines on a Young Lady's Photograph Album'), 'where my childhood was unspent' ('I Remember, I Remember'), 'unfingermarked again' ('Maiden Name'), 'untalkative, out of reach' ('Here'), 'A quite unlosable game' ('Annus Mirabilis'), 'Unmendably' ('The Mower'). The word 'unsatisfactory' occurs four times, all in the same poem, 'Reference Back', and nowhere else. The short poem 'Solar' has three such words ('unfurnished', 'unrecompensed', 'Unclosing'). 'An Arundel Tomb' also features three prominent 'un-' words in a rising sequence of emotional impact: 'undated', 'unarmorial', and most emphatically, 'Untruth'. The distinctive 'unresting' occurs in 'The Trees' in a fulsome celebration of the annual resurrection, 'afresh', of the leaves: 'still the unresting castles thresh'. Larkin then ironically 'quotes' himself ten years later in 'Aubade' in an opposite context: 'Unresting death a whole day nearer now /... / Flashes afresh'.

It may seem surprising that Larkin's idiolect is so varied and inventive. He cultivated the reputation of a plain, even a prosaic poet. In fact, however, he employs a high proportion of terms which are quite out of the way of common usage. Among words which occur only once after 1945 are archaisms such as 'accoutred', 'simples', 'blazon', 'losels', 'sizar'; neologistic coinages such as 'undeciduous', 'parishfuls', 'stooging', 'blort', 'soppy-stern'; and words of ephemeral out-of-the-way jargon such as 'the four aways', 'Bri-nylon', 'Freshman Psych', 'the knock'. Studied poeticisms ('emaciate', 'blent', 'prinked', 'thronged', 'terminate', 'momently', 'natureless', 'Immensements', 'lucent') are answered by studied vulgarisms ('yowl', 'snaggle-toothed', 'arselicker', 'hair-dos', 'pissing themselves', 'ratbags', 'wanking'). There are numerous hyphenated compounds, some memorable for their clumsy precision, some with an elevated Keatsian feel: 'spray-haired', 'Fast-shadowed', 'Luminously-peopled'. 'innocent-guilty-innocent', 'sun-comprehending', 'century-wide', 'Rain-ceased', 'gentle-sharp'. Seamus Heaney's assertion that Larkin's is 'a stripped standard English voice', offering 'the bright senses of words worn clean in literate conversation' is highly inaccurate.[19]

Each of the hitherto taboo sexual vulgarisms which moved into acceptable polite usage during the 1960s and 1970s is carefully placed. 'Stuff' in the vulgar sense is used only once, in 'Toads' (*Stuff your pension*). 'Sod' occurs twice but in different idiomatic forms: 'What does it prove? Sod all' ('Send No Money'); 'that spectacled school-teaching sod' ('The Life with a Hole in it'). 'Cock' and 'balls' occur only in 'Sunny Prestatyn'; 'arse' only in 'Vers de Société' ('In a pig's arse, friend'). 'Shit' occurs in 'The Dance' ('some shoptalking shit'), but since this poem was not published during Larkin's lifetime, he was not inhibited from using the word again in 'The Life with a Hole in it' ('the shit in the shuttered château'). 'Fuck' and 'fucked' occur only in 'This Be The Verse', 'fucking' in 'Annus Mirabilis'. Significantly, in 'Love Again', at the very end of his career, he did not re-use this word as he might well have done. He wrote not 'someone else fucking her'. Instead he employed a word as yet unused in his *oeuvre*: 'Someone else feeling her breasts and cunt'. This late poem also shows his only use of the hitherto suppressed and most intimate taboo word, 'wanking'.

Even on the middle-ground of common usage, quite unremarkable words may lodge themselves in the reader's memory because of their distinctive contexts. 'Swerving' appears after 1945 only in its threefold repetition at the beginning of 'Here'. 'Wonderful' appears only in 'Reasons for Attendance' ('The wonderful feel of girls'); 'welcome' only in 'The Importance of Elsewhere' ('difference... made me welcome'). 'Useful' appears only in 'Wild Oats' ('useful to get that learnt'). Neil Powell has remarked on Larkin's 'ability to know when a 40-watt word will be more telling than a 100-watt one'.[20] It might seem a mere accident that, in the course of only 176 poems written after 1945,[21] 'detest' appears only once ('Poetry of Departures'), and 'extinction' does not occur earlier than 'The Old Fools' and 'Aubade'. But in an idiolect as verbally overdetermined as Larkin's there is little room for accident. He seems to write always with the partly-completed *oeuvre* in mind. He waits for the right time to use a word, will not use it until that time comes, and then, if at all possible, never uses it again. An internal verbal censor forbids repetition, except in deliberate self-reference, as in the case of 'Toads' and 'Toads Revisited', or of 'unresting' and 'afresh' in 'The Trees' and 'Aubade'.

Larkin's phrase-making is equally distinctive. His noun phrases are particularly rich and inventive, even on the simplest level of adjective-plus-noun: 'sad scapes', 'a vast unwelcome', 'Threadbare perspectives', 'stone fidelity', 'rabid storms of chording', 'Lonely horizontals', 'Far-reaching singleness'.[22] More elaborate noun-constructions aim at a pensive tenuousness, an impression beyond expression: 'A slight relax of air where cold was', 'how things ought to be', 'this frail / Travelling coincidence', 'the wind's incomplete unrest', 'the sudden shut of loss'.[23] Or they express overflowing emotion: 'Its bright incipience sailing above', 'all they might have done had they been loved', 'Far / From the exchange of love to lie / Unreachable...'.[24] Frequently the deliberate clumsiness of such phrases seems designed to draw attention to the artifice of the verbal device itself, its ultimately hopeless struggle to capture non-verbal reality.

One characteristic kind of noun phrase is introduced by the pronoun 'what', gesturing with clumsy meditativeness at an elusive state of being or intangible emotion: 'what since is found / Only in separation', 'What will survive of us', 'what it started as', 'what meeting made us feel', 'What morning woke to'.[25] In 'The Whitsun Weddings', 'what [the train] held' makes ready to loose itself on London, as each of the watching faces in the wedding-parties seems to define 'Just what it saw departing'. In 'Ambulances' the failing identity of the dying patient becomes 'what cohered in it across / The years', confronting 'what is left to come'. In later poems the 'what' phrase is frequently a passionate circumlocution for the unknowable fate that governs our lives. In 'Send No Money' the poet suffers the blows of 'what happened to happen'. In 'Dockery and Son' our lives are dictated by 'what something hidden from us chose'. In 'The Life with a Hole in it' one element in the locked stasis of existence is the reductive 'what you'll get'. In 'Aubade' death becomes, with euphemistic dread, 'what's really always there', or 'what we know'.

Even the most basic elements of the language may take on an audible Larkinesque inflection, the verb 'to be' for instance: 'what I am', 'all we are', 'being here'.[26] The present participle 'being' (used thirty-six times after 1945, in twenty-five poems) introduces a number of particularly memorable phrases. The world caught in the young lady's photograph album moves the poet simply by 'being over'. The couple in 'Talking in Bed' are an emblem of two people 'being honest'. In 'The Whitsun Weddings' the couples are transfigured by 'all the power / That being changed can give'. The Old Fools are confused, 'trying to be there, / Yet being here'. In the same poem this simplest of phrases, 'being here', is yoked, to unforgettable effect, with the embarrassing epithetical extravagance of 'the million petalled flower of...'. 'Being' carries an extra charge when used to indicate age or ageing. An early poem is titled 'On Being Twenty-six'. In 'Love Songs in Age' the widow is nostalgically overcome by 'the unfailing sense of being young'; in 'Sad Steps' the ageing poet yearns for 'the strength and pain / Of being young', and in 'Money' he quips dryly 'You can't put off being young until you retire'. In 'The Old Fools' he reflects: 'Perhaps being old is having lighted rooms / Inside your head'. And in 'Aubade', what he fears is not simply 'death', nor 'dying', but, more chillingly the oxymoronic state of 'being dead': being without being.

The result of this concentrated economy of diction is a kind of 'copyrighting' of words. A poet who today gives prominence to a word beginning with 'un-' needs to ensure that it does not sound like a feeble echo of Larkin. Even words of such commonplace currency as 'here' and 'wardrobe', have become difficult to use in a poem without reminding the reader of 'Here' and 'Aubade'. The overall economy of Larkin's diction is such that even his most neutral phrases may come to haunt the memory, so that after reading him, the reader's own everyday speech seems full of quotations: 'You can see how it was'; 'I was late getting away'; 'What does it prove?'; 'useful to get that learnt'; 'your mum and dad'; 'a couple of kids'; 'somewhere like this', 'they're for it', 'We shall find out', 'Work has to be done'.[27] It is this sense of intimate familiarity, deep in Larkin's diction, which gives his work the 'much-loved' quality which some critics find suspect.

Form and genre

The economy which governs Larkin's diction extends also to his forms and genres: 'As a guiding principle I believe that every poem must be its own sole freshly created universe' (*RW* 79). Each poetic 'device' creates a distinctive verbal world through a unique combination of expressive elements: diction, rhyme/rhymelessness, stanzaic/non-stanzaic pattern, metre, voice (dramatized first person or meditative third person), genre, or blend of genres.

Larkin rhymes, for instance, with more inventiveness and complexity than any other poet of the twentieth century. As he said in an interview: 'I think one would have to be very sure of oneself to dispense with the help that metre and rhyme give and I doubt really if I could operate without them' (*FR* 21). This might seem a limitation, an admission of old-fashioned traditionalism. But the picture is not so simple. Larkin continues: 'some of my favourite poems have not rhymed or had any metre, but it's rarely been premeditated' (*FR* 21). Whether or not one accepts his denial of premeditation, the general expectation of rhyme in his work certainly makes his choice not to rhyme momentous and highly expressive. Twenty-seven of his mature works show no detectable rhyme,[28] and a number of others show minimal rhyme.[29] Their rejection of the warm reassurance of rhyme feels like a deliberate gesture of impersonal seriousness. It is in his unrhymed poems that Larkin comes closest to the spiritual or religious impulse.

In 'Wedding-Wind' mainly unrhymed tetrameters and pentameters, with the occasional intensifying rhyme, create a Lawrentian effect of ecstatic elevation. The abstract symbolist meditations, 'Oils' and 'Dry-Point', however, reject any hint of rhyme. The characteristic unrhymed form of Larkin's maturity has short, two- or three-stress lines. 'Solar' achieves an impersonal austerity by the scrupulous denial both of rhyme ('face/centre/sky/stand/unaided'), and also of metrical regularity. 'Going' and 'Nothing To Be Said' strike a note of gnomic gravity, heard again in a softer, more relaxed form in 'Afternoons'. The blank rhymelessness of 'MCMXIV' is movingly alleviated by a single rhyme at the fourth and eighth line of each octave stanza; 'The Explosion' is severely unrhymed. The rhymelessness of 'Dublinesque' contributes to a tone of uncanny solemnity, while in 'Livings II' staccato unrhymed trimeters serve to articulate the lighthouse-keeper's fierce anathema on society. In his hedgehog elegy, 'The Mower', the chilling absence of rhyme seems to imply a self-inflicted penance.

In the rhymed poems which make up the majority of Larkin's work, rhyme and pararhyme create the widest spectrum of effects: ornamental richness, fluent ease, jokey facility, brutal crudity. Context and tone are all-important, and similar kinds of rhyme may be used to widely different ends. Perfect rhymes may be unobtrusively harmonious as in 'The Trees', or pat and garish as in 'Annus Mirabilis'. Perfect double rhymes create a tone of playful cosiness in 'Poem about Oxford' ('note-case/Boat Race', 'cake-queues/breakthroughs'), but of black comedy in 'The View' ('fifty/shifty'; 'lifetime/unwifed, I'm'). In 'Best Society' pararhymes create a delicate musicality ('wrong/thing'; 'expressed/ just'; 'if/chafe'); in 'Here' they impart a sensuous chromaticism ('pheasants/presence'; 'cluster/water'; 'stands/ascends'). 'The Importance of Elsewhere' subtly clashes imperfect rhymes in an evocation of the poet's benign 'difference' in Ireland ('home/welcome'; 'speech/ touch'; 'faint/went'). The doubled half-rhymes of 'To My Wife' sound emotionally drained ('nothing/flapping'; 'regalia/failure); 'Toads', in contrast, stages a riot of farcical misrhyming ('bucket/like it'; 'toad-like/hard luck'; 'blarney/money'). The half-rhymes of 'Reasons for Attendance' are distinctly queasy ('glass/face/happiness'), an effect only intensified by the perfect rhymes of the final stanza, which instead of restoring concord, strike a note of sore irony: 'and both are satisfied, / If no one has misjudged himself. Or lied.'

In 'Poetry of Departures' and the first and third stanzas of 'Wild Oats' a shift in the final lines from half-rhyme ('hand/sound; epitaph/ off; *everything*/purifying') to full rhyme ('approve/move') makes for a satisfying effect, like the final consonant chord in a piece of music. Similarly, in 'Latest Face' and 'Church Going' a deviation into para-rhyme towards the end of the stanza prepares the way for a concluding return to full rhyme (go on/.../die/has gone/sky'). 'Best Society', 'At Grass', 'An Arundel Tomb', 'Faith Healing' and 'High Windows', however, all close, in a distinctively Larkinesque way, on beautifully unexpected dissonances ('palm/am', 'home/come', 'prove/love', 'loved/disproved', 'glass/endless'). This is a device which the poet reserves for his most intimately emotional conclusions.

Each stanza-form is shaped to its subject, either preserving the same line-length throughout or anticipating closure with a shorter line. In an extreme gesture the pentameters in 'Next, Please' and 'The Old Fools' shorten brutally at the end of each stanza to a dimeter: 'But we are wrong'; 'We shall find out'. 'Essential Beauty' has the extraordinary form of two identically-rhymed sixteen-lined stanzas, all the lines being pentameters, except the ninth (a tetrameter) and fifteenth (a trimeter). Clearly Larkin's notion of beauty involves a complex harmonious underlying shape, though the reader can scarcely be expected to 'hear' the precise regularity of this scheme. Even more elusively intricate are the patternings of 'I Remember, I Remember', which imposes a nine-line rhyme-scheme on a five-line stanza, and 'The Building', which imposes an eight-line rhyme-scheme on a seven-line stanza, making each stanza uniquely different from the others.

The four sonnets which Larkin published during his lifetime create quite disparate internal dynamics.[30] 'Spring' has a flowing

'Shakespearean' octave (*abab cdcd*) and a sestet which denies neat closure by bringing forward the expected final couplet (*effgeg*). 'Whatever happened?' follows Shelley's 'Ode to the West Wind' in combining sonnet with *terza rima*, four interlinked tercets being followed by a couplet (*aba, bcb, cdc, ded, ff*). 'Friday Night in the Royal Station Hotel' is playfully distorted, with a nine-line 'octave', ending resonantly on the new rhyme-word 'Room', which is then dully half-rhymed with 'home' in the five-line 'sestet'. 'The Card-Players' has a slight variant on the classic 'Petrarchan' octave (*abba cddc*), which then spills over surprisingly into the sestet without a break. The rhyme scheme is then concluded after only five further lines, with a neat 'Shakespearean' couplet ('farts/hearts'), leaving the final, typographically isolated fourteenth line to leap out in an exclamation of brutal euphoria: 'Rain, wind and fire! The secret, bestial peace!' Every poem by Larkin, it seems, has not only its own theme and imagery, but its own unique form. His remark, 'Form holds little interest for me. Content is everything', is either the most misleading judgement any artist has made on his own work, or it is startling proof of the truism that form is content.[31]

Some of Larkin's poems fall into established genre categories. 'Solar' is the single prayer in his *oeuvre*. 'An April Sunday brings the snow' is his only orthodox mourning elegy. 'Myxomatosis' and 'The Mower' are very different animal elegies. 'Church Going' is an updated graveyard meditation in the tradition of Gray. 'The Old Fools' is a Keatsian Ode to Senility. 'Broadcast' has elements of the medieval 'blazon' or poem focused on parts of the beloved's body ('your face among all those faces… / Your hands, tiny in all that air'. The 'Toads' poems, 'A Study of Reading Habits', 'Naturally the Foundation will Bear Your Expenses' and 'Posterity' give distinctive inflections to the dramatic monologue form of Browning and Eliot. In poems with regular metres, iambs are overwhelmingly the norm. However there are three notable exceptions. 'The Explosion' mutes the incantatory trochees of Longfellow's *Hiawatha* to elegiac effect. 'Poem about Oxford' and 'We met at the end of the party' revive the anapaestic metre of the informal eighteenth-century verse epistle to convey mature, unillusioned intimacy.

'Wires' is an 'emblem', a version of the seventeenth-century pattern-poem of wings or altar. The cattle approach the electrified wires in the first four lines (*abcd*), and then rebound from them in the next four (*dcba*), the central *d* rhyme being on the same word 'wires', making a two-strand fence against which the young cattle blunder. A poignant echo of this patterned wit is evident in the late poem, 'The Winter Palace', whose six isolated couplets, each typographically separated on the page, create a reductive image of defeat. It is as though the poet, his inspiration guttering, were struggling to impose on his words the simplest of formal schemes.

'Going' is Larkin's only riddle (it was originally entitled, punningly, 'Dying Day'). It is also clearly a belated 'Imagist' poem, written decades after the brief Imagist movement had ended. It follows exactly the formula laid down in HD's most mannered works, such as 'The Pool' and 'Sea Rose': rhymelessness, confident brevity, symbolist imagery, abrupt sentences, varying line-lengths and a culminating rhetorical question.[32] Moreover, the way the initial regular iambs collapse into virtually unmetrical free verse at the end embodies, with the concentration of a Poundian *image*, the sensation of fading consciousness.

As Jacques Derrida said, 'there is no *genre*less text.'[33] On the other hand the greatest artists submit to genre only to master it. 'Lines on a Young Lady's Photograph Album' is a highly original variation on the seventeenth-century seduction poem. 'The Whitsun Weddings' is an unusual collective *epithalamium*, celebrating not one, but many weddings, while 'The Dance' offers the wryest negative take on the *epithalamium* genre. 'The Dance' also, I believe, falls into the Romantic category of the deliberate 'fragment', whose incompletion is a calculated effect. 'Deceptions' and 'Sunny Prestatyn' are deeply refracted *Liebestod* elegies, variations on the 'death and the maiden' theme. Like 'Sunny Prestatyn', 'The Card-Players' is a picture-poem, recalling as it does a Dutch genre painting; in German it would be called a *Bildsonett*. 'Absences' is the most elliptical of sublime odes, and 'Here' infuses elements of this genre into a topographical poem concerned with the poet's home (like Thomas's 'Fern Hill' or McNeice's 'Carrickfergus'). In 1946 the young Larkin wrote two *aubades* (poems greeting the dawn), one upbeat and in a woman's voice ('Wedding-Wind'), the other despairing and in a man's voice ('At the chiming of light upon sleep'). He returns to the genre only after three decades when his final definitive self-elegy also takes this form.

The economy of Larkin's forms and genres, the predominance in his *oeuvre* of the *hapax* principle ('its own sole freshly created universe') is difficult to parallel elsewhere in literature. In music, however, Maurice Ravel shows a similar scrupulosity, composing one opera for adults and one for children, one brooding single-movement piano concerto for left hand, one extrovert three-movement piano concerto for two hands, one triptych of solo piano pieces, one quartet, one piano trio,

one mature violin sonata, one work for the unprecedented combination of harp, flute, clarinet and string quartet, a unique bolero, a single
archaic pavane. In each case the artist transforms the 'given' genre
with his own original touch, then moves on to another. Larkin is this
kind of writer. His mature volumes contain, it has been said, 'a remarkable percentage of the definitive poems of his time.'[34] This is, largely,
because he consciously aimed to make his version of any genre he
touched 'definitive'.

Oeuvre

The 112 mature poems which Larkin himself saw into print after 1945,
twenty-nine in *The Less Deceived*, thirty-two in *The Whitsun Weddings*,
twenty-six in *High Windows*, and twenty-five more in magazines and
newspapers, constitute the strictest and most definitive of *oeuvres*.
Larkin was very scrupulous about what he published, and his three
major mature collections are works of art in their own right. The
sequencing of the poems is as finely devised as that of the words and
phrases within each poem. Asked in an interview 'Do you take great
care in ordering the poems in a collection?', he answered 'Yes, great
care', adding with an affectation of casualness: 'I treat them like a
music-hall bill: you know, contrast, difference in length, the comic,
the Irish tenor, bring on the girls' (*FR* 55). The three mature volumes
invite reading from cover to cover. They draw the reader into an
unfolding emotional narrative: from 'Lines on a Young Lady's
Photograph Album' to 'At Grass'; from 'Here' to 'An Arundel Tomb';
from 'To the Sea' to 'The Explosion'. Moreover the three phases of life
which they embody seem organic and natural: the hard opening buds
of *The Less Deceived*, followed by the delicate flowers of *The Whitsun
Weddings*, then the ripe or overripe fruits of *High Windows*.

Poems echo and dialogue with each other within and across the
volumes. In *The Less Deceived* the tragic 'Deceptions', expressing guilt
over the destruction of a woman's hopes, is reimagined in the comic
'If, My Darling', depicting a man's failure to live up to the woman's
domestic fantasy. The date poems 'MCMXIV' in *The Whitsun Weddings*
and 'Annus Mirabilis' in *High Windows* both project historical myths,
one tragic and focused on the Great War, the other comic and contemporary. 'Water', a light-toned poem about religion in *The Whitsun
Weddings*, is followed in *High Windows* by an elemental pagan prayer,
'Solar'. 'Naturally the Foundation will Bear Your Expenses' in *The
Whitsun Weddings*, speaks in the voice of a cynical British scholar

happy on the academic circuit; 'Posterity', in *High Windows*, speaks in the voice of an idealistic American scholar, unhappy with his lot. In *High Windows* the tension between self and society is given sombre symbolist treatment in 'The Card-Players' and ironic social treatment in 'Vers de Société'. Readers familiar with Larkin's work will readily add further parallels and sequences.

However, only three years after the poet's death, this consciously crafted *oeuvre*, with which a generation of readers had become familiar, was overwritten by a new, larger version with different resonances. In the *Collected Poems* of 1988 (revised in 1990), Anthony Thwaite reorganized the poems, as far as possible, into the order in which Larkin wrote them, according to the poet's own dates. Since, as Thwaite says, 'the earliest poems which strike his characteristic note and carry his own voice' were written in 1946, the work up to 1945, including *The North Ship*, was relegated to a section at the end of the volume.[35] One effect of this new chronological arrangement was to replace artfully deliberate poetic sequences with the dynamics of process, revealing a poet wrestling with words, not always successfully, in order to translate his personal plight into impersonal art. The 1988/90 volume, for instance, throws into focus the poetic crises at the beginning, middle and end of Larkin's career, which had been virtually invisible in the lifetime publications. It reveals the poetic silence of eleven months which followed the death of his father and the publishers' rejections of 1948. The subsequent outpouring of 1950 (twenty poems, fifteen of which he published) can be seen to usher in his full maturity. There is a sense of arrival in 'At Grass', written, appropriately, in January 1950, the month after he had, by his own account, abandoned his novelistic ambitions.[36] A second, mid-career crisis is apparent, fourteen years later, when he left 'The Dance' unfinished and suffered a second creative block of six months. Finally, when his *oeuvre* seemed to have been completed with the publication of the third mature volume, he added the most eloquent of postscripts, the self-elegy 'Aubade', enacting, as he grimly put it, 'The death-throes of a talent' (*SL* 574). After this deliberate full-stop he wrote only a tiny handful of explicitly belated poems, to be published in magazines or left in typescript.

Equally momentously, the *Collected Poems* of 1988 included more than sixty post-1945 works which had, for whatever reason, remained unpublished during Larkin's lifetime. Anthony Thwaite wrote in his introduction that eight of the 'new' poems, 'An April Sunday brings the snow', 'The March Past', 'Mother, Summer, I', 'Far Out', 'Letter to a Friend about Girls', 'The Dance', 'When first we faced, and touching showed', 'The Winter Palace', and 'several others... deserve to stand with his best already known work'.[37] He might have added 'Deep Analysis', 'At thirty-one, when some are rich', 'The View', 'Morning at last: there in the snow', and 'Love Again'. Many welcomed this enlarged *oeuvre*. Derek Walcott was delighted with the new 'ample Larkin', a 'fecund, if not voluminous poet'.[38] He found it surprising that Larkin should have left so many good poems unpublished. Other readers were offended by the volume's apparent disregard for Larkin's 'intentions', and remained loyal to the orchestrated sequences of *The Less Deceived*, *The Whitsun Weddings* and *High Windows*. Some accused Thwaite of releasing 'second-rate material, by Larkin's standards'.[39] More recently one commentator has suggested that the posthumous enlargement of Larkin's *oeuvre* in the *Collected Poems*, the *Selected Letters* and *Trouble at Willow Gables*, has rendered 'the totality of Larkin's work... less than the sum of its parts'.[40]

In 2003 Faber and Faber bowed to this faction, and the 1988/1990 *Collected Poems* was allowed to go out of print. A new *Collected Poems*, confusingly identical in title and editor with the 1988 version, re-presented the slim volumes as Larkin himself had published them, beginning with *The North Ship*, and with appendices for the thirty-five (juvenile and mature) poems published separately in magazines and newspapers. This restoration of the *oeuvre* as it had existed at Larkin's death was greeted in some quarters as 'the book that should have been published sixteen years ago'.[41]

Larkin himself, however, had always been aware that after his death more of his poems would see the light. Indeed he clearly intended this to happen. From an early age he carefully preserved his poetic manu-scripts and, from 5 October 1944 to November 1980, he wrote (and carefully dated) virtually all his complete and incomplete drafts in a series of eight workbooks. The first of these he presented to the British Library as early as 1964. Moreover he gave Maeve Brennan a copy of the unfinished 'The Dance', and left a tape-recording of himself reading it. In 1975 he suggested to Betty Mackereth that she might make some money by selling her typescript of the unpublished poem 'When first we faced, and touching showed': 'Flog it to Texas if it seems embarrassing.'[42] He inserted typed fair copies of 'When first we faced', 'Morning at last: there in the snow' and 'Love Again' in the final workbook. His signals to posterity could scarcely be clearer. Thwaite records that Larkin 'often referred... to work which would have to be left for "the posthumous volume" of his poems'.[43] It is true that, at the very end of his life he suffered a loss of creative nerve. In his notoriously 'repugnant' (self-contradictory) will, his purist super-ego inserted a clause requiring his executors to destroy his unpublished work 'unread'. Fortunately, in another clause, his poetic ego gave them full permission to publish what they wished (Motion xvi).

Moreover the disputants on both sides failed to acknowledge that Larkin's 'intention' had by no means always been the decisive factor in determining whether a poem saw print at the time he wrote it. One of the crudest elements in the poet's plight is the role of the publisher's reader. An important group of early mature poems, for instance, had remained unpublished despite the poet's best efforts. In 1947–8 he submitted twenty-five poems for publication, under the title *In the Grip of Light*, a phrase which he told James Sutton 'seems to sum up the state of being alive' (*SL* 144). The volume, however, failed to appear, for no better reason than that Faber and Faber, John Lane, J. M. Dent, Macmillan, Methuen and John Lehmann all rejected it. Nine of the poems in this collection, including 'Going' ('Dying Day'), and 'Wedding-Wind', were subsequently published by George and Jean Hartley in *The Less Deceived* in 1955. However, fourteen of them, including the beautiful early mature works 'Deep Analysis', 'And the wave sings because it is moving', 'Two Guitar Pieces', and 'At the chiming of light upon sleep', remained unpublished. It is a strange twist of literary history that Faber rejected the brilliant *In The Grip of Light* after so readily accepting *A Girl in Winter* two years earlier.

At the time Larkin's response was to turn publisher himself. In 1951 he paid for a hundred copies of *XX Poems* to be printed in Belfast, only two pieces being carried forward from the *In the Grip of Light* typescript (he was developing fast at this point). Fifteen of these poems were later reprinted in *The Less Deceived*, but five remained unpublished outside this most limited of editions until 1988.[44] Thwaite refers to the 'hammer-blows of successive rejections' which hit Larkin in 1948, and concludes: 'Much later, when he had established a high reputation, he could not bring himself to publish anything about which he felt any doubt', even when friends urged him to publish.[45] Indeed, only the most private and self-critical of poets could have failed to retrieve such early works as 'An April Sunday brings the snow', 'Best Society', 'The local snivels through the fields' and 'Autumn' for publication, or left unpublished such later works as 'Far Out', 'Letter to a Friend about Girls', 'The View' and 'Morning at last: there in the snow'. All these poems are omitted from the 2003 *Collected Poems*, as 'unpublished' during Larkin's lifetime. It is unfortunate that editorial principle was not stretched to allow the inclusion of an appendix of the poems first published in 1988, some of which are today among Larkin's best-known works.[46] As it is, history repeated itself with a second rejection by Faber, this time of a larger number of better poems than in 1948.

Until the appearance, in the fullness of time, of *The Complete Poems*, edited by Archibald Burnett, it is only in the *Collected Poems* of 1988/1990 that the reader can follow Larkin's mature creative development in all its developing complexity: its shifts and significant silences. The plight of the writer is a life-sentence, to be served as well as written. The *oeuvre* to which Larkin devoted his life does indeed possess the cogency of a single, spontaneous sentence. He sometimes took many months to complete a piece, but it is inconceivable to imagine him, like Yeats and Hughes, returning to rewrite a poem at a later date, or, like Wordsworth and Auden, continuing to manufacture inferior verse into a long twilight. Each poem records its own irrecoverable moment in its own unique way. The mature lifetime publications of the 2003 *Collected Poems* may offer the fullest and most elegant *précis* of his life's sentence, but the richer, more complex sentence of his life's work, as represented in the 1990 *Collected Poems*, provides a more exact register of the shifting phases of his poetic plight.

2
Poetry as a Living

Professing poetry

According to convention the lyric poet is above the world of getting and spending: either surveying the world from an ivory tower or starving in a garret. Lyric poetry is, like love, the province of the amateur. The great ages of the lyric poem are the seventeenth century when courtier or clergyman poets circulated their work in manuscript with no thought of payment, and the Romantic period when young idealists burnt themselves out in exile from respectable society. Poetry cannot be measured in material terms. It is valueless because it is invaluable. Poetic authenticity may even seem guaranteed by the fact that it is worth nothing in material terms. A. E. Housman published *A Shropshire Lad* at his own expense. Wallace Stevens boasted: 'My royalties for the first half of 1924 amounted to $6.70', adding: 'I shall have to charter a boat and take my friends around the world.'[1] Larkin forgot to mention money to the publisher of *The North Ship*, and never received a penny from him. Poetry is 'professed' as a selfless vocation, it cannot offer the gainful employment of a 'profession'.

Today this unmercenary version of the poet's plight may seem out of date. As Marx has taught us, culture is economically determined, and the artist like any other productive worker supplies a commodity to the market. 'No man but a blockhead ever wrote, except for money' said Samuel Johnson briskly, at a time when poetry was yielding preeminence to the more saleable novel and biography.[2] Johnson would have appreciated the twentieth-century witticism: 'Beethoven only did his LPs for the bread.' And so, in some moods, would Larkin. In the 1940s he fantasized a future career for himself as a successful novelist, 'writing 500 words a day for six months, shoving the result off to

21

the printer and going to live on the Côte d'Azur' (*RW* 49). And when, in 1983, I thanked him for signing my copy of *Required Writing*, he responded: 'Oh. Don't thank *me*. I get forty-nine and a half pence for every one of these they sell, you know.'

However, financial reward for his writing came late, and Larkin was only too aware that it was not his poems that brought in the money. Instead it was secondary literary work, particularly his editing of *The Oxford Book of Twentieth Century English Verse*. For his own poems he received merely 'medals and prizes and honorary-this-and-thats' (*RW* 62). The low commercial viability of poetry still makes the phrase 'professional poet' sound very uncomfortable, even an oxymoron. To speak of the 'profession of poetry' is to evoke contradictions. Either the poet should not stoop to the level of a professional, or he or she is deluded to aspire to it. On the one hand Christopher Ricks can speak of the 'more-than-profession of artist',[3] on the other hand Larkin's line-manager, the Vice-Chancellor of the University of Hull, jokingly complained of paying the poet 'a librarian's salary to write poems' (Motion 302). One may devote one's life to poetry. But this is not the same thing as devoting one's 'working life', full-time, to a profession.

In his interview with Neil Powell in 1967 Larkin addresses the poet's plight in a world defined by work and money:

> Some people try to make a living out of it – I don't just mean a financial living; but you can't write poetry all the time, and you can't live on the proceeds of it, and therefore you must do something else.
>
> (*FR* 28)

He says 'try to make *a* living out of it', rather than 'try to make *their* living out of it', adding 'I don't just mean a financial living'. The strange turn of phrase manages to encompass at the same time both the practical business of 'living by' poetry and the romantic vocation of 'living for' poetry: writing to live *and* living to write. With 'Movement' common sense he finds the second task as problematic as the first.

On the one hand it is impractical to try to live by poetry. The time and effort it demands is not matched by the financial reward it brings. Short lyric poems require long devotion, and a slim volume may contain the product of a decade or more of patient work. Even Eliot's *The Waste Land*, the most monumental of twentieth-century poems, was not long enough to fill a publishable volume, and scholarly notes had to be concocted to fill the empty pages. Few poets ever achieve significant sales. Oxford University Press's recent decision to discontinue its contemporary poetry list is only one symptom of poetry's failure to achieve a secure place in the modern economy: 'you can't live on the proceeds of it'. The poet needs a 'day job'.

On the other hand, less romantically, 'you can't write poetry all the time.' Trying to live entirely for poetry leaves one with time on one's hands: 'I've always found, myself, that you can't write poetry for more than say a couple of hours. After that, you're going round in circles. What do you do with the rest of the day?' (*FR* 114). The poetic plight, for Larkin, involves a great deal of waiting: 'I've never... gone out to look for it. I waited for it to come to me, in whatever shape it chose' (*RW* 74). So, however the poet earns a living, he or she needs 'something else' to do while waiting.

Had Larkin succeeded in his early ambition to become a novelist, the situation would have been different. In later life he made a wry joke of his failure, concluding that novels 'were just too hard for me' (*RW* 49). But on one level he always envied his friend Kingsley Amis who actually achieved a more sober version of this fantasized career, working as a university lecturer until he could earn enough to become a full-time writer. Larkin had set out with the same aim:

> I was brought up to think you had to have a job, and write in your spare time, like Trollope. Then, when you started earning enough money by writing, you phase the job out. But in fact I was over fifty before I could have 'lived by my writing' – and then only because I had edited a big anthology.
>
> (*RW* 62)

Writing fiction both provides one with a full-time occupation and, unlike poetry, is quite likely to yield enough money to live on.

The task for the poet, as Larkin sees it, is to find something which will both occupy his or her time, and also provide a living, while allowing him or her to wait for 'the experience. The beauty' to come (*RW* 68):

> The question is whether you do something as like poetry as possible or as unlike it. And that depends on your temperament. You can earn your money talking about poetry in universities or hopping from one foundation to another or one conference to another – or you can go away and be something very different like an accountant...
>
> (*FR* 28)

Many twentieth-century poets chose the first of these options. Secondary literary activity has for centuries been the means by which a poet may make money and so gain the standing of a professional.

Alexander Pope ensured his financial security by translating Homer and editing Shakespeare. Larkin edited a big anthology. And in the twentieth century the unprecedented growth of higher education offered a new expanded and institutionalized version of this secondary work. Within the education system the poet could now make a profession of being a poet: 'You can earn your money talking about poetry in universities' (*FR* 28). For Robert Crawford the increasing interdependence of poetry and 'talking about poetry' has become the defining characteristic of the 'modern poet'. Modern poetry is 'a poetry of knowledge' and the modern poet is expected also to be an expert on the subject of poetry. He or she becomes a 'writer in residence', a 'professor of poetry', or even a teacher of 'creative writing'.[4]

The first two poetic generations of the century, that of T. S. Eliot, and that of W. H. Auden, saw an unprecedented revolution in the world of poetry. And each threw up a different model of how to make a living out of it. The Modernists, Eliot and Pound, saw English literature become a university subject of study. Their response to the challenge of the new professionalism of science and technology was to claim their own professional expertise. In a curious intensification of Matthew Arnold's notion of poetry as a didactic 'criticism of life' the writing of poetry itself was absorbed into the New Criticism. Inspiration became professional expertise and the mystique of the ancient shaman or bard was transferred to the poet-critic. The modern poet claimed professional authority over culture. Pound and Eliot, if to a large extent unintentionally, turned poetry into an educational instrument of a kind which would have puzzled Tennyson, Browning or Hardy. In his influential essay of 1919, 'Tradition and the Individual Talent', Eliot saw the poet's function as to comprehend all past culture and bring it up to date. The poet must:

> write not merely with his own generation in his bones, but with a feeling that the whole of the literature of Europe from Homer and within it the whole of the literature of his own country has a simultaneous existence and composes a simultaneous order.[5]

As this notion of poetry gained acceptance the 'difficult' works of Pound and Eliot were increasingly canonized as 'exam-poems, testing the audience, and demanding in turn the attention of the reader as student'.[6] Such 'bookish', 'library fuelled' poetry, 'points forward to the research university full of graduate students devoting all their time to a verse of labyrinthine difficulty'.[7]

Thus reified, the work of Pound and Eliot came to offer an intimidating model for their successors. Already by 1927 Laura Riding and

Robert Graves in their *A Survey of Modernist Poetry* are neurotically burdened with the new professionalism:

> Modern civilization seems to demand that the poet should justify himself not only by writing poems but furthermore by proving with each poem the contemporary legitimacy of poetry itself – the professional authority of the term 'poet' in fact. And though in a few rare cases the poet may succeed even now in writing by nature without historical or professional effort, he is in general too conscious of the forced professionalization of poetry to be able to avoid justifying himself and his work professionally, that is, critically, as a point of honour.[8]

Yeats's poetry had celebrated the abounding, glittering jet of 'life's own self-delight'; the Modernist poet has the more daunting task of 'historical and professional effort'; 'the modernist poet does not write for the school-room: if for anything at all, for the university.'[9] The following year H. W. Garrod, the Professor of Poetry at Oxford, himself a scholar rather than a poet, was sadly accepting the new rigour which was expected of him: 'The age of elegant amateurism is either dead already or dying. Very soon, it will be no longer possible for any of us to escape the duty of knowledge.'[10] Rescued from the plight of garret or irrelevant ivory tower the poet is forced into the academy; and as Les Murray puts it: 'All academies are police academies'.[11]

Larkin, who felt, simply, that 'poetry is a matter of emotion' (*FR* 27), stands against this 'forced professionalization of poetry'. For him poetry is not a matter of 'knowledge', and certainly not of 'duty'. He is suspicious of poets as academics, and of difficulty as a measure of literary value:

> But if the poet engages in this exegesis and analysis by becoming a university teacher, the danger is that he will begin to assume unconsciously that the more a poem can be analysed – and therefore the more it needs to be analysed – the better poem it is, and he may in consequence, again unconsciously, start to write the kind of poem that is earning him a living.
>
> (*RW* 89)

He sees dangers in the poet devoting too much energy to criticism. The 'campus poet', he argues,

> by acting like a critic... may come to think like a critic; he may insensibly come to embrace what I think of as the American, or

Ford-car, view of literature, which holds that every new poem somehow incorporates all poems that have gone before it and takes them
a step further.

(RW 89)

Larkin cannot but acknowledge that 'the modern poetic audience... is
a *student* audience, pure and simple' (*RW* 81), but he still insists that:
'at bottom poetry, like all art, is inextricably bound up with giving
pleasure, and if a poet loses his pleasure-seeking audience he has lost
the only audience worth having, for which the dutiful mob that signs
on every September is no substitute' (*RW* 81-2).

Larkin has often been criticized for the 'philistine' anti-Modernism
expressed in the Introduction to *All What Jazz* and elsewhere. But the
reader needs to bear in mind the iron grip of 'difficult' Modernism on
readers of poetry in the middle years of the last century. James Fenton
engagingly recalls the climate of criticism in the 1960s:

> I remember people saying about W. H. Auden that he had, as it were,
> had his encounter with Modernism, absorbed what he wanted, and
> then moved on in his own sweet way. And this wasn't considered
> good enough. It was as if he hadn't quite taken Modernism seriously.[12]

As an undergraduate in the 1960s I was already reading Larkin in my
spare time. However, I was aware that this was only a pleasurable holiday from my application to the duty of knowledge, as I laboriously
decoded the obscurer parts of *The Waste Land* and the *Cantos*. The more
opaque the literary allusion, the more abstruse the outdated anthropology, the more tenuous the foreign allusion, the more serious my task
appeared. Today an infinite hypertext is available to the student at the
click of a mouse. Eliot's own prophetic self-questioning springs to
mind: 'Where is the wisdom we have lost in knowledge? / Where is the
knowledge we have lost in information?'[13] In this context Larkin's
extravagant, irritable wit offered a heady release:

> You've got to work at this: after all, you don't expect to understand
> anything as important as art straight off, do you? I mean, this is
> pretty complex stuff: if you want to know how complex, I'm giving
> a course of ninety-six lectures at the local college, starting next week,
> and you'd be more than welcome.

(RW 293)

Poetry, like jazz, he complains, has moved into 'the culture belt', and universities have become 'the accepted stamping ground for the subsidized acceptance of art rather than the real purchase of it'. The poet may not be able to make a living by selling his work, but the only genuine readers are in the open market-place. The 'artist-audience nexus' has been distorted (*RW* 294).

However, having established its professional credentials in the 1920s, poetry itself did not follow the difficult route suggested by Riding and Graves. The major poet of the 1930s was not William Empson, but W. H. Auden, a poet of spontaneous fluency, whose best work is breathtakingly lucid at first reading. It was Auden who in his later career promoted a new and different version of the Modernist professionalization of poetry. In the years following the Second World War, as the education system resumed its expansion, and international travel became easier, a poet could 'make a living out of it' by 'hopping from one foundation to another or one conference to another', reading his or her work, or giving critical lectures. Auden was one of the first to take advantage, in the 1950s, of this new 'poetry circuit'. As Charles Osborne explains:

> Auden... began to give readings of his poems at universities and colleges. He was one of the first poets to do so on a regular and frequent basis, and could fairly be said to have played his part in bringing into existence that travelling circuit which gave employment to so many poets, British and American, during the fifties and sixties.[14]

Universities now seemed the natural habitat for the poet, and 'talking about' literature was firmly established as an institutionalized profession. Most practitioners of this new profession were scholars, with expertise in 'academic literary criticism'. But no conference on contemporary literature would be complete without an original poet or two, with a licence to behave badly or disrupt proceedings from the margins. And literary festivals offered an alternative, less strenuous forum.

Auden lamented: 'It is a sad fact about our culture that a poet can earn much more money writing or talking about his art than he can by practising it'. However, he was not, in reality, very sad about this situation. His poem 'On the Circuit', though sharply self-mocking, shows a frank enjoyment of this peripatetic lifestyle, so well suited to his temperament, among 'pelagian travelers, / Lost on their lewd conceited way / To Massachusetts, Michigan, / Miami or L. A.' The poet seems also

pleasantly lost, and content that his way should be as lewd and conceited as theirs. He depicts himself sitting 'In airborne instrument',
playfully parodying the ominousness of his 1930s manner, in which
airmen overlooked obscurely threatened landscapes. This postwar airborne visitation, however, has no sinister undertone:

> Predestined nightly to fulful
> Columbia-Giesen-Management's
> Unfathomable will,
>
> By whose election justified,
> I bring my gospel of the Muse
> To fundamentalists, to nuns,
> To Gentiles and to Jews...[15]

He is aimiably delighted with his ecumenical role as the secular priest
of a godlike literary foundation.

Larkin's attitude towards the literary 'circuit' is contradictory, and it
is also intimately involved with his ambiguous attitude towards Auden,
one of the major influences on his youthful work. Early 'English'
Auden, the Auden of *Look, Stranger!* and *Another Time*, was for Larkin 'a
superb, magnetic, wide-angled poet... the poetry was in the blaming
and warning' (*FR* 40). The later Auden he called 'the great American
windbag' (*FR* 296), full of 'flatulent abstractions' (*FR* 344). One element
in his antagonism seems to be envy at the ease with which the older
poet took to his role in 'the cultural entertainment industry'. It is characteristic of Larkin that his own poetic treatment of this theme is indirect and ambiguous. Nowhere in Larkin's poems do we find the direct
attack on the institutionalization of poetry which he so pungently
expresses in his interviews and reviews. There is, for instance, no parody of Modernist obscurantism, no satire on Pound or Empson. This
was Larkin's explicit policy. He strove to appeal to the widest audience:
'I have always tried to keep literature out of my poems as a subject'
(*FR* 85). The speaker in Larkin's poem about the circuit, 'Naturally the
Foundation will Bear Your Expenses' (1961), is consequently not a poet
but a careerist academic.

The poem is more character study than satire, and although its persona is, as Larkin said, 'a shit' (*FR* 58), like the shit in the shuttered
château in 'The Life with a Hole in it', he is a shit whose impudent
Audenesque irreverence the poet seems to find attractive. As he hurries

to catch his Comet on an expenses-paid jaunt, leaving a British
November for the sunshine of Bombay, he muses on his next project:

> I pondered pages Berkeley
> Not three weeks since had heard,
> Perceiving Chatto darkly
> Through the mirror of the Third.

There is a touch of English sniffiness in Larkin's pronunciation of
Berkeley as 'Barkeley' on the 'Listen' recording of 1964, but the poem's
aim is not really a destructive moral critique. Larkin elucidated hesi-
tantly: 'Certainly it was a dig at the middleman who gives a lot of talks
to America and then brushes them up and does them on the Third and
then brushes them up again and puts them out as a book with Chatto'
(*FR* 25).[16] His explanation is very conditional: 'Certainly it was a dig';
the 'dig', it seems, is not the most important element. On the 'Listen'
recording he concedes that the poem has been read as unsuccessful
'light verse', and concedes 'That may be so'. He cites the origin of the
poem as 'a mixture of finding that a number of my friends had gone to
India and hearing, as I usually do, the broadcast of the service at the
Cenotaph on what used to be called Armistice Day'.[17] There is some
obfuscation here, and an unconvincing show of the conservatism
expected of him ('as I usually do', 'what used to be called Armistice
Day').

He claimed also that this poem is 'as serious as anything I have written' (*FR* 25). The seriousness, however, is not a matter of moral earnest-
ness or censure. Motion's view of the poem as 'a piece of savagery'
seems wide of the mark (Motion 311). Asked in an interview about
'Posterity' and 'Homage to a Government' Larkin said:

> I shouldn't call myself a satirist, or any other sort of -ist. The poems
> you mention were conceived in the same way as the rest. That is to
> say, as poems. To be a satirist, you have to think you know better
> than everyone else. I've never done that.
>
> (*RW* 73)

The relationship between poet and persona is not one of simple irony.
The poet is not concerned to assert his moral superiority over this shit.
It is significant that in the middle of his description of the 'dig at the
middleman' he slips into a querulous defence of the character's dislike

of the Remembrance Day ceremonial: 'Why he should be blamed for not sympathizing with the crowds on Armistice Day, I don't quite know' (*FR* 25). Larkin seems unsure whose side he is on.

The speaker sees himself, in an elegant poetic touch, 'dwindling' into the distance:

> – But I outsoar the Thames,
> And dwindle off down Auster
> To greet Professor Lal
> (He once met Morgan Forster),
> My contact and my pal.

The strained, Byronic *Don Juan* rhyme, 'Auster/Forster', with its classical reference to the benign South Wind, 'Auster', betrays the character's facile scholarship. But it is nevertheless entertaining, and the poet enjoys its ingenuity as much as his persona does. The speaker of Auden's 'On the Circuit' shows a similar euphoria as he leaves his latest audience 'dwindling' below him:

> Another morning comes: I see,
> Dwindling below me on the plane,
> The roofs of one more audience
> I shall not see again.
>
> God bless the lot of them, although
> I don't remember which was which:
> God bless the U.S.A., so large,
> So friendly, and so rich.[18]

There is a poetic dialogue here. The twinkling irreverence of Larkin's poem is distinctly Audenesque, and it might not, perhaps, be too fanciful to suggest that 'Auster' could have been generated in Larkin's mind as a portmanteau of 'Wystan Auden'. Had Auden's self-satire been written before Larkin's poem, 'Naturally the Foundation' would clearly be Larkin's 'Homage to W. H. Auden', the younger poet's version of 'On the Circuit'. In fact, Auden's poem seems to have been influenced by Larkin's, which he will have read in its first publication in *Twentieth Century* in July 1961. In both poems the speaker enjoys his plane-bound elevation with self-satisfied euphoria. The rhymes are similarly jokey, and the appearance of 'dwindling' in Auden's poem sounds like an echo. Larkin selected 'On the Circuit' for his *Oxford Book of Twentieth Century English Verse* and, prompted by the ordeal of having to give a rare public lecture himself, cited it in his Shakespeare Prize speech in Hamburg in 1976 to illustrate 'the miseries of the lecture tour'. Revealingly, he exaggerated the negativity of Auden's poem in his speech: 'This is of course very funny, but I think it is rather dreadful too; the lecture circuit suddenly comes to resemble one of those other circuits described in Dante's *Inferno*' (*RW* 90).

Despite their similarities, Larkin's and Auden's 'circuit' poems are very different in effect. Where Auden dramatizes himself with bracing candour and a sense of the absurd, Larkin pours a murky mix of contempt and envy into a fictional character quite distinct from himself. The poet, indeed, is rhetorically absent from the poem. Later in his career Larkin began a series of first-person poems punningly entitled 'Livings', focusing on the means by which particular characters make their way in life. His intention was to write a longer series, but only three were completed. The felicitous title focuses attention on a characteristically Larkinesque kind of poem which he had inaugurated as far back as 'Wedding-Wind' in 1946: a first-person evocation of the feel of being alive, capturing a character at a moment of epiphany. The poetic point in each case is to catch the existential plight of 'living', not to explicate any historical or social theme. 'Naturally the Foundation' is this kind of poem. Though its speaker is an academic, it is not so much a poem about the profession of literature as a celebration of a particular mode of being for its own sake.

Larkin's sensibility was very different from Auden's. Auden found it natural to dramatize his own personal situation in the public terms of large ideas and historical perspectives. His successor in this respect was Robert Lowell, in poems such as 'Beyond the Alps' and 'Memories of West Street and Lepke'. Larkin is more private. One reason he gave for this was his early shyness, particularly his stammer: 'I wasn't a happy child: I stammered badly, and this tends to shape your life. You can't become a lecturer or anything that involves talking... I still stammer' (*FR* 48). It is not difficult to imagine that had he not suffered from this impediment, and had he not become increasingly deaf, Larkin could have overcome his objections and created a distinctive place for himself on the poetry circuit. In the privacy of the recording studio he produced some of the best readings by any poet of his own work. Moreover some of his works make perfect 'performance poems': the 'Toads' poems, 'I Remember, I Remember', 'MCMXIV', 'Sunny Prestatyn' and

'The Trees', for instance, while in 'Annus Mirabilis' he shows that he can, on occasion, place himself with Audenesque impudence, in 'History': 'Sexual intercourse began / In nineteen sixty-three / (Which was rather late for me) –'.

There is a deep ambiguity in Larkin's attitudes towards the role of the poet as self-publicising performer on the academic or arts-festival circuit. He repeats that it is a matter of 'temperament'. Echoing Auden, he says: 'you *can* live by "being a writer", or "being a poet", if you're prepared to join the cultural entertainment industry, and take hand-outs from the Arts Council (not that there are as many of them as there used to be) and be a "poet in residence" and all that' (*RW* 61-2). His dismissiveness ('the cultural entertainment industry') is contradicted by his apparent disappointment at the diminishing funding opportunities. He himself, indeed, was a prime mover in securing the Compton Poetry Fellowship for Hull University in 1969. The experiment was unsuccessful in stirring interest among students (Motion 379). However, over the following four years it did provide a means of paying C. Day Lewis (then Poet Laureate), Richard Murphy, Peter Porter, Ian Hamilton and Douglas Dunn for their poetry, without requiring that they pretend too hard to be teachers or scholars.

But such a role was not for Larkin himself. Whatever the reasons for his diffidence, a more public Larkin would have been a different poet. His formal perfectionism, often relying on a slight verbal nuance or subtle word-play, yields far more on private reading than in the auditorium. As he said: 'Hearing a poem, as opposed to reading it on the page, means you miss so much – the shape, the punctuation, the italics, even knowing how far you are from the end' (*RW* 61). He also claimed to be repelled by the way the 'confessional' poets of the 1960s and 1970s dramatized their breakdowns and failed relationships. His own poetry is, however, not notably reticent; 'Talking in Bed' is as painfully revealing as any poem by Lowell or Plath. But recited from a platform, its intimate quality would be lost. The poet's physical presence before the audience would risk transforming intimate musing into embarrassing autobiography.

> I remember saying once, I can't understand these chaps who go round American universities explaining how they write poems: it's like going round explaining how you sleep with your wife. Whoever I was talking to said, They'd do that, too, if their agents could fix it.
>
> (*RW* 71)

The danger is that poetry readings throw the focus on to the poet as a personality, marginalizing the poetry itself: 'this fashion for poetry readings has led to a kind of poetry that you *can* understand first go: easy rhythms, easy emotions, easy syntax. I don't think it stands up on the page' (*RW* 61). 'Performance poetry', as written by Roger McGough, Benjamin Zephaniah, Ian Macmillan and Pam Ayres, may be enjoyable and entertaining. But its techniques and aims are not Larkin's. 'I don't want to go around pretending to be me' (*RW* 51).

At the Hamburg ceremony in 1976 Larkin reviewed his achievement with self-punishing humility: 'I have to admit with some shame that I have never read my poems in public, never lectured on poetry, never taught anyone how to write it, and indeed this is only the second time since 1945 that I have been abroad' (*RW* 90). There is little irony here. Three years earlier, in 1973, Charles Monteith had written to indicate that he and Auden were willing to nominate Larkin for the Oxford Professorship of Poetry. Larkin declined firmly, but with a note of genuine regret:

> To know that Auden and yourself are willing to nominate me is the biggest compliment I have been paid for many years. I only wish I felt your confidence was justified, or could do something to justify it. But as you will know – and you know me a good deal better than Auden does – I have really very little interest in poetry in the abstract; I have never lectured about it, or even written about it to any extent, and I know that I could never produce anything worthy of such a distinguished office and audience.
>
> (*SL* 470)

His instinct was sound. Larkin's critical prose is brilliant, but it is all in the form of short reviews, interviews, or statements of his own practice. His most extended series of reviews deals with jazz. It would have been torment for him to attempt to produce a series of reflective lectures on poetry to match Auden's *The Dyer's Hand*.

Librarian-Poet

Larkin, then, refused, or was unable by temperament, to make a full-time profession of poetry. He was, nonetheless, wholly committed to his art. Larkin was plighted to poetry in the fullest sense of the word, as his helplessly stubborn avoidance of marriage, children, and property-ownership indicates. In the early poem, 'The Spirit Wooed' (1950), he adopts the pose of humble attention to a muse:

> Once I believed in you,
> And then you came,
> Unquestionably new...
>
> You launched no argument,
> Yet I obeyed...

He fears that the spirit has withdrawn because he was over-eager, and resigns himself to his plight with the abjection of the courtly lover, submitting to a 'pause' in inspiration 'Longer than life, if you decide it so'. As Larkin develops, his tone becomes brisker and in 'Reasons for Attendance' (1953) his aestheticism is impatient of its own preciosity. An offhand, 'Movement' diffidence '(Art, if you like)' replaces the earlier religiose fervour ('Yet I obeyed'), but there is no irony in the poet's commitment: 'It speaks; I hear'. Like the church bell of religion this bell of secular aestheticism proclaims his higher calling. He refuses to 'attend' the party and 'attends' instead to the bell of art. Even in the late 'Vers de Société' (1971), where Larkin throws the saddest doubt on his antisocial artist's vocation, it is not the time spent sitting alone by his lamp which he regrets, but advancing age, which leaves him 'company' as a poor substitute for the creative solitude he can no longer use. In cynical mood he might cite Auden to the effect that 'in the end, art is small beer' (*FR* 40), but the sentiment did not come naturally to him.

Larkin's frequent self-deprecatory comments have led to him being seen as a limply 'unpretentious' poet.[19] In fact few poets in the century took their poetic pretensions more seriously. He professes his calling on the most primitive level, where the word 'profess' is a near-synonym for 'confess' and the poet resembles a religious devotee. Robert Frost's nice discrimination seems relevant here: 'To be a poet is a condition, not a profession'.[20] By profession Larkin was an unpoetic librarian at the centre of a busy institution of higher education; by condition he was a poet, living at the margins:

> you can go away and be something very different like an accountant
> – I believe Roy Fuller is something like that, Wallace Stevens was an
> insurance man; I'm a librarian, I never see a book from one year's
> end to another.
>
> (*FR* 28)

The divorce between profession and condition is neatly caught in the odd wording: 'you can go away and...'; the two modes of living or the two 'professions' are in separate psychological and spiritual places.

Larkin depicted his career in librarianship as a lucky accident. Spurred into action by a letter from the Ministry of Labour in 1943, and failing to secure a post in the Civil Service, he happened to answer an advertisement for a librarian in Wellington, Shropshire:

> looking back it was an inspired choice. Librarianship suits me – I love the feel of libraries – and it has just the right blend of academic interest and administration that seems to match my particular talents, such as they are. And I've always thought that a regular job was no bad thing for a poet.
>
> *(RW 51)*

At the time, however, the youthful Larkin was not at all sure that librarianship was a suitable occupation for 'a man of acute sensibility and genius'. On taking up the Wellington post he wrote in a letter to his friend Jim Sutton: 'I intend to devote myself to writing and doing my boring job without enthusiasm or slackness. I only took it on account of being able to write in the intervals: it's not so easy, I must say, but it's possible.'[21] His writing comes first, and his day-job is a necessity to which he must submit without enthusiasm, but also, as one would expect of the son of the Coventry City Treasurer, without slackness.

Wallace Stevens, another 'nine-to-five man', argued that 'It gives a man character to have this daily contact with a job'.[22] Larkin's version has less moralism about it: 'a regular job [is] no bad thing for a poet'. The poet's day-job gives him an anchor in the 'real world' of ordinary, unliterary people with ordinary jobs. Larkin's greatest poems avoid literariness, on the principle that readers are not themselves poets. He is no airy-fairy *littérateur*, but a 'regular' citizen. 'My job as a University Librarian', he told one interviewer, 'is a full-time one, five days a week, forty-five weeks a year... But you wouldn't be interested in all that' (*RW* 57). His tone, however, is laconic and ambiguous. Behind the belligerent claim of responsible citizenship there lurks the wry resignation of his earliest years as a librarian to his 'boring job'. He himself, deep down, as vagrant poet, is not 'interested in all that' either.

Nevertheless, when, in 1959 Larkin was included for the first time in *Who's Who*, he gave his occupation as 'librarian', on the principle that 'a man is what he is paid for' (Motion 294). This, however, was the point in his life when he was most absorbed with his professional commitment to librarianship, having overseen Phase One of the new Library building at Hull, reworking the original inadequate plans and making himself an expert on various technicalities of design and construction. Librarianship was never after this to be so satisfying for him. Moreover, he could, perhaps, by this stage, four years after the publication of *The Less Deceived*, afford to class himself as a 'librarian', safe in the knowledge that only a tiny minority of readers would be led to his entry in *Who's Who* by his librarianship. Later he adopts a very different tone, complaining about the disproportionate rewards of his two professions:

> The only thing that does strike me as odd, looking back, is that what society has been willing to *pay* me for is being a Librarian. You get medals and prizes and honorary-this-and-thats – and flattering interviews – but if you turned round and said, Right, if I'm so good, give me an index-linked permanent income equal to what I can get for being an undistinguished university administrator – well, reason would remount its throne pretty quickly.
>
> (*RW* 62)

Nevertheless he took his day-job very seriously: 'on the whole I have always enjoyed being a librarian. It's a very good job and I have tried to do it well' (*FR* 114). Following his death the Library Association published a collection of essays on librarianship dedicated to his memory.[23] There are some, indeed, who feel that his poetry has unjustly eclipsed his achievement in librarianship. Father Anthony Storey, former Catholic chaplain at the university, comments: 'I think it's a mistake having on his gravestone: "Philip Larkin: Writer"; "Philip Larkin: University Librarian", that was his triumph: building that library. That was his great aim: to make the University intellectually respectable.'[24] Similarly Sir Brynmor Jones, Vice-Chancellor of Hull University from 1955 until 1973, commented after Larkin's death: 'I think people who have written about him have made too much of his poems and not enough of him as a librarian.' It is scarcely surprising in view of this relative evaluation that he and Larkin 'were never close friends'. The Vice-Chancellor found his librarian 'totally uncommunicative', though 'very charming' (Motion 302). Theirs was a relationship of the purest professionalism.

Larkin's relations with John Saville, left-wing Professor of Economic History, showed a similar pattern. Despite jocular references to his 'seditious' projects, Larkin gave ready support to Saville's efforts to build up the Library's Archive of Labour History, assisting in the acquisition of the early archive of the National Council for Civil Liberties and the papers of the political cartoonist 'Vicky' (Victor Weisz), as well as other important documents. As Saville says 'his very conservative politics did not confuse his role as a librarian', and 'in all matters in which I was somehow or other involved, he remained the dedicated librarian.'[25] They would occasionally lunch together and once Larkin gave Saville a Pee Wee Russell record. Their 'distant but friendly' relations were a model of productive professional co-operation.

A different kind of professionalism is evident in Larkin's relationship with Brenda Moon, his Deputy Librarian between 1962 and 1979. While working out her notice in Sheffield prior to moving to Hull, she chanced upon 'Breadfruit' in its first publication in *Critical Quarterly*. 'This was a terrible shock. I hardly knew what the words meant, but they unnerved me'. However, in Hull she came to value Larkin's 'extreme honesty as well as his kindness'.[26] She found the librarian she worked with a more vivid person than the poet. He was, she says: 'so much more than he appeared in his publications'.[27] Unsurprisingly, perhaps: 'We almost never spoke about his poetry.'[28]

Larkin's library colleagues are agreed on his unusual ability to command respect while at the same time remaining friendly and approachable. At first he was called 'Sir' by many, but with a reference to the popular film at the time 'To Sir with Love', giving its formality a slightly subversive undertone.[29] Pauline Dennison, Assistant Librarian 1963–95, recalls: 'He always liaised and consulted; he was fair-minded and willing to listen. Above all, he never failed to express appreciation and give encouragement. In short, he was a gentleman'.[30] His secretary, Betty Mackereth says: 'He was a very good boss. He took an interest in people; he spoke to people.'[31] Peter Crowther, Sub-Librarian 1972–89, remembers 'the very many occasions on which he made dull staff committee meetings bearable by his hilarious wit and his ability to mimic people'.[32] For many years he paid out of his own pocket for an annual staff Christmas dinner. His happiest years as a librarian were in the late 1950s and early 1960s. After Phase Two of the building was completed in 1970, his more youthful and extensive staff became more distant from him; he became increasingly deaf and was alienated by the new technology. In his final years funding cuts coincided with his failing health to fill him with gloom. 'Larkin's library' as the students called it in their protest against funding cuts, was no longer his.

In one particular area his role of librarian bore an intimate relationship to his role as a poet. In 1963, after he had been approached twice by American libraries concerning his own papers, Larkin helped in the setting up of an Arts Council committee to purchase the manuscripts of living British poets for the National Collection in the British Library. He served on the Advisory Panel from 1963, and was its chairman from 1967–79 (Motion 340). His essay 'A Neglected Responsibility', delivered to the Standing Conference of National and University Libraries (SCONUL) in 1979, attempted to alert British librarians to the problem of contemporary British poetry manuscripts being bought up by libraries in the USA.

To some readers the separation between Larkin's two professions seems artificial. For them his sensibility is of a piece; a man is, indeed, what he is paid for, and his poetry is that of a librarian. Like that of a 'bricklayer-poet', or a 'housewife-poet', his work is properly to be understood in the context of his job. A. Alvarez sees him as belonging to a group of 'academic-administrative' poets.[33] Seamus Heaney, one of the few recent poets to have succeeded in making his living out of poetry, politely implies that the work of the 'nine-to-five-man who had seen poetry'[34] is insufficiently spiritually 'corroborative' to achieve the transcendence essential to the 'redress of poetry'. He is not 'the poet who would be most the poet'.[35] Larkin, interestingly, felt that the works of the professional poet Heaney were too 'litty' (*SL* 659). More recently Larkin's 'so boring writing practice' has been seen as reflecting 'the monotony of the administrative jobs in the economy of that time'.[36] However, though Larkin was prepared to describe himself in *Who's Who* as a 'librarian', he would not have described himself as a 'librarian-poet', or 'poet-librarian'. Jean Hartley describes 'his distaste at the thought of any link between his profession as a librarian and his life as a poet'. And she remembers how he would wincingly relive the official opening of Phase One of the Library building in 1960, mimicking the Welsh lilt of the Vice-Chancellor: 'This is Mr Larkin our poet-librarian,' and then the Queen Mother's piping reply: 'Oh, what a lovely thing to be.'[37]

Robert Crawford sees Larkin as a 'modern poet' with an intrinsic relationship to academe: 'Larkin's 'poetic *oeuvre*', he writes, 'is inextricably bound up with his work in academia.' 'Working as a university librarian kept Larkin out of seminars; yet it situated him unignorably in academe.'[38] This analysis needs careful qualification. Larkin certainly worked in academe and felt it 'suited' him. He could also be said to have undergone a kind of 'professional' training in poetry, reading English Literature at Oxford as an undergraduate. Moreover, for most of his life he worked in a university, and was intimate with a university lecturer in English, Monica Jones. To this extent he does indeed belong in Crawford's category of the 'modern poet'. However this version gives a misleading impression of the poetry. Larkin was not an academic in any sense of the word. Though he worked on a campus, he was not a 'campus poet'. He had nothing to do with the English Department of his university, and refused to read his poetry or speak about it in academic contexts.

Above all, Larkin does not write a 'poetry of knowledge', as do Eliot and Empson. The characteristic Larkinesque position, indeed, is resolutely inept and inexpert. In 'Ignorance', he meditates:

> Strange to know nothing, never to be sure
> Of what is true or right or real,
> But forced to qualify *or so I feel*,
> Or *Well, it does seem so:*
> *Someone must know.*

He aligns himself with the bored, uninformed common man. He claimed, with comic exaggeration: 'I read everything except philosophy, theology, economics, sociology, science, or anything to do with the wonders of nature, anything to do with technology – have I said politics? I'm trying to think of all the Dewey decimal classes' (*RW* 53). Nor, he continues, does he read foreign poetry or even much poetry by his English contemporaries. He insists that he is an administrator:

> The academic world has worked all right for me, but then, I'm not a teacher. I couldn't be. I should think that chewing over other people's work, writing I mean, must be terribly stultifying. Quite sicken you with the whole business of literature. But then, I haven't got that kind of mind, conceptual or ratiocinative or whatever it is.
> (*RW* 60)

Librarianship in itself does not involve the reading or studying of books or archives. It is a matter of managing their storage and distribution, and, in Larkin's case, also overseeing extensive building projects: 'I'm a librarian, I never see a book from one year's end to another' (*FR* 28). His current successor bears the title 'Director of Academic Services', the phrase 'and Librarian' being appended in deference to the University Statutes.

The comment that Larkin 'liked simultaneously to inhabit an academic milieu and to mock it',[39] may be true of his prose, but his poems almost never evoke 'an academic milieu'. Larkin goes to great lengths to preserve the primitive role of the poet as 'a man speaking to men' and to women, rather than a spokesman for, or critic of a clerisy: 'I have always tried to keep literature out of my poems as a subject', he insists, drolly conceding 'A Study of Reading Habits' as the single exception (*FR* 85). Larkin may write, inevitably, for a student readership. But librarians, academics, students can also be general or common readers. As D. H. Lawrence's Birkin asks: 'Am I a teacher because I teach, or a preacher because I preach?' As well as being academics, accountants, librarians, engineers, stockbrokers, plumbers or accountants, we are also people. It is in these unspecific terms that Larkin defines his theme and his audience.

In this spirit several of his most popular poems focus precisely on the strains between 'the man' and 'what he is paid for'; between the satisfying state of living and the annoying task of making a living. In 'Poetry of Departures' the poet expresses abject admiration for a character who '*chucked up everything / And just cleared off*'. It is important that this adventurer has no excuse of genius for this 'audacious, purifying, / Elemental move'. He is no D. H. Lawrence or Paul Gauguin. As the stereotypical imagery indicates, the poem concerns a common, unliterary plight: 'everyone's' boring job and 'everyone's' fantasy of escape. Similarly, the speaker of 'Toads' and 'Toads Revisited' is a generic middle manager. He works in an office and has a secretary, but no reader could guess from the text whether he is an insurance broker, an advertising executive, a bank employee or a librarian. Apart from the private joke about lecturers living off their wits (which Monica Jones no doubt relished) there is no hint of academe:

> Why should I let the toad *work*
>   Squat on my life?
> Can't I use my wit as a pitchfork
>   And drive the brute off?
> ...
>
> Ah, were I courageous enough
>   To shout *Stuff your pension!*
> But I know, all too well, that's the stuff
>   That dreams are made on...

The poet acknowledges a radical *déformation professionelle*. 'What he is paid for' has become more real to him, or to his own inner, servile toad, than his stereotypical dreams of 'The fame and the girl and the money'. And like most people in his position, having let off steam, he returns sulkily to his orderly life of books, china and pension.

Larkin's own job security and pension were the focus of much apparent anxiety for him. Graham Stroud, a former administrative manager at Hull University, with whom Larkin used to chat in the 1970s reports that:

> There was a period when Philip became convinced that the University would dispense with his services... he seemed obsessed. He would say that he was of little importance, did very little and that the University could save a lot of money by getting rid of him... He was afraid of the prospect of being made redundant, but more, of the shame and embarrassment that would go with it.[40]

Stroud confesses, however, to having little or no interest in poetry, and ingenuously reports that Larkin 'half-admitted' to him 'that he couldn't see what people saw in his poetry anyway'.[41] It seems likely that Larkin was playing to a particular audience here. There was always an element of histrionic exaggeration in his anxiety over his job. 'I was over fifty before I could have "lived by my writing"... and by that time you think, Well, I might as well get my pension, since I've gone so far' (*RW* 62). His is the common lot of pensionable humanity. In the event, as he himself forecast, death pre-empted his professional *curriculum vitae* and he died in post at 63. The pension remains undrawn.

'Toads Revisited', written eight years later than 'Toads', adopts a more resigned tone. The poet is at first puzzled to find that he is not enjoying an idle stroll in the park as much as he should: 'The lake, the sunshine, / The grass to lie on'. This should feel 'better than work'; but it doesn't. Instead of delighting in his freedom he finds himself grateful that he is not like the other visitors to the park: 'Palsied old step-takers, / Hare-eyed clerks with the jitters, // Wax-fleshed out-patients', and others too 'stupid or weak' to have a job. The price of living without having to make a living is, apparently, loneliness and failure. 'Think of being them!' he intones with horror (*CP* 147). The poem's opening lyricism turns with a slight inflection into emptiness and despair:

> Watching the bread delivered,
> The sun by clouds covered,
> The children going home;
> Think of being them,
>
> Turning over their failures
> By some bed of lobelias...

The poem is, however, no conservative call to the reader to get on his or her bike. What the poet finds contemptible is not unproductive idleness, but, with shocking candour, age, madness, illness and weakness. 'Think of being them' he repeats, this time more pensively, without an exclamation mark, aware that he himself could well share their plight. He can console himself with his nine-to-five job for the time being. But this is not, with prose logic, because he is making himself useful to society and can look forward to a secure pension, but more simply and poetically, because he still has time, and being is good. The euphoric epiphany with which the poem concludes blends wry resignation with a zestful joy in simply being alive. Shadowed by mortality, boring ordinary life becomes very precious:

> No, give me my in-tray,
> My loaf-haired secretary,
> My shall-I-keep-the-call-in-Sir:
> What else can I answer,
>
> When the lights come on at four
> At the end of another year?
> Give me your arm, old toad;
> Help me down Cemetery Road.

His profession is, after all, a kind of living, as well as a hated means of making a living.

There is one poem in Larkin's *oeuvre* in which he does deal specifically with poetry as a means of making a financial living. 'Posterity' presents us with a character who is succeeding in making a living out of the poet's own poetry. With wicked irony, however, this is not the poet himself, but an academic: 'Jake Balokowsky, my biographer'. If anything, Jake is more uncomfortable with his work than the narrator of the 'Toads' poems: 'I'm stuck with this old fart at least a year':

> 'I wanted to teach school in Tel Aviv,
> But Myra's folks' – he makes the money sign –
> 'Insisted I got tenure. When there's kids –'
> He shrugs. 'It's stinking dead, the research line;
> Just let me put this bastard on the skids,
> I'll get a couple of semesters leave
>
> To work on Protest Theater.'

Robert Crawford sees Jake as a satirized representative of the academic racket:

> Though there may be self-loathing in 'Posterity', more apparent is the poet's detestation of a particularly American-accented academic mill, against which, in one sense, his poetry is aimed; yet in another way, Larkin knows that his work is also aligned with the system in which pages are microfilmed and students learn 'crummy textbook stuff from Freshman Psych'.[42]

But this drastically simplifies the poem's irony. Only on the most superficial level is this an English poet's defence of his work against an American 'academic mill'. As far as Jake is concerned the poet is indeed aligned with 'the system'; he needs to complete the biography in order to gain tenure. But Jake is no champion of this system; he is its victim. His plight is similar to that of the poet himself, both being fouled up by the gulf between their dreams and hard reality. The poet does not satirize Balokowsky from a superior position. Like the speaker of 'Toads', Jake too labours grudgingly at his uncongenial work for the sake of money and security. Perhaps, once he has secured his living by gaining tenure, he will earn himself the chance to live, finding fulfilment in Protest Theater or in teaching school. Perhaps this, also, is such stuff as dreams are made on, and Myra's folks or the kids will keep him still tied down.

As Yeats says, said poetry is made out of the quarrel with ourselves, and, different though he seems, Jake is the poet's intimate alter ego. His description of his subject conveys the poet's own self-judgement:

> Not out of kicks or something happening –
> One of those old-type *natural* fouled-up guys.

The poet is not at all sure that he knows better than Jake. This is no satire, but a poem of playful self-irony. Jake's boring job is to write the biography of the author of 'Toads'. With delightful wit the poet's life becomes Balokowsky's living. The toad with whom Jake is walking down Cemetery Road is Larkin.

Money

Jake's 'tenure', his 'hold' (Latin *tenere*) on living, depends on the dollar. We have to make money in order to live. We do not, however, live by making money and anyone who lives only to make money should get him or herself 'a life' instead. It is money which reduces the poetry of living to the prose of making a living. The wage-slave Arnold in 'Self's the Man' gets his money 'for wasting his life on work'. Wordsworth put the same thought in a more elevated idiom: 'Getting and spending, we lay waste our powers'.[43]

Robert Graves expresses the common view that money is poetry's opposite. 'If there's no money in poetry neither is there poetry in money.'[44] Poetry is, by implication, the more valuable of the two and the poet should treat money with the contempt it deserves. The poet follows St Paul: *Radix malorum est cupiditas*, 'the love of money is the root of evil'. Like Karl Marx, poets are alert to the distinction between life as an end in itself, and life abstracted to a medium of exchange: the inhuman resource of money. Money may be necessary, but only those sad people who have no real life to speak of live in terms of money. As Schopenhauer put it: '*Money* is human happiness *in abstracto*, consequently he who is no longer capable of happiness *in concreto* sets his whole heart on money.'[45] It is clear, surely, where Larkin, the poet of 'living', must stand on this issue.

But this is too easy. Moralists and sentimentalists may reduce money solely to its nasty literal component. But money, crudely literal, yet also the locked promise of so much potential living, is a metaphor, with both real and imagined dimensions. Indeed, as a medium of exchange with no use value, money is the most natural of all metaphors. Its embodiment of happiness in the abstract is the very stuff of the poetic dream. Against Robert Graves's 'neither is there poetry in money' we may set Wallace Stevens's: 'Money is a kind of poetry.'[46] And Larkin's poem 'Money' is on the side of Stevens's lyric insight rather than Graves's moralism.

Money, personified in the poet's quarterly bank or dividend statements, 'reproaches' him:

> 'Why do you let me lie here wastefully?
> I am all you never had of goods and sex.
> You could get them still by writing a few cheques.'

You are making a living, money tells him; so why are you not living? But the poet cannot understand how to construct concrete happiness out of the abstract happiness of his money. He looks at what other people do:

> They certainly don't keep it upstairs.
> By now they've a second house and car and wife:
> Clearly money has something to do with life.

In common speech life and money are so metaphorically interchange-able that the *faux naïf* last line here sounds tautologous. Of course money has something to do with life. We make our living by making money. We 'spend' our lives, just as we 'spend' our money. We 'mort-gage' our futures to a bank or to a political ideal. 'Substance' is both bio-logical matter and metaphorical wealth; clearly the speaker of this poem is a 'man of substance'. But the poet is still comically stumped by the puzzle of the connection between the two.

Is this perhaps simply the result of his age? Larkin had turned fifty a few months before he wrote the poem. Money, perhaps, cannot give him the only things really worth having: youth, health and the fresh idealism that goes with them. 'You can't put off being young until you retire', he declares, turning flat prose, with breathtaking virtuosity, into echoing pentameter. But this is not simply a poem about ageing. Larkin's images of 'life': 'sex', 'the car', 'the wife', have a dismissiveness which he had felt even in his youth. As he wrote in an early letter: 'My great trouble, as usual, is that I lack desires. Life is to know what you want, & to get it. But I don't feel I desire anything' (*SL* 152). The reduc-tive sterility of the phrase 'goods and sex' is not simply the product of sour grapes. He has never really needed more 'goods', while 'sex' bought with a few 'cheques' would sound farcically inadequate at any age.

The poet is fascinated by money, not with the banal obsessiveness of the miser who loves it, nor with the censure of the moralist who spurns it, and certainly not with the ambitions of *l'homme moyen sensuel* in quest of goods, sex, house, car and wife. Money inspires him, as a poet, with metaphorical awe. For him, money really is 'a kind of poetry':

> I listen to money singing. It's like looking down
>   From long french windows at a provincial town,
> The slums, the canal, the churches ornate and mad
>   In the evening sun. It is intensely sad.

In 'Toads Revisited' the poet succeeded, against the grain, in lyricizing his profession. Here, in this more profound poem, money 'sings' of its own accord, and its lyrical song is an elegy for living: 'It is intensely sad'. James Fenton's description of the finale of this work as a 'beau-tiful stunt' is accurate, but there is perhaps a real philosophical logic to it.[47] Though this image of the human plight has the surreal quality of a painting by Magritte, its allegory can be spelled out in quite pro-saic terms. Money, like the alleys, canals and churches of a provincial town, is a machine for living in. But, however much we daily elide the two, however clear it is that money has something to do with life, the literal and figurative parts of the metaphor refuse quite to hold together. Money is not itself life, nor can its sad song tell us anything about living. So Larkin's beautiful but empty townscape is a very precise image of what exactly it is that money, and poetry, have to do with life: everything, and nothing.

3
Loves and Muses I

Life into art

Poetry, T. S. Eliot asserts, is 'not the expression of personality but an escape from personality.'[1] Wallace Stevens concurs: 'Poetry is not personal.'[2] In a different tone, but to similar effect, D. H. Lawrence urges 'Never trust the artist. Trust the tale.'[3] Virginia Woolf asserts that Shakespeare achieved greatness by getting his work 'expressed completely':

> We are not held up by some 'revelation' which reminds us of the writer. All desire to protest, to preach, to proclaim an injury, to pay off a score, to make the world the witness of some hardship or grievance was fired out of him and consumed.[4]

Literature is a matter of texts, not authors. 'The death of the poet', Auden tells us in his celebrated elegy, 'was kept from his poems', and Yeats 'became his admirers'.[5] With elegant Gallic hyperbole Roland Barthes takes demystification to its furthest point. The author's plight, he believes, is precisely to have no plight, no unique 'manner of being': 'it is language which speaks, not the author; to write is... to reach that point where only language acts, "performs", and not "me".'[6] The author is textually dead even as he or she writes.

All these assertions of impersonality are, of course, ambiguous. Eliot, for instance, slyly reasserts the traditional romantic plight by adding: 'But, of course, only those who have personality and emotions know what it means to want to escape from these things.'[7] D. H. Lawrence's fiction can be close to raw autobiography; he insisted that his readers would be 'in the thick of the scrimmage', and advised those who wanted 'a safe seat in the audience' to read someone else.[8] Similarly,

47

though Woolf's depiction of Mrs Ramsay in *To the Lighthouse* is artistically dispassionate, the work was also an act of private therapy. Only when she had completed the novel did her dead mother stop haunting her dreams. Auden's elegy observes how political events in mad Ireland 'hurt' Yeats into poetry.[9] Having declared the death of the author, the author Roland Barthes continued to collect royalties on his original and distinctive books, until a road accident gave his famous *reductio* an entirely personal significance.

Larkin shows a similar contradiction. He insisted on the autonomy of each poem's 'sole freshly created universe' (*RW* 79), but he also acknowledged that his poetry was 'nothing if not personal',[10] and held that 'The poet's task is to move our feelings by showing his own' (*FR* 30). At times he could make the most ingenuous connections between life and art: 'I should feel it false to write a poem going overboard about someone if you weren't at the same time marrying them and setting up house with them' (*FR* 23). At other times he maintained that art and life were quite separate: 'I don't really equate poems with real-life as most people do' (*SL* 366). In technical terms the focus of this ambiguity is the lyric poet's flexible 'I', which the prose writer Julian Barnes so envies: 'when I say "I" you will want to know within a paragraph or two whether I mean Julian Barnes or someone invented; a poet can shimmy between the two, getting credit for both deep feeling and objectivity'.[11] The dramatized, fictionalized 'I' of the poet lays claim to 'objectivity', rising free from the muddle of his or her personal plight. But, equally, the intensity of lyric poetry comes from its 'deep feeling', with the implication of personal experience.

I. A. Richards, in his early New Critical classic, *Practical Criticism*, attempted to ensure impersonal textuality by giving his students poems to analyse without author's names or dates. However, readers remain, quite properly, interested in contexts. We find it illuminating to know who wrote a particular poem, how it relates to his or her other works, whether it is early or late, whether it shows the influence of any other writer. We might feel that such an interest in the narrative of the *oeuvre* is a purely literary and aesthetic matter. But it is difficult, in practice, to draw a line between purely literary intertext and impure biographical context. We puzzle over what 'real life' event lies behind the change of tone from one poem to the next. We want to know more about the particular people to whom poems are addressed.

Some poems, indeed, are inextricable from the poet's biographical situation. Robert Lowell's 'Memories of West Street and Lepke', for instance, will mean very little to the reader until it is explained that

Lowell was imprisoned as a conscientious objector in West Street Gaol, where the murderer Lepke was on death row. In this case the text requires contextual placing before it can be properly apprehended. Writers frequently demand biographical reading, living in such a way as to feed their art, or even writing the scripts of their lives before living them. Yeats occupied, and wrote about, a tower from which he surveyed the tides of Irish history. Sylvia Plath's suicide, in Larkin's view, fulfilled the self-destructive myth with which her poetry had experimented. Larkin himself projected a self-conscious artistic myth to mediate between his personal experience and his impersonal art, depicting himself as the bachelor hermit of Hull who finds essential beauty in advertisement-hoardings and profundity on the railway.

One aim of these two chapters on Larkin's poetry of intimacy, therefore, is to contextualize particular poems within the relationships which generated them. His refusal of marriage left him free to relate to different women in various, inconsistent poetic voices, and his poems of intimacy enact a number of very diverse relationships. The story they tell, however, is a poetic one. The personal plight of the man supplies the raw materials for his impersonal art; it cannot 'explain' that art. Sometimes, as we shall see, the demands of art contradict the biographical context, or detach a poem entirely from its 'real life' occasion. My aim in these chapters, therefore, is not to illustrate Larkin's love life through his poems, even less to explain his poetry in terms of biography. Biographical contexts are of relevance; but poetry belongs exclusively to texts. To that extent Barthes is right. The poet, in so far as he is a poet, 'lives' only in his poems. The personal plight of the man coping with his emotions must be translated into the impersonal plight of the artist coping with his medium of words.

Larkin's rhetoric of intimacy covers a wide spectrum from Hardyesque realism to Yeatsian archetype. In Hardy's poems women appear as real people: his dead sister, her young arm awave in the apple-tree whose branch is now burning in his hearth, Lizbie Brown glimpsed and missed years before, his early love Tryphena, and his first wife, Emma, the 'woman much missed' of the great elegies of 1912–13. Larkin achieves a similar impression of specific real human relationships. On the face of it his is a literal world of social realism, of mothers, wives, lovers, friends, entanglements. But Larkin's world is mediated, in a way unknown to Hardy, through what Roland Barthes would call 'modern mythologies'.[12] His is a world of familiar clichés: loaf-haired secretaries, 'bosomy English roses' and 'friends in specs', 'your mum and dad', 'my darling' and 'a couple of kids'.[13] This world may seem far from the archetypes projected by Decadent and Modernist poets: Yeats' Helen of Troy and Crazy Jane, Eliot's hyacinth girl, Lady of Silences, and Thames maidens. However, Larkin is not as far from the romantic-decadent mode as he might at first appear. Ancient and modern myths, archetype and stereotype, are not as far apart as they may seem. A mere change of tone may convert realism into symbolism. In poems such as 'Love Songs in Age', 'Lines on a Young Lady's Photograph Album', 'Talking in Bed', and 'The Large Cool Store', Larkin could be said to blur stereotype and archetype. Moreover, his work, as we shall see, has its own original versions of the Romantic types of virginal muse and threatening *femme fatale*.

The seven women with whom Larkin shared an intimacy inspired very different poems. The number of poems is small, but once they are separated out, each group can be seen to distil a particular relationship, with its own verbal texture and its own development through time: sometimes brief, sometimes decades-long. For convenience and at the risk of reduction, I have characterized each relationship in terms of the social-realist type which the poems depict, or which they transcend or transfigure. Thus the poet's sad, exasperating mother appears as 'your mum', who fucks you up.[14] His relationship with Ruth Bowman is a broken engagement ('Parting, after about five / Rehearsals').[15] Winifred Arnott is addressed in the language of flirtation ('From every side you strike at my control').[16] 'Whatever Happened?' records an erotic affair with Patsy Strang. The poems related to Monica Jones give a miniature epitome of an unorthodox marriage, or what would now be called a 'long-term partnership' ('the homeliness / Of den, and hole, and set').[17] The relationship with Maeve Brennan is a prolonged courtship ('[I'm falling in] "Love Again"'). And the affair with his secretary, Betty Mackereth, is a late fling ('We met at the end of the party').

'Your mum'

'Mother, Summer, I', completed in August 1953, about the time of Larkin's thirty-first birthday, is close to direct autobiography. In two plain, indicative stanzas the young poet describes how his mother, 'who hates thunderstorms', only loses her 'worried summer look' with the onset of rain and frost. He, her son, 'though summer-born / And summer-loving', is also easier 'when the leaves are gone'. He cannot confront the 'Emblems of perfect happiness' of summer days. Like her, he awaits: 'A time less bold, less rich, less clear: / An autumn more appropriate.' It is a moody, self-involved poem. Though addressed by a son to his mother it shows no explicit affection; its tone is cold and detached, with a touch of resentment. Nevertheless, it is an expression of extreme intimacy, even identity. The poet accepts that his temperament is like his mother's. Though the son is in the summer of his life, he joins her in spirit in the autumn of hers, before his time.

'Mother, Summer, I' achieves its objectivity by a strict reduction of elements. A single image of the seasons is wittily deployed with a hint at the elegiac theme of time. 'Reference Back', completed two years later in 1955, and once again prompted by Larkin's August birthday, enlarges this snapshot. It opens more ambitiously with a dramatized scene, enacting the resentment of the earlier poem with greater immediacy:

> *That was a pretty one,* I heard you call
> From the unsatisfactory hall
> To the unsatisfactory room where I
> Played record after record, idly,
> Wasting my time at home, that you
> Looked so much forward to.

The transferred epithets sulkily blame the hall and room for the poet's own sense of unsatisfactoriness. But pulling against this selfishness is a sad sympathy for the mother. The son feels guilty for shunning her, thereby compelling her to force this clumsy contact through a misconceived praise for his jazz. The form is also more artistically complex, the two regularly-rhymed eight-line stanzas of the earlier poem being replaced by a more original structure of unequal sections, using full and half-rhyme in uneven couplets to convey the speaker's restless mood. In the second couplet, for instance, the rhyme with 'I' is satisfied prematurely by the first syllable of 'idly', acting out the son's idleness by leaving the second syllable trailing. Then the following couplet dramatizes the mother's disappointment by faltering from the stressed 'you' to the unstressed 'to', and from tetrameter to trimeter.

The son reflects that every time he hears the music in future he will remember how Oliver's *Riverside Blues* 'made this sudden bridge / From your unsatisfactory age / To my unsatisfactory prime.' The parallel repetition of 'unsatisfactory' repeats the same repetition as in the first section with surly but also rueful over-insistence, while the unsatisfactoriness of the communication between mother and son is underscored by the failed rhyme 'bridge/age'. His initial impulse to blame her for spoiling his music for him is lost as the distances in space between hall and bedroom, mother and son, open into the awesome distances in time between her age, his prime, and the recorded notes played by 'those antique negroes' the year after he was born. As space fades into time the poem modulates into an abstract, philosophical register, and, like the opening of an organ stop or an expected *tutti* from the orchestra, the line lengthens to spacious pentameter:

> Truly, though our element is time,
> We are not suited to the long perspectives
> Open at each instant of our lives.
> They link us to our losses: worse,
> They show us what we have as it once was,
> Blindingly undiminished, just as though
> By acting differently we could have kept it so.

The grating, isolated final word of an abrupt tetrameter, 'worse', is clashed subtly with 'was' at the end of the following, longer pentameter line. The penultimate line is introduced by a reversed foot in a sudden emotional fulsomeness:

> /   x | x / |
> Blindingly un...

The perfect rhymes of the final couplet ('though/so') create a quietly ironic singsong, complicated by the lengthening of the second line from pentameter to plangent alexandrine. This complex orchestration of emotion transforms an adolescent gripe against an unsatisfactory mother who thinks that *Riverside Blues* is 'pretty' into a moving meditation on youth and age. The poem has opened with 'I' and 'you', but ends with an unlocalized 'we' which encompasses not only the poet and his mother, but also the reader.

The biographical context of 'Mother, Summer, I' and 'Reference Back' is Larkin's dysfunctional family. Larkin's father's secretary reports that Eva Larkin was 'a pleasant, unobtrusive person'. Her husband, however, was 'very much the male chauvinist. He thought that women were of little account, their only functions to be decorative and to wait on men' (Motion 11). The poet's response to his parents was ambivalent. On the one hand he inherited his father's masculine impatience with women, and his mother's maunderings confirmed his life-long fear of marriage:

> I suppose her age had something to do with it, but the monotonous whining monologue she treated my father to before breakfast, and all of us at mealtimes, resentful, self-pitying, full of funk and suspicion,

must have remained in my mind as something I mustn't *under any circumstances* risk encountering again. Once she sprang up from the table announcing her intention to commit suicide.

(Motion 14)

On the other hand he inherited his mother's passive helplessness before life's demands. Ten years before writing 'Mother, Summer, I' the twenty-year old poet had described looking into a mirror and detecting both his parents' features in his own: 'I realized that I contain both of them... It intrigues me to know that a thirty-years struggle is being continued in me, and in my sister too. In her it has reached a sort of conclusion – my father winning. Pray the Lord my mother is superior in me.'[18] His response was to identify himself with his mother.

Following his father's death in 1948 Larkin bought a house for Eva in Leicester, and spent the next two years living with her in a state of exasperated repression. Not until October 1950 did he escape to his new post as Assistant Librarian in Belfast. This escape resolved the crises in both his personal and his poetic career. For the first time he was free to live and write as he wished. However, he remained loyal to his mother, visiting her once a month all his life, once a fortnight in her final years, writing her thousands of trivial, reassuring letters, and having childish rows with her for which he later abjectly apologized: '*Please* forgive me. You do everything to make my visits enjoyable and then I have to go and upset everything' (Motion 258). A fundamental element in Larkin's personality was a desire not to hurt those who were emotionally dependent upon him: 'she's my mother after all, and it's my duty, yes ma dooty, to look after her if she can't look after herself... I suppose she arouses in me strong alarm and hostility because she makes me feel guilty for not looking after her' (Motion 384).

The third poem in this 1950s series, 'Love Songs in Age', nicely illustrates the transformation of personal plight into impersonal art. It was begun in July 1953 at the same time as he was writing 'Mother, Summer, I', though not completed until three and a half years later (Motion 230). Clearly his mother figured in the poem's inception. Motion indicates that its completion was also prompted by his mother, citing a letter of January 1957 in which Larkin describes his Christmas visit to Leicester and goes on to reflect more generally on marriage (Motion 279). It is intriguing then, that on the 'Listen' recording of *The Whitsun Weddings* the poet flatly denies any personal inspiration:

Every so often one does write a poem that has no personal basis in one's own experience at all, and I can't imagine what led me to write a poem about Victorian or Edwardian love songs. I can't even remember wanting to write it or completing it. However here it is.[19]

The poet would seem to have little reason to suppress any personal motive here. His comment is, moreover, true to the poem's tone, which moves beyond the personal context of 'mother' and 'I' to a dispassionate third person and an anonymous personification of widowhood. At some point in the poem's long development the personal inspiration was left behind and its subject became impersonal. Though it belongs poetically to the same sequence as 'Mother, Summer, I' and 'Reference Back', this is a much more 'objective' poem.

The speaker is no longer a participant in the text, indeed he is virtually effaced; for all the text tells us the narrator could be a woman. The focus is entirely on the widow's thoughts: 'She kept her songs, they took so little space, / The covers pleased her...'. The long perspectives of her life are casually inscribed on the sheet-music: one song being bleached by the sun, one marked by a vase, another mended 'when a tidy fit had seized her'. The phrase 'tidy fit' seems to imply youthfulness, but 'coloured by her daughter' leaps across the decades to her maturity. The years have passed, and the songs have 'waited' for the moment when she finds them, just as the poem has waited until now to describe the part the music originally played in her life:

> ... the unfailing sense of being young
> Spread out like a spring-woken tree, wherein
> That hidden freshness sung,
> That certainty of time laid up in store
> As when she played them first.

The theme of time, which gave 'Reference Back' its climax, is now complicated by the additional theme of romantic love, absent in the earlier poems. The stanzaic form and rhyme-scheme are more conventional than those of 'Reference Back', but the emotional progression is more refined, taking the reader through three, rather than two stages: the first plainly descriptive; the second evoking the woman's past life, and the third acknowledging the failure of love's promise to 'solve, and satisfy, / And set unchangeably in order.'

The poem's sole freshly created universe is achieved, in technical terms, largely through variations on the single device of anacrusis: in classical metrics 'a syllable at the beginning of a verse before the just rhythm' (*OED*), analogous to an *appogiatura* or up-beat in music. Thus the poem changes emotional gear at the end of the first stanza with the anticipatory pause after 'and stood...', imitating the woman's sudden arrested surprise, and giving the second stanza the feel of a startled rush of emotion.

> ... and stood

> Relearning how each frank submissive chord...

But then the second stanza continues to take breath with further end-of-line anacruses: 'ushered in / Word after sprawling hyphenated word'; 'wherein / That hidden freshness sung'; 'even more, // The glare of that much-mentioned brilliance, love'. With each anticipatory intake of breath the emotional shock of the sudden long perspective is renewed with a fresh wave of emotion. The final anacrusis sinks to a quiet mono-syllabic sigh ('So'):

> So
> To pile them back, to cry
> Was hard, without lamely admitting how
> It had not done so then, and could not now.

It is an exquisite effect, achieved with the simplest of means. By the end of the poem the ear has come to expect the repeated anacruses, so that even the slight pause after 'how' at the end of the penultimate line seems to echo the earlier anticipations. But by now what is ushered in is merely, with sad predictability, the expected concluding couplet rhyme.

In 'Mother, Summer, I' the poet asserted his identity with his mother; in 'Reference Back' he moved from sulky resistance to final empathy. Here without the intervention of any identifiable mediating voice the reader is drawn into the drama of the widow's feelings. Intimacy is not asserted, as it was in 'Mother, Summer, I'; it is enacted by the poem's rhetoric. Paradoxically, the exclusion of the poet's 'I', and the move from a specific mother and jazz-loving son to a generic widow and Victorian and Edwardian songs, gives an even greater sense of the poet showing his own feelings. Though a more impersonal poem than its predecessors, it is charged with a felt emotion beyond theirs.

This paradoxical sequence of increasingly intimate yet also increasingly objective poems seems to have produced a poetic, and perhaps also a psychological catharsis. After 'Love Songs in Age' the poet no longer draws so explicitly on his mother for his subject matter. Her presence can be detected, however, in the meditations on love, marriage and transience of such middle and late works as 'The Whitsun Weddings' (1958), 'Home is so Sad' (1958) and 'To the Sea' (1969). In 'This Be The Verse' (1970) Larkin generalizes his dysfunctional family into a reductive aphorism: 'They fuck you up, your mum and dad.' In the 1970s his mother's growing senility colours his obsession with death in such poems as 'The Building' (1972), and 'The Old Fools' (1973), while her death in 1977 provides the impetus for the completion of 'Aubade'.

One poem, however, 'Heads in the Women's Ward', bears the impress of a more specific occasion. In January 1972 Eva Larkin fell and broke her leg, and Philip and his sister arranged for her to move into a nursing home where she spent the remaining five years of her life. Like 'Love Songs in Age', 'Heads in the Women's Ward', written in March 1972, excludes explicit personal reference. The rows of senile heads, with staring eyes, open jaws, and bearded mouths are described dispassionately, in simple tetrameter couplets. Then, in a pared-down, starker version of 'Reference Back' the poet opens out the long perspective:

> Sixty years ago they smiled
> At lover, husband, first-born child.
>
> Smiles are for youth. For old age come
> Death's terror and delirium.

The final singsong couplet seems to come from a cruel nursery rhyme, suitable perhaps for the second childhood of an audience of sufferers from Alzheimer's Disease. Its combination of 'deep feeling' with 'objectivity' is frightening.

The broken engagement

In 'Reference Back' the son rebuffs the mother on the personal level of domestic affection, only to reunite himself with her on the impersonal level of aesthetic contemplation. She appears in 'Mother, Summer, I' as an unsatisfactory entanglement, but then, in 'Love Songs in Age', as muse, the inspiration for poetic transcendence.[20] This familiar polarity informs much of Larkin's poetry of intimacy. The pearl of poetry is secreted around the grit of domestic involvement. At one extreme there is a vivid sexual politics of resentment and guilt; at the other an identification with the woman's otherness which effaces the poet and offers glimpses of transcendence.

Larkin's earliest poetry of love in the 1940s however, shows a quite different pattern. In what appears in retrospect as a false start, he attempted a bold reconciliation of domestic entanglement with poetic muse in positive images of commitment, even marriage. In 'I see a girl dragged by the wrists', written in early 1944, the poet expresses envy of a breathlessly self-abandoned girl, laughing as she is dragged across 'a dazzling field of snow' in courtship horseplay. 'Deep Analysis', completed in April 1946 goes further and adopts a female voice:

> I am a woman lying on a leaf;
>   Leaf is silver, my flesh is golden,
> Comely at all points...
>
> Why would you never relax, except for sleep,
>   Face turned at the wall...
>
> Your body sharpened against me, vigilant,
>   Watchful, when all I meant
> Was to make it bright, that it might stand
>   Burnished before my tent?

Female nagging is elevated into a moving plea by biblical and Lawrentian imagery, with touches of Yeats: 'comely', 'your straight sides', 'burnished', 'assuaged', 'only your grief under my mouth'. Such an abject feminine plea is remarkable in a poem written by a young man of twenty-three.

The biographical context to this poem is Larkin's relationship with Ruth Bowman, whom he met shortly after taking up the post of librarian in Wellington, Shropshire, in 1943. He was just twenty-one; she was a sixteen-year old schoolgirl. Over the following seven years he earnestly discussed the depth of his love for her in letters to his Lawrentian friend, James Sutton, while deriding her as 'the schoolcaptain' in letters to the sceptical Kingsley Amis. The relationship survived his move to Leicester in 1946 when he became Assistant Librarian at the University College there, and later her move to London for her teacher training. Then, in the traumatic weeks following the death of his father in Spring

1948, they became engaged. The tone in which he related this to his friend Sutton is awkward with apprehension:

> To tell you the truth I have done something rather odd myself – got engaged to Ruth on Monday… we have gone on seeing each other until the point seemed to arrive when we either had to start taking it seriously or else drop it. I can't say I welcome the thought of marriage…
>
> (*SL* 147)

After a further two and a half years of indecisions the engagement was finally broken off when Larkin left for his new post as Assistant Librarian at Queen's University, Belfast.

'Deep Analysis', written when Larkin had known Ruth Bowman just over two years, begins the long sequence of poems which constitute his 'marriage debate'. Though the poem reads perfectly well without biographical placing, its empathetic identification with the woman can be seen, contextually, as the young poet's attempt to persuade himself into marriage. Five months later, in 'Wedding-Wind', an *aubade*, or song greeting the dawn, he ventured further. The poet effaces himself, and the poem celebrates the woman's joyful submission to the flux of nature: wind, flood, night, day, clouds and storm. She has lain overwhelmed by happiness through her wind-blown wedding night, while her husband attended to the frightened horses. Now day has come, and her man, an archetypal 'He', is away looking at the floods, while she carries a chipped pail to the chicken run, her apron 'thrashed' by the wind:

> Can it be borne, this bodying-forth by wind
> Of joy my actions turn on, like a thread
> Carrying beads? Shall I be let to sleep
> Now this perpetual morning shares my bed?

'Wedding-Wind' was completed on 26 September 1946, and its poetic self-persuasion worked all too well. Within days of completing the poem his relations with a real potential wife abruptly dispelled this romantic euphoria. Philip received a letter from Ruth suggesting that she might be pregnant (Motion 153).

The poetic result, 'At the chiming of light upon sleep', written eight days after 'Wedding Wind', on 4 October 1946, is another *aubade*, but one which dreads rather than welcomes perpetual morning. It is an overwrought symbolist meditation on Eros and Thanatos in which the selfish masculine 'I' is to the fore. The poet emerges into consciousness at first light, dreaming of 'a green world' of:

> Unchanging holly with the curled
> Points, cypress and conifers,
> All that through the winter bears
> Coarsened fertility against the frost.

His dream provides a sanctuary of wintry repression with 'no flowers'. But now the daylight thaw provokes procreative desire, and trapped in the cycle of nature he sees that the ecstasies of sex are merely a manifestation of the death instinct:

> flowers are generation,
> And the founding, foundering, beast-instructed mansion
> Of love called into being by this same death
> Hangs everywhere its light.

From blossom comes fruit, and from fruit, decay and death. The young poet resorts to garish biblical imagery to express his terror at this threat to his self-contained selfhood:

> Unsheath
> The life you carry and die, cries the cock
> On the crest of the sun: unlock
> The words and seeds that drove
> Adam out of his undeciduous grove.

The speaker's life, his words, his seeds are only temporarily his until Nature orders him to procreate and die. In unsheathing his life in unprotected sex he commits the original sin, and his wages are death.

This archetypal opposition, between a benign unsexual world of stasis and control (which may be male or female) and a malign world of procreative flux and decay, underlies, in various forms, much of Larkin's early and middle work. It is the pattern of all his early fiction. In the 'lesbian' Brunette Coleman stories of 1943 men are excluded in a closed, idyllic world of femininity. In *Jill* Kemp's aesthetic dream of schoolgirl innocence is shattered when he comes into physical contact with the real-life Gillian. *A Girl in Winter* reverses the gender roles but with an even more emphatically sterile outcome, as sex with Robin freezes Katherine's summer dream into an icy vision of winter. Larkin's inability to complete his next two novels, *No For An Answer* and *A New World Symphony*, seems to result from his determination to reject the unrealistic poetic dreams of his early protagonists, and instead to engage with life in a prose of hard realism. And this new artistic realism was matched on the personal level by his engagement to Ruth, now seen in more realistic terms than those of 'Wedding-Wind'. Larkin's repeated draftings of the 'seduction fiasco' between Sam and Sheila in *No For An Answer* show the imaginative problems of this failed attempt at maturity.

The opposed male and female *aubades* of 'Wedding-Wind' and 'At the chiming of light upon sleep' offer a fascinating artistic contrast. Both deal in archetype, and both adopt an artificial, literary tone. The poet's fictional dream of womanhood in 'Wedding-Wind', however, is more poetically successful than the urgent tangle of first-hand emotions with which the poet wrestles in the later poem. 'Wedding-Wind' achieves a unified (if strained) tone of exaltation by effacing the male author. 'At the chiming of light upon sleep', in contrast, demands extra-textual explanation. Its blurred welter of archetypal images and psychoanalytical hints betrays subjective emotions not fully under the writer's control. Because of its impersonal artifice, 'Wedding-Wind' succeeds where the personal confession of 'At the chiming of light upon sleep' fails. The events of Larkin's life, however, had closed off the poetic route indicated by 'Wedding-Wind'. The poetic way forward must lie, for better or worse, through 'At the chiming of light upon sleep'.

Already, months before writing these poems, in April 1946, Larkin had drawn their poetic lesson. In a letter to Sutton he admitted a strengthening suspicion

> that in my character there is an antipathy between 'art' and 'life'. I find that once I 'give in' to another person, as I have given in not altogether voluntarily, but almost completely, to Ruth, there is a slackening and dulling of the peculiar artistic fibres that makes it impossible to achieve that mental 'clenching' that crystallizes a pattern and keeps it still while you draw it... this letting-in of a second person spells death to perception and the desire to express, as well as the ability.
>
> (*SL* 116)

'Waiting for breakfast, while she brushed her hair', written in December 1947, formulates this dialectic for the first time in his work in terms of the traditional poet's plight, torn between ideal muse and real woman. Significantly the muse is drained of the usual female human attributes, and imaged as a 'tender visiting, / Fallow as a deer or an unforced field'. Equally importantly the call to aesthetic disengagement is not seen, as in 'Deep Analysis' and 'At the chiming of light upon sleep' in terms of a hard masculine 'clenching', but as a delicate, unsexual openness to the beauty of the world. The poet gazes at the 'undisturbed excitement' beyond the window, as

> [t]he colourless vial of day painlessly spilled
> My world back after a year, my lost lost world
> Like a cropping deer strayed near my path again...

The muse is 'jealous' of the woman brushing her hair, and will refuse to return until the poet has 'sent / Her terribly away'. This poem gives the young Larkin's version of the plight of the Decadent artist, caught, like Oscar Wilde or Thomas Mann, between life in society and anti-social art. Its rejection of domestic commitment marks an important step in the development of Larkin's poetic personality, and he signalled its importance in his *oeuvre* by adding it to the reissue of *The North Ship* of 1966, even though it post-dates all the other poems in that volume.

To marry would be to sacrifice 'art' to 'life', and destroy his very ability to write:

> Time & time again I feel that before I write anything else at all I must drag myself out of the water, shake myself dry and sit down on a lonely rock to contemplate glittering loneliness. Marriage, of course (since you mentioned marriage), is impossible if one wants to do this.
>
> (*SL* 116)

He put it to Ruth in the simplest terms: 'How will I be able to write when I have to be thinking about you?' (Motion 180). A woman might be his muse, his poetic inspiration, but only, as in 'Wedding-Wind' and *A Girl in Winter*, as an object of contemplation. His muse could not be his wife.

Larkin does not, however, always see his anti-social impulses in high-flown aesthetic and philosophical terms. In his letters to Sutton he frequently depicts the problem simply as one of 'selfishness', under-mining his Lawrentian commitment to 'life'. After announcing his engagement in May 1948 he writes: 'I suspect all my isolationist feelings as positively harmful and certainly rather despicable. "Are you a bloody valuable vase, man, to be kept so carefully?"' He describes his engagement as 'a sincere chance of "opening out" towards someone I do love a lot in a rather strangled way' (*SL* 147). Against this is pitted his unhappy experience of marriage: 'let me remember that the only married state I intimately know (i.e. that of my parents) is bloody hell. Never must it be forgotten' (Motion 151). As he put it later, in 'Love': 'My life is for me.' His marriage-debate poems of 1946–64 divide between those, like 'Reasons for Attendance' and 'Latest Face', in which the rejection of marriage is seen as his artistic duty, and those, like 'Love', 'Self's the Man' and 'Wild Oats', in which it seems merely 'selfish'.

As his relationship with Ruth neared its end this questioning of his motives threw the poet into the crisis fictionalized in 'Deceptions' (1950), which describes a man's attempt to free himself from the conventions of 'bridal London' by means of rape. This poem signals Larkin's move away from the romantic imagery of the 1940s and towards a new imagery of social realism. However it is still a very 'literary' work. One hidden intertext is indicated by the poem's original title, 'The Less Deceived' (later transferred to the entire volume). We need Larkin's extra-textual explanation to tell us that this is derived from a scene in *Hamlet*. The prince tells Ophelia 'I loved you not', and she replies 'I was the more deceived.'[21] The title is a dry private allusion. Philip's and Ruth's relationship in 1948–50 had been plagued, like that of Hamlet and Ophelia, by the ghost of his father, leading him to torment her to distraction. The poem, as it were, takes up the argument, apologetically, on Hamlet's behalf.

The second, more explicit allusion, however, evokes a more provocative parallel, from sociology rather than high art, dramatizing the story of a London prostitute recorded in *London Labour and the London Poor* by Henry Mayhew. This historical contextualization might be expected to depersonalize the poem. Instead, however, the riddling title and the long prefatory quotation create a clutter, as though the poet were apprehensive about approaching his subject. As he offers his useless consolation to the Victorian victim across the slums and years, the impression is not one of detached elegy, but of unresolved guilt. The recollections of the ageing prostitute in Mayhew's account are reduced in the poem to one stark moment of violence, and the poet's intrusion as spectator on her isolation, 'out on that bed', gives the poem an immediacy which sounds strangely staged. The poet's clumsy attempt to lay claim to his share of her grief is disconcerting. His 'I's are insistent, even embarrassing ('I can taste the grief'; 'I would not dare /

Console you if I could'). This embarrassment, however, is not a mistake on the poet's part, but a calculated effect. He is quite aware that his apology for her rape sounds rhetorical and strained, and that the abstract argument over degrees of deception is irrelevant to the social reality of her situation:

> For you would hardly care
> That you were less deceived, out on that bed,
> Than he was, stumbling up the breathless stair
> To burst into fulfilment's desolate attic.

Significantly the final, most poetically resonant line of the poem belongs to the rapist rather than the victim. Its eloquent expression of failed transcendence confirms a scathing self-critical negativity.

If we may short-circuit between biography and art here, it seems that Larkin, determined to 'open out' to Lawrentian 'life' and reject 'clenched' masculine selfishness, has chosen an extreme metaphor, accusing himself of using Ruth's body, like a rapist. He unhappily acknowledges a sympathy with the man in the poem, who is interpreted as a misguided artist, a voluptuary in search of the ultimate sensual-aesthetic experience. By thus casting his choice of art over life as a rape, Larkin expresses shame for his behaviour, and also (perhaps) makes his boldest attempt to show that his mother is 'superior' to his father in him. Unfortunately this bold subtextual self-inculpation is all too easily read, textually, as simple masculine special-pleading. Janice Rossen comments, not unreasonably, that the poet's argument that it is 'really worse for the rapist because he is less undeceived than the girl ... seems academic and cruel', and detects a 'callousness' in the poem.[22] More crudely, Joseph Bristow argues that by throwing the weight of responsibility for the man's crime on 'desire' the poet offers 'an apology for rape'.[23] Bristow interprets the miserable self-contempt of the speaker as a subtextual desire to abuse the woman. This is wildly off target. But the hectic confusion of Larkin's miscalculated metaphor of rape does hint at an edgy bad faith on his part. If we read it biographically as an apology to Ruth, then it is an apology which is not entirely wholehearted.

'No Road', written less than a month after Larkin arrived in Belfast, moves further into unambiguous 'Movement' mode, rejecting elaborate literary layering in favour of the plainer imagery of a road-sign. In another stark difference the 'biographical' context of the poem is established, in clear view, as part of its text, rather than being buried in the subtext. Consequently precise biographical details seem irrelevant. This is a perfectly 'expressed' work of art. The poet looks back at the disused road between himself and his beloved, 'so little overgrown, / Walking that way tonight would not seem strange, / And still would be allowed.' The final truncated couplet generates a tone of miserable resignation, conjuring the subtlest psychology out of the simplest of technical devices: 'Not to prevent it is my will's fulfilment. / Willing it, my ailment.' The half-hearted singsong of 'My will's fulfilment' exactly catches the poet's mixture of stubbornness and angry self-disgust. The pentameter then slips by means of a drearily playful internal rhyme ('will's... / Willing') into a discordant trimeter, faltering to a premature conclusion on an excruciatingly 'bad' double-rhyme ('fulfilment/ ailment'). The two lines concentrate no fewer than ten high short 'i' or 'e' syllables, and seven 't' sounds, in an expression of dismissive distaste. Impersonality is achieved here not through selfless transcendence of the poet's personal plight, but through a scathing rhetoric of self-contempt.

'To My Wife', written some months later in March 1951, again adopts an image taken from commonplace demotic speech, being spoken by a husband who has preferred the single bird in the hand to the numerous tease-birds flapping in the bushes. He has surrendered the Yeatsian 'mask-and-magic-man's regalia' of poetry, and 'my wife' has become 'my boredom and my failure'. The apparent misogyny of its reference to 'your face' and 'your few properties' is countered by his glum fellow feeling with the woman: 'No future now. I and you now, alone.' But this dispirited poem has not fully worked its way free of the biographical tangle of its occasion.

The aftershocks of Larkin's broken engagement continued to reverberate through the 1950s, in declarations of masculine selfishness and derisive images of marriage, until in 1962 Larkin offered his final postscript in the form of 'Wild Oats'. Already at this time he was writing the large, generous, reflective poems of his *Whitsun Weddings* manner, but this poem deliberately preserves his *Less Deceived*, 'Movement' tone. The plight of the speaker in 'Wild Oats' is that of a typical young man of the period. There is no allusion to artistic commitment, and the broken engagement is presented in terms of the stereotypes of the seaside postcard: weedy weaklings, bosomy English roses, and their mousy friends. The tone is a brisk, masculine demotic. 'Faces in those days sparked / The whole shooting-match off'. It is the 'friend in specs I could talk to' that the speaker takes out, and, in this caricature version, he meets 'beautiful' only twice. 'She was trying / Both times (so I thought) not to laugh'. This is a calculated simplification of the facts. The bosomy rose is based on Ruth Bowman's friend Jane Exall, with whom Larkin conducted a brief correspondence after breaking off his engagement with Ruth (Motion 118).[24] Though Amis had encouraged his friend to seduce Jane in order to make Ruth jealous, Larkin held back for fear of emotional and physical complications (*SL* 136). The poem, however, does not risk such complexities, maintaining a stereo-typical pose of masculine self-deprecation.

Its tone is, however, complex. Tension grows between the surface of social comedy and the emotional reality beneath, glimpsed in the 'seven years' of the relationship, with its 'four hundred letters' and 'ten-guinea ring / I got back in the end'. In the final lines the strain between offhand comic tone and implied depth becomes painfully audible:

> Parting, after about five
> Rehearsals, was an agreement
> That I was too selfish, withdrawn,
> And easily bored to love.
> Well, useful to get that learnt.

An uneasy personal edge subverts the comedy. The speaker's phrasing ('Parting... was an agreement') shows him still resentful of the negative image of himself which he has been reluctantly forced to accept as the price of disengaging himself from the relationship: 'Well, useful to get that learnt.' His tone recalls the trapped bitterness of his letters of over a decade earlier: 'Ruth returned and demanded that we continue being friends, so that is what we are continuing being' (*SL* 153).

During the time of Larkin's relationship with Ruth Bowman, he was in the process of maturing both personally and poetically. A greater number of poems is associated with her than with any other woman in his life, and they show a wider range of styles: from the early archetyp-alism of 'Wedding-Wind', through the expressionistic distortions of 'Deceptions', to the sophisticated stereotypes of 'Wild Oats'. They ini-tiate two related themes in his work: his personal plight between selfishness and commitment, and his aesthetic plight between muse and entanglement. In the case of the next intimacy with which we are concerned, however, this tension is exhilaratingly dispelled, as Larkin encounters the first woman who appeared to him almost unambigu-ously in the light of a muse.

Flirtation

The speaker in 'To My Wife' regrets that 'for your face I have exchanged all faces'. 'Latest Face', written a month earlier, in February 1951, four months after Larkin's arrival in Belfast, shows the consequences of the opposite choice. The speaker has, in the words of 'To My Wife', 'elected nothing' and so inhabits a liminal world of 'Matchless potential'. This latest face is one of many. It exacts no obligations and so can be admired in and for itself:

> Admirer and admired embrace
> On a useless level, where
> I contain your current grace,
> You my judgement...

In the most refined and insubstantial of flirtations the pair co-operate in the aesthetic event of their unselfish, 'useless' meeting. Unlike his engagement to Ruth this relationship generates no conflict between the poet's selfishness and the woman's desires. Indeed the poet's aestheticism transcends gender. The face does not necessarily belong to a woman, and, as far as its text is concerned the poem could celebrate a homosexual or an asexual encounter. The 'Precious vagrant' which the poet addresses is not 'My Wife' or 'My Darling', but a depersonalized and objectified 'face'.

'Latest Face' is an extreme romantic paean to the passing moment, and, as in Keats's great odes, it is transience itself which confers value. The lasting attributes of life, 'Bargains, suffering, and love', are rejected in favour of 'this always-planned salute'. The husband in 'To My Wife' saw 'No future now'; the speaker in this poem looks forwards, though he confines himself resolutely to the short perspective. Incipience is all. Aware, however, that our element is time, he becomes apprehensive: 'will / The statue of your beauty walk?' he asks, in an allusion to the myth of Pygmalion. The protagonists of Larkin's two completed novels created ideal partners in their imaginations, only to be disappointed when their creations crossed the threshold into real life. This poem is similarly nagged by speculation as to what might ensue should a 'real' relationship develop. Will the poet be forced to 'wade' behind his living statue, until 'Something's found – or is not found – / Far too late for turning back.' The poet fears that an ordinary, untidy, bargained-for relationship might develop. With uncharacteristically obscure expression he envisages 'Denial of you' ducking and running out of sight to leap out 'And murder and not understand'. The wording leaves it unclear what is murdered without being understood. Is it the poet's precious freedom, destroyed by unforeseen love and commitment, or is the real woman behind the face, in an echo of 'Deceptions', destroyed by his callous aestheticism?

'Latest Face' is the first of a group of poems written in the four years between February 1951 and January 1955, in which woman as inspirational other returns to Larkin's work. The euphoric empathy of 'Wedding-Wind' is recalled, but in a provisional form and in a male voice. The biographical context for these poems is the happiness which Larkin had found in the privacy of his top-floor flat in Belfast. Though emotionally wary following his failed engagement, as a twenty-eight-year old Assistant Librarian surrounded by female staff he could scarcely avoid new liaisons. In particular he was attracted by Winifred Arnott, a twenty-one-year-old library assistant who had arrived at the Library at the same time as himself. It is Winifred's name which appears over and over again on the last page of the draft of 'Latest Face'. When, at the end of 1952, Winifred announced her engagement to be married, Philip's interest was only heightened: 'He became a whole lot more affectionate once I'd got engaged.'[25] On one level he was jealous; on another, deeper level, he felt freed from the possibility of serious entanglement. This possibility was, in any case only slight, as Winifred recollects: 'He was a working colleague, seven years older than me, already balding. I was 21. I didn't think of him like that. We were flung together in Belfast, both being English.'[26] This short-lived, unconsummated one-sided relationship offered the poet a delightful opportunity to dramatize himself in the plight of hapless servant of the muse.

All the women who feature in Larkin's poems, with the exceptions of Monica Jones and Patsy Strang, could be said to serve as his muse at some point in their relationships. This role, however, was filled pre-eminently by two women: Winifred Arnott and Maeve Brennan. In 'Waiting for Breakfast' the muse had taken a non-human, vaguely animal shape. Now, in this less fraught relationship, she could take the traditional sublimatedly erotic, human form. From Dante's Beatrice and Petrarch's Laura, to Eliot's hyacinth girl and Yeats's Maud Gonne, the literary muse is by definition out of reach, longed for, but never attained, in an arrangement sometimes deliberately devised by the poet as an artistic strategy. Larkin's relationship with Winifred Arnott was, on his side, a highly poetic affair. Thus, in 'He Hears that his Beloved has become Engaged', written two years after 'Latest Face' in January

1953, and dedicated to Winifred's fiancé ('for C. G. B.'), it is not rivalry for the beloved's hand which makes the speaker jealous. The poet is not concerned to possess her person, but to celebrate her transient youth and beauty for its own sake. Not wishing to spoil her perfection the poet sits tight while the successful suitor barges in, clumsily joining the woman in the dance, in the poet's indignant italics: *'fancying you improve her'*:

> Where's the sense
> In saying love, but meaning interference?
> You'll only *change* her. Still, I'm sure you're right.

The sulkiness of the final phrase recognizes that the engaged couple, the woman as much as the man, dwell in the world of 'real untidy air', of 'Bargains, suffering, and love'. Neither she, nor her fiancé, shares the poet's aesthetic vision.

Dante's Beatrice was a disembodied symbol of spiritual purity; Yeats's Maud Gonne was a latter-day Helen of Troy whose 'high beauty' was above the poet's reach. The woman in 'Lines on a Young Lady's Photograph Album' (1953) is apparently very different. She is a 'real girl in a real place'. This poem, with its self-parodic persona and its focus on the sentimentalities of the photograph album is frequently seen as a work of 'Movement' social realism. But, under his disguise as 'dirty young man', the speaker remains a haunted, alienated artist in the Decadent tradition. He is like Thomas Mann's Tonio Kröger, on the margin of society, looking in, entranced by the unreflecting *bourgeois* Hans and Inge. This woman is a twentieth-century muse of real life, beautiful precisely because of her perfect ordinariness. Thus photography performs a self-contradictory function in the poem. It is the agent of an empirical reality beyond the distortions of art:

> But o, photography! as no art is,
> Faithful and disappointing! that records
> Dull days as dull, and hold-it smiles as frauds,
> And will not censor blemishes...

On the other hand, for the poet these 'disappointing' frauds and blemishes of photography only enhance the beauty of reality. The religious 'grace' of the divine muse is secularized in a celebration of 'empirically true' commonplaces: 'what grace / Your candour thus confers upon her face!' The word 'candour' is carefully chosen for its etymological resonance, implying both plain-speaking and, archaically, innocence,

Its root in the Latin word for 'brilliant whiteness', is also appropriate
to the context of black-and-white photography. The poet may even,
perhaps, have the light of a flashbulb in the back of his mind.

However, as well as an ode to the muse of the more-than-art of
photography, this is also a strange kind of love poem. Ever since the
Middle Ages the Platonic idealism of the address to the muse has been
blended ambiguously with flesh-and-blood eroticism. In the cavalier
love poems of Jonson, Suckling and Marvell the lover couches his
seduction as the worship due to a pure, spiritual being. Larkin's contribution to the genre playfully bourgeoisifies the aristocratic conventions, recasting the earlier poet's sublimated erotic address to his 'lady'
as a comic flirtation with a modern 'young lady', a phrase with a quite
different resonance. The traditional pleading for the 'mistress' to pity
the plight of her despairing servant is reformulated as the admirer's plea
merely to see her photographs. His conquest is a mock-heroic one:

> At last you yielded up...

But what is yielded up is not her heart or her body but, in this modern world of advertising and commodification:

> ...the album, which,
> Once open, sent me distracted.

He possesses not the flesh-and-blood 'real girl', but a book full of simu-
lacra of her, which he ventures, with delicious suggestiveness, to 'open'.
This, indeed, seems the height of his desire; he wishes to penetrate no further. The language suggests pornography: 'My swivel eye hungers from
pose to pose'. The poet's autoerotic desires are amply satisfied by mere
images of the woman herself, and the poem lacks the aggression or slyness
which usually characterizes the seduction genre. The rape of 'Deceptions'
is reduced to the harmless, and unacted impulse to steal 'this one of you
bathing'. Despite its subject-matter this is, after all, not an erotic poem.

Significantly the disappointment of photography does not lie in its
failure to match warm-blooded reality. To the poet the photographs
seem more real than the woman herself. What excites him, paradoxically, is that the 'real girl' in the photographs no longer exists:

> Or is it just *the past*? Those flowers, that gate,
> These misty parks and motors, lacerate
> Simply by being over; you
> Contract my heart by looking out of date.

By a brilliant inversion the photographs' very empirical truth becomes an unchanging Platonic Form, which we, trapped in our element of time, can never regain. Like the images on Keats's Grecian urn the photographs freeze the fleeting moment into a timeless pastoral:

> In pigtails, clutching a reluctant cat;
> Or furred yourself, a sweet girl graduate;
> Or lifting a heavy-headed rose
> Beneath a trellis...

The photographs are the most real thing about the woman; more real than her flesh, which is already ageing. Their message of permanence, like the similar consolation of Keats's urn, 'Beauty is truth, truth beauty', cannot ultimately satisfy. They offer a cold pastoral, the more achingly beautiful for its distance: 'Smaller and clearer as the years go by'. The ageing body is, of course, more empirically true than the unageing image, but this unpoetic logic is suppressed. The pattern is that of Oscar Wilde's *Picture of Dorian Gray*, though Larkin is a purer aesthete than Wilde in not building any moral disapproval into his preference for the unageing image over the ageing reality.

In the traditional *carpe diem* poem the passing of time is an argument for action. In Larkin's anti-*carpe-diem* poem what is seized, instead, is the elegiac poignancy of the past moment. The poet does not exhort the young lady, as Thomas Herrick exhorted the 'Virgins' to 'make much of Time' and 'goe marry', nor, as Marvell exhorted his coy mistress, to 'sport us while we may'.[27] For him it is already too late. Elegy subsumes seduction. The strategic male desire for physical conquest is replaced by sympathy. The poet's only design on the woman is to meditate 'without a chance of consequence' on the growing gulf between her mortal body and the pristine 'empirical' truth of her images, now for ever 'out of date'. He joins the woman on the useless level of her past 'that no one now can share', no matter 'whose your future'. His detached but intimate fellow-feeling weirdly unites aestheticist philosophizing with sentimental pathos.

'Maiden Name' repeats the pattern of 'Lines on a Young Lady's Photograph Album'. Its attempt to welcome the marriage which so 'thankfully confused' the woman with someone else, is again overwhelmed by elegy. The closed-off youthful identity preserved in the name becomes, like the photographs, a perfect unchanging symbol of 'the past':

> since you're past and gone,
>
> It means what we feel now about you then:
> How beautiful you were, and near, and young,
> So vivid, you might still be there among
> Those first few days, unfingermarked again.

Like a work of art, or a newly-taken photograph, her 'unfingermarked' perfection is spoiled by handling. The dramatized 'I' of 'Lines on a Young Lady's Photograph Album' is replaced, in this more meditative work, by a collective 'we' of admirers. Sympathetic and intimate though his tone is, the poet's posture is still one of extreme aestheticism. The phrase 'our faithfulness' carries no moral implications, loyalty being owed only to the 'scentless, weightless, strengthless' old name. The poet insists, with a faint echo of Keats's Ode, that, despite her marriage, this name is not 'wholly / Untruthful'. He is determined to cling to the illusion that beauty is truth.

The response of the real-life muse to these poems was what one might expect. When *XX Poems* was printed in April 1951, including 'Lines on a Young Lady's Photograph Album', Larkin gave her a copy, inscribed 'For Winifred: This poem and 19 others.' But his aestheticist philosophy held no appeal for her. By the time 'Latest Face' and 'Lines on a Young Lady's Photograph Album' were published in *The Spectator* in 1954, Winifred was too busy with her wedding arrangements to be interested: 'He was a bit miffed that I didn't take much notice of them. I felt "Oh what a bore. I don't want any more of this. I've left him behind." I didn't want to think about it.'[28] She is still to this day offended at the flirtatious tone of 'Lines on a Young Lady's Photograph Album': 'I never, ever, *ever* flirted with Philip'. And she still smarts at his adjective 'sweet': 'I wasn't "sweet"'! On April Fool's Day 1954 she sent him a cool thank you, insisting that, as far as she was concerned her past was not over. On 7 April he replied, saying that he was 'glad, at long last, the two poems eventually got published and you saw them', and continued:

> I'm glad you feel more settled about your future life – frightful as marriage is, it's worse if you don't embrace it whole-heartedly. I shall put away my inconvenient emotions and wish you nothing but good.

> (*SL* 225)

Now, half a century later, after two marriages, and with three children, three stepchildren and eight grandchildren, Winifred Dawson is
even more unsympathetic to the idea that her married life has been
laden with 'depreciating luggage'. In 'Photograph Albums Revisited'
published in 2002, she gives her considered response, in verse.[29] She
takes issue with the poet's backward-looking elegy on her life, which,
after all, in 1953, was only just beginning:

> For you my past is over, but for me the future waits,
> That peacock-fan whose closing-up you feared,
> Call it dilution or increase, whatever you wish,
> Like a bud in May it will burst open
> In an explosion of diversity and colour.
> Husbands, children, stepchildren, grandchildren, friends,
> Cousins, cats, cars, canals: a cornucopia of pleasures,
> The brilliance of the world revealed in a dozen larger, newer albums.
> I have jumped in with both feet and found myself not drowning, but
> waving.

Intriguingly, however, her poem also celebrates Larkin's 'legacy' to her,
'late in life', when the reflected fame of having been his 'Young Lady',
and the now public romance of what was then his private life, brings
her into contact with lovers of his poetry, and also with the poet's other
muses. Half a century after their brief encounter she participates in
Philip Larkin Society annual birthday walks, '[w]ith friends who've
traced your documented footsteps'. In her recent albums:

> soon appear
> Pictures of those you never thought I'd meet,
> Of Ruth and Maeve, who came before and after,
> Now here together with me, eating a pub lunch in a sunny garden;
> And places that you never guessed I'd visit.

Winifred seems admirably suited to the long perspectives which the
poet so dreaded.

As in *Jill* the real Gillian is not the dream. The poet's vision is, as
Larkin says, without hope of consequence, or as Auden put it, 'poetry
makes nothing happen'.[30] Winifred, as a real girl, made things happen,
while the poet sat tight. The poet cannot engage with Winifred
Bradshaw, nor Win Dawson; nor would her 'larger, newer albums'

appeal to him. His service is to the muse: the 'Unvariably lovely' Winifred Arnott, 'unfingermarked again' in her smaller, clearer world of *'the past'*, when photography was so expensive that snaps were tiny. Quite unconsciously she confirmed Larkin's sense of his own poetic plight. Andrew Motion accurately registers the impact of Winifred on Larkin's poetry: 'Exciting but separate, she helped him reaffirm his devotion to "Art" rather than "Life"' (235). However, her own devotion was to life. As she implies in her poem, Larkin could have got himself a life; instead he chose poetry.

There remains one further poem in the group addressed to Winifred, in a startlingly different style from the others. While composing 'Lines on a Young Lady's Photograph Album' Larkin wrote to Winifred that it 'can't make up its mind whether it's going to be serious or not' (*SL* 209). Later he wrote a sincere and 'serious' version of the comic plight of 'He Hears that his Beloved has become Engaged' and 'Lines on a Young Lady's Photograph Album'. 'Long roots moor summer to our side of earth', dated the day of Winifred's wedding, 12 June 1954, addresses her as a woman rather than as a muse, and eschews the Decadent wit and elegiac subtleties of the other works addressed to her. Its self-dramatization is tragic rather than comic and it reverts to the organicist imagery of 'Wedding-Wind' and 'At the chiming of light upon sleep'. In fervent sound-writing reminiscent of Gerard Manley Hopkins the poet awakes to find summer already taller than 'the green / River-fresh castles of unresting leaf'. He goes on to develop a wholly positive vision of procreative nature:

> It unfolds upward a long breadth, a shine
>
> Wherein all seeds and clouds and winged things
> Employ the many-levelled acreage.

In an echo of 'Mother, Summer, I' the poet acknowledges his in-adequacy in the face of this gorgeous vision of summer, not with 'clenched' self-possession, but with passionate despair:

> Where can I turn except away, knowing
> Myself outdistanced, out-invented? what
> Reply can the vast flowering strike from us,
> Unless it be the one
> You make today in London: to be married?

Lacking the brilliant literary wit of 'Lines on a Young Lady's Photograph Album' this poem is usually ignored. It might be felt that its style is one which Larkin had already left behind him. But this is too simple. Though it remained unpublished and he did not even send a copy to Winifred, it is a moving and beautiful work. Moreover its nature imagery persists in later poems. His last great poem, 'Love Again', finds him still isolated in the same sterile plight, unable to identify the element which 'spreads through other lives like a tree', or to say why it 'never worked' for him, while others participate naturally, elsewhere, in a world of spontaneity and love.

An affair

'Whatever Happened?' (1953), the most enigmatic poem in *The Less Deceived*, offers a very different lesson in the complicated process by which life is objectified in art. Part of its expressive force derives from its show of suppression and reticence. Like 'Deceptions' it gives signs of being a coded metaphor for an incident too private or traumatic to be treated explicitly. But in this case the poet's artistic control is more complete. The first line stubbornly refuses to answer the question of the title, merely transforming its words into an indicative euphemism: 'At once whatever happened starts receding.' Whatever happened is so decidedly best forgotten that the poet will not tell us what it was. The vivid consequences of the undescribed event, 'trousers ripped, light wallets, and lips bleeding', evoke a scenario from a story by Somerset Maugham or perhaps Graham Greene. Travellers or holiday-makers from a cruise-ship have paid a port-visit during which a brawl has occurred in bar or brothel. Oddly, these travellers remain a plural 'we' throughout the poem. The speaker seems to be avoiding 'I' in an attempt to dilute his own personal implication in this obscure disaster. As the travellers view the receding coastline they think to themselves 'Perspective brings significance', and snap some photographs: 'What can't be printed can be thrown away.' But as time passes significance fades and the sordid affair recedes completely, becoming 'just a latitude' on the map.

   The tone is one of worldly-wise retrospection and the structure maintains careful control: an unorthodox sonnet consisting of four *terza rima* stanzas followed by a concluding couplet (*aba*, *bcb*, *cdc*, *ded*, *ff*). The detached tone and overdetermined form are, however, subverted by the vagueness of the central event. A verdict is delivered in authoritative tones: '"Such coastal bedding always means mishap."' But this unattributed moralizing lacks the inevitable conviction its tone seems to imply. The technical term 'coastal bedding', denoting submerged reefs, threatens to send the metaphor awry, implying that it is the ship, not the passengers, which has got into difficulties, though an awkward pun on 'bedding' preserves a sexual implication. All this carefully-enacted obfuscation suggests a traumatic repression on the part of the speaker. Though the final two lines break through the pretence with expressionist violence, they still explain nothing:

> Curses? The dark? Struggling? Where's the source
> Of these yarns now (except in nightmares, of course)?

Instead of a neat conclusion the couplet offers four questions, and attempts to relegate the event to the status of a 'yarn', a nightmare whose source is buried in psychology.

On the purely textual level this is a powerful poem, evoking, through skilfully vague literary allusions, a familiar kind of panic at being caught off-guard in unaccustomed surroundings. However, its reticence is not merely an artistic strategy. The poem does have a context which the poet is withholding from the reader, and it is easier to respond to the poem if the reader is aware of this context. Andrew Motion associated the poem with Larkin's feelings over Winifred Arnott's engagement (235). However, in tone and texture this is a quite different kind of relationship from that dramatized in 'Latest Face' and 'Maiden Name'. The poem was, in fact, occasioned by a different liaison altogether: the poet's brief 'coastal bedding' of Patsy Strang in 1952–3. Patsy was very different from the other women in Larkin's life: married, in a 'semi-detached' way, to a lecturer in philosophy, sexually adventurous, from a wealthy South African background, well-connected (her husband would inherit a title), highbrow, and herself an aspiring writer. Winifred Dawson (Arnott) comments: 'I was frightened of her. She would have quite despised me as a middle-class virginal wimp. She was experienced and sophisticated and rich.'[31] She was a complete contrast, also, to the witty, down-to-earth Monica Jones.

Motion says that Philip's relationship with Patsy 'was the most happily erotic of all his affairs' (Motion 222). But happy eroticism was not a combination for which Larkin had much talent. Nor was Patsy, unlike Winifred, a happy person. Winifred and Philip would frequently discuss 'why Patsy was so miserable'. Winifred also remembers Philip stating emphatically: 'As far as I'm concerned other men's wives are completely banned.' Her verdict is that 'Patsy seduced him.'[32] The correspondence between them does indeed show the poet being swept off his feet, exhilaratingly, but also dangerously. He never felt quite happy with the secrecy and risk of discovery which, for her, gave spice to adultery. After a secret visit which she paid to Belfast from a holiday on the mainland in July 1952 he wrote to her apologetically: 'I reproached myself silently for being in such a gibbering funk as to have come near to spoiling such a happy weekend, such as I've never had before.'[33]

At the end of that month she wrote that she was pregnant by him, but before he could reply she suffered a miscarriage. The episodic letter in which he responds to both events shows his anxious adjustment to the situation. Of the pregnancy he says: 'After feeling sorry & alarmed & guilty, I find it rather thrilling.' On learning of the miscarriage, however, he reassures her: 'I fancy you should be thankful... you wd have got pretty tired of "a lifetime of deceit", which really is what it would've turned out to be.'[34] There is no hint from either side that he might acknowledge his paternity. The letter is illustrated with drawings of a walrus smiling down on a baby walrus, and, following the miscarriage, a drawing of the walrus waving good-bye to the baby. The love affair lasted another year, but it never regained its initial heady excitement. It finally came to an end in August 1953, when Patsy wrote to say that she would be remaining in Oxford while her husband took a job in Newcastle (they divorced shortly afterwards). Larkin wrote a valedictory letter of vivid and warm regret, ending: 'But oh dear, oh dear! You were so wonderful!' (*SL* 208). The past tense ('were') is carefully chosen, and the 'oh dears' carry a hint of ambiguity. Fascinating and stimulating though she was, Patsy was no inspiring muse.

The poem was completed three months later, on 26 October 1953, only a month after 'Lines on a Young Lady's Photograph Album'. Its imagery can be readily 'decoded' in terms of the real-life affair. Patsy's cosmopolitan, South African background suggests the exotic setting, his guilt and sense of violation (she had read his diaries without permission) are translated into the battered confusion of the travellers, and 'What can't be printed can be thrown away' brutally hints at her miscarriage. The poem's obscure symbolism is successful in objectifying an easily recognizable psychological state; but it was not dictated solely by artistic imperatives. This obscurity was, it seems, essential if Larkin wished to publish the poem (it appeared in *The Fantasy Poets 21*, then in *The Less Deceived*). He needed to render it opaque to such readers as Colin Strang, Winifred Arnott and Monica Jones. On 1 November 1953 he sent Patsy a copy, with slightly different wording from the final

version, and with the title 'The story of an occurrence and a disoccurrence'. He datemarked his letter gloomily *'All Hallows'*, lightly speculated on whether he had lung cancer and fended off her attempt to
reignite the affair: 'if a "wrong" thing becomes harder to do, it seems
wronger in consequence and – well, we have our obligations. I wish I
could write this without sounding priggish & unfriendly...' (*SL* 215-17).

To read this work simply as a biographical *poème à clef* is inadequate.
The affair with Patsy was its occasion and suggested its imagery. But
Larkin has made a virtue of necessity and taken artistic advantage of
the reticence imposed upon him to recast its theme in impersonal,
symbolic terms. As he explains in his letter:

> Having typed it out, I think its fault is being just another poem
> about ships & journeys when we know it all means something dif-
> ferent. In case it isn't clear, it treats of the way in which the mind
> gets to work on any violent involuntary experience & transforms it
> out of all knowledge... I have tried to keep the wording ambiguous,
> so that 'whatever happened' could be sexual as well as violent.
> (*SL* 216)

The rhetorical disruptions and contradictions of the poem have been
articulated to form an artistic depiction of repressed trauma. As his
wording hints, there is a hidden subtext ('something different', 'In case
it isn't clear'). But it is not essential to decode this in order to understand the poem.

A month after 'The story of an occurrence and a disoccurrence', he
sent Patsy another sonnet in more conventional form: 'Autobiography
at an Air-Station'. After thanking her for her latest poem, he writes:

> I know the feeling, in fact I wrote a very light poem about it myself
> wch I'll transcribe.
> > Delay, well, travellers must expect
> > Delay. For how long? No one seems to know.
> > With all the luggage weighed, the tickets checked,
> > It can't be *long*...
>
> (*SL* 219-20)

The travellers kick their heels wondering whether to make friends
with each other, but decide against it since it might spoil their chances
in the race for seats: 'You're best alone', he concludes portentously,
'Friendship is not worth while'. As dusk falls the poet is left in a familiar

Larkinesque plight, on the edge of life, in transit, 'staled, / Hypnotised, by inaction.'[35]

With Patsy Strang as his intended reader Larkin writes in an elusive, symbolic manner. Though she had qualified at Oxford as a doctor, she was determined to be a writer herself, and had lived in Paris. Their letters discuss French poetry, cinema and the latest art exhibitions. In these two poems we catch a glimpse of an unfamiliar Larkin: mannered, world-weary, cosmopolitan, even 'difficult'. It is a tone which is echoed thirteen years later, in 'Friday Night in the Royal Station Hotel' (1966), another unusually-structured sonnet concerned with the alienation of transit. Otherwise Patsy Strang's personality disappears from his poetry in 1953.[36] They continued to correspond and, after her marriage to the poet Richard Murphy in 1955 Larkin would sometimes write to them jointly. By the time she died in 1977 the relationship had faded to the exchanging of irregular letters. He wrote grimly to Amis: 'Did you know Patsy was dead? I forget if I told you on the phone. Found literally dead drunk, it seems – empty Cointreau bottle, ½ empty Benedictine bottle. Fascinating mixture, what' (*SL* 571).

4
Loves and Muses II

'My wife'

'If, My Darling', completed in May 1950, adopts a tone of combative humour new to Larkin's poetry at the time. In the title, a comma isolates the heavily-stressed 'If', suggesting a direct address to the woman: a question, or a threat. Is she perhaps herself the, or an, intended reader? Then in the poem's first line the same words are edgily recapitulated, but without the comma, to introduce the consequences of her foolhardiness, as if to say: 'well, she's asked for it.' The poem deploys the coarsest post-war stereotypes of prim young lady and anti-social bachelor with an aggressive edge which seems designed to provoke protest. My darling's quaint, sentimental world is patently a wilful caricature. The mahogany claw-footed sideboards, the fender-seat, the prissy 'small-printed books for the Sabbath', the bibulous butler and lazy housemaids belong to an archaic world of ridiculous Victorian propriety. We might reflect that we have only the male poet's word that this is indeed what his darling expects of him.

Moreover, his own antithetical junk-shop of masculinity, though less simply a matter of caricature, is itself wilfully grotesque:

> She would also remark
> The unwholesome floor, as it might be the skin of a grave,
>
> From which ascends an adhesive sense of betrayal,
> A Grecian statue kicked in the privates, money,
> A swill-tub of finer feelings.

The higher call of art is caricatured in 'A Grecian statue kicked in the privates', and his 'finer feelings' are no better than pigswill. Abstract concepts jostle against lavishly crude images, with obscure leaps of association. Mixed metaphor becomes a governing principle of style as, in a brilliant display of 'bad writing', the poet stumbles over his images in his eagerness to make his inner room seem as sordid as possible. The varying light is 'Monkey-brown, fish-grey' (what shade is monkey-brown?) 'A string of circles is 'infected' (how can a circle be infected?) and the circles loiter 'like bullies, about to coagulate' (how do bullies, or circles for that matter, 'coagulate'?) The reader cannot but sympathize with this latter-day Alice, trapped inside the poet's unwholesome head, stopping her ears against

> the incessant recital
> Intoned by reality, larded with technical terms,
> Each one double-yolked with meaning and meaning's rebuttal.

Such insight, the speaker warns, in an obscurely sexual image, might 'knock my darling off her unpriceable pivot'.[1] But the poet seems to be protesting too much, and is perhaps more on his darling's side than he admits. His display of self-disgust reveals itself, on reflection, as a clumsy attempt to see things her way. It is, also, perhaps, meant to make her laugh. Is this a bizarre seduction poem, aimed indirectly at a woman of humour and intelligence? Carroll's Alice, one recalls, rose to the challenge, kept her composure and took charge of the chaos around her.

Less than a month after completing this poem Larkin persuaded himself into a miserable final proposal of marriage to Ruth Bowman, which he withdrew after three weeks. But 'If, My Darling' does not fit into the context of Philip's feelings for Ruth. Its new demotic energy and humour give it a very different texture from his other anti-marriage poems of the time, while the cliché endearment, 'my darling', has a companionable familiarity not appropriate to the woman implied in 'Waiting for breakfast' and 'No Road'. Moreover, the poet's anxiety over his darling's possible response when she discovers the worst reflects a relationship at an early stage of negotiation rather than at its exhausted conclusion. It seems relevant here that Larkin's affections at this time were transferring themselves to Monica Jones. Shortly after the final break with Ruth Bowman in July 1950, two months after this poem was written, he slept with Monica Jones for the first time. The *Alice in Wonderland* 'floating skirt' of this poem might suggest Monica's bell-skirts,[2] while his darling's cosy mental furniture recalls Margaret Peel in Amis's *Lucky Jim*, a novel in whose composition Larkin played a part. Monica's full name was Monica Margaret Beale Jones.

'If, My Darling' shows Larkin in his most Amisian clowning vein. Monica Jones's own verdict on Amis, however, was as cruelly incisive as his on her: 'Kingsley wasn't just making faces all the time, he was actually trying them on. He didn't know who he was' (Motion 169). Larkin, in contrast, did decidedly know 'who he was', and in many crucial ways he was like Monica: abrasive, humorous, sceptical, but also sensitive and vulnerable. Though her response is not recorded, it is not difficult to imagine her wry smile at the exuberant posturings of 'If, My Darling'. As Motion says of the couple: 'Both relished each other's combination of diffidence and resilience' (Motion 169). Behind the extravagant self-critical rhetoric of the poem can be glimpsed the possibility of a playfully combative relationship quite different from that in the poems associated with Ruth.

Larkin said in an interview: 'of course most people do get married, and divorced too, and so I suppose I am an outsider'. He claims the romantic isolation of the artist, plighted to poetry and so alienated from society (*RW* 65). Or, in more selfish terms, he knows what he can stand, and has got out as early as he could. In fact Larkin participated more than he admits in the common plight of connubial humanity. The poems concerning his engagement to Ruth show a distress beyond that of many divorces, while his developing loyalties and routines with Monica came to resemble a marriage in everything except day-to-day cohabitation. It was, as Anthony Thwaite said, 'just like a marriage'.[3]

Larkin had met Monica Jones in the autumn of 1946 when he took up the post of Assistant Librarian at Leicester University College, where she was an Assistant Lecturer.[4] But it was not until four years later that they shared a bed. Monica Jones was the only woman in Larkin's life whose literary background and inclinations matched his own. They had been exact contemporaries at Oxford, though they never met there, and both achieved first-class degrees in English. Augusta Bax, the university lecturer in Larkin's unfinished novel, *A New World Symphony*, bears a close physical resemblance to Monica Jones and shares her creator's fierce sense of privacy and wry distaste for her parents' family life. Philip and Monica shared a quirky, sceptical literary intimacy, as is shown by their copy of Iris Murdoch's *The Flight from the Enchanter*, whose title is altered into a critical verdict on the novelist's work: *The Shite from the Non-Enchanter*, and whose text is extensively altered to produce three hundred pages of obscene innuendo. Though Larkin never showed anyone his poetic work in progress, Monica is unique in having participated to some small extent in the drafting of his poetry, giving him the word 'blazon' in 'An Arundel Tomb' (he asked her for 'something meaning a sign, two syllables') (Motion 275). For all these reasons Monica could never have been Larkin's muse. A muse must be, like Winifred Arnott or Maeve Brennan, different, exotic, unliterary.

Over the following decade their relationship settled into a pattern. Monica made few demands on him and they met usually at monthly intervals. During his five years in Belfast, and also after he moved to Hull in 1955, Philip would combine visits to his mother in Leicester with visits to Monica. Monica visited him in Belfast in 1952 and they travelled around Northern Ireland. The following year they went to Skye, beginning a sequence of annual holidays which continued until 1979, usually to the extremities of the British Isles: Sark in the Channel Islands, Shetland, the Highlands, or the West of Ireland. By 1965 he could say to her in a letter: 'I think of myself "coming home at holiday time" just like the aimless undergraduate of twenty-five years ago' (Motion 357). It was on a winter holiday with Monica in January 1956 that they visited Chichester Cathedral, and the emotion of 'An Arundel Tomb' owes something to his feeling for her. The brisk afterthought in the workbook also bears the mark of her acerbic intelligence: 'Love isn't stronger than death just because statues hold hands for 600 years' (Motion 274). Appropriately *The Less Deceived*, published in 1955, was dedicated 'To Monica Jones'.

In late 1959 both Monica's parents died, and in March 1960 Larkin wrote movingly to his mother, that she was 'very depressed and low. I sometimes wonder if she will ever get over all this: her work seems to weigh her down so much and she feels so alone in the world' (Motion 303). His difficulties in coping with her inconsolable grief must have deepened the mood of 'Talking in Bed', the date of which, August 1960, suggests that it is an anniversary poem, marking ten years since the couple first slept together. By this time Monica Jones had been the only person with whom Larkin had talked in bed since the end of his brief affair with Patsy Strang, seven years earlier, and was to remain so until 1975, fifteen years later. For two decades, between the ages of 31 and 52 Larkin was, in sexual if not emotional terms, a monogamist. The poem's text, however, rises free of any specific occasion or relationship, reviving, in distilled form, Larkin's early archetypal style. The protagonists are indicated only by the impersonal 'two people' in line three, reducing starkly in line eight to 'us'. The poem's subject is the plight of marriage as Larkin had defined it in 'To My Wife': 'No future now. I and you now, alone'; the shared physical proximity of domestic routine, in sickness and in health, for better or for worse, with all its dissimulations, boredoms and tolerances.

It is both an embarrassingly personal poem, and also icily detached. It must have caused many a reader to wince with recognition. Perfect formal control and a neutral indicative tone combine to give it the impact of an aphorism; though, on reflection, its intellectual wit is surprisingly ingenious. The exact formulation of its title is startlingly original; not 'Alone together', 'Silences' or 'Bed Time', but the matter-of-fact present-participle noun phrase: 'Talking in Bed'. The rhyme-scheme is hyper-exact and conclusive, the first three stanzas being tercets with interwoven rhymes, a variant on *terza rima* (*aba, cac, dcd*), while the final stanza chimes three times on the same plangent diph-thong, 'find/kind/unkind', 'kind/unkind' being a *rime riche* on the same word. This highly formal pattern imparts a laconic facility to the poem, but it also ironically counterpoints the confused dissatisfactions of the emotions it describes.

The words 'Talking' and 'Lying', paralleled at the beginnings of the first two lines, make a painfully obvious pun, while the phrase 'Lying together' blends recrimination and self-reproach. Their lying, in both senses of the word, is a mutual activity. The problem is the simplicity of their situation, which permits no evasion. Like the couple in 'An Arundel Tomb' they are 'An emblem of two people being honest', which 'goes back so far'. It goes back, indeed, as far as the first two people, Adam and Eve, who lay together after eating the fruit, and then lied together in a vain attempt to escape the consequences of their sin. A more elusive word-play opens the second stanza. 'Yet more and more time passes silently' can be read either with the stress on 'more and more', giving the meaning: 'As time goes on more time passes with the lovers remaining silent'; or it can be read with the stress on 'time', giving a plainer, secondary meaning: 'More and more time goes silently by'. In Larkin's poetry the simple elegiac reductions of mortality are never far from the surface.

The enclosed, indoor scene is now located, as in a surrealist paint-ing, against a deftly evoked nightscape of mutability and indifference in which 'the wind's incomplete unrest' builds and disperses the clouds, as 'dark towns heap up on the horizon'. But the sentimental antithesis between inner warm intimacy and outer cold indifference fails to convince. The phrase 'incomplete unrest', though describing the physical state of the clouds, applies equally to the lovers' emo-tions. The sudden personalisation of focus in 'us' again seems to pit the lovers against an uncaring world, as 'this' with its hard initial con-sonant and high 'i' sound crushes the paralleled, weaker, lower vowel of 'us':

/ /
None of this cares for us.

But the lovers still fail to achieve togetherness:

> Nothing shows why
> At this unique distance from isolation
>
> It becomes still more difficult to find
> Words at once true and kind,
> Or not untrue and not unkind.

By a wilfully contrived wording the poet makes their closeness to each other sound like distance: 'this unique distance from isolation', while the juggling word-play of the last two lines forces an emotional gulf between the grammatically identical meanings of 'true' and 'not untrue', and 'kind' and 'not unkind'. The double negatives which dominate the poem should cancel themselves out: 'incomplete unrest' should mean 'complete rest'; 'distance from isolation' should mean 'togetherness'; 'not untrue' should mean 'true'; and 'not unkind' should mean 'kind'. But they don't.

'Talking in Bed' marks the end of a phase in Larkin's relationship with Monica Jones. In 1960 his feelings for Maeve Brennan deepened into love, following her success in the Library Examinations for which he had coached her. Philip and Monica's shared routines continued: his visits to Leicester, their annual holidays, and after 1961 visits to the house she bought at Haydon Bridge, overlooking the River Tyne. Though Maeve's strict Catholicism prevented that relationship from developing physically, Philip and she were in constant contact in the library and she became his intimate companion. In April 1961 he suffered a mysterious physical breakdown and was sent to London for tests. No cause was diagnosed, but the strain of this new situation must surely have been a factor (Motion 313-14). The following years saw the poet locked in an uncomfortable triangle, declaring his love to Maeve in Hull while denying the closeness of the relationship to Monica in Leicester. In 1964 it seemed that the women would force him to choose between them. But the crisis passed and the situation remained unresolved. In a letter to Monica of 1965 Larkin echoes 'If, My Darling': 'I've always tried to get you to see me as unlikeable, and now I must be getting near success'. He praises her for rising above the possessiveness of marriage:

> I feel that as long as I was faithful, you could somehow accept the unsatisfactoriness of our relation – we might not be married legally, but we were different and perhaps superior – at least your sacrifice of

yourself to me was superior to frog-marching me or anyone to the altar rails. But when I am unfaithful – not technically but spiritually – you can only feel duped and made light of, quite apart from the awful upsetting emotion... (Motion 356)

The problem, he concedes, is 'my fault'. He is unable to cope with the usual adult responsibilities.

'Scratch on the scratch pad' (1966) confirms his diagnosis. With its 'Rabbit *memorabilia*', 'Handkerchiefs and horoscopes', 'Spectacles' and 'Steeple hats', it takes refuge in childhood imagery, translating the couple's domestic routines into a sentimental animal game based on the Beatrix Potter stories. Monica was 'Dear Bunny' or 'Bun' in his letters. It is a delicate, wan poem, too intimately personal to generate much impact outside the relationship which produced it. It remained unpublished during Larkin's lifetime and Thwaite annotates it 'unfinished?'

'Poem about Oxford', also unpublished until after the poet's death, is however a more substantial work. It was written during the happy months in 1970-1 which Larkin spent at Oxford, working on the *Oxford Book of Twentieth Century English Verse*, and revisiting the scenes of his youth. A draft of the poem is inserted in the manuscript of his early novella, *Michaelmas Term at St Bride's*, written in 1943, which he must have reread at this time. He also inscribed the poem on the flyleaf of an illustrated history of Oxford which he gave to Monica for Christmas in 1970, and it is explicitly dedicated 'for Monica'. It is probable that it was intended as another anniversary poem, ten years on from 'Talking in Bed'.

'Poem about Oxford' is very much an 'occasional' piece, prompted by his memories of the long-vanished city they 'shared without knowing'. The form is not the densely compact interwoven rhyme of 'Talking in Bed', but the favoured metre for occasional verse in the eighteenth and nineteenth centuries, anapaests in alternate rhyme. Unlike 'If, My Darling' it projects no fictional *personae*, and unlike 'Talking in Bed' it makes no attempt to generalize the relationship into an archetypal plight. This is an unusual poem in Larkin's *oeuvre*, whose 'we' is explicitly confined to the poet and the woman addressed. Their shared experience unites them against others who do not share their memories. Its uniquely frank privacy makes this in many ways Larkin's most intimate poem.

One form of intimacy is the indulgence of shared prejudices. Both speaker and addressee are 'glad' to leave Oxford, unlike the arselicker who stays. From Hull and Leicester, two places with less social 'tone' than Oxford, they mock the reverential nostalgia of many Oxonians for their Alma Mater. The tone is dictated by the poem's addressee; Monica scorned Oxford pretension, while at the same time being fiercely proud of her Oxford background. Betty Mackereth remembers calling at 105, Newland Park with a bottle of champagne for Larkin's birthday. They invited her to join them and, touching glasses, Monica led the toast to 'Oxford Firsts!'[5] Aside from 'more durable things' (such as their Firsts) the poet lists the casual social externals of their shared place and time: not the Cambridge of Girton and King's but the Oxford of St Hugh's and St John's.

> To all that it meant – a full notecase,
> Dull Bodley, draught beer, and dark blue,
> And most often losing the Boat Race –
> You're added, as I am for you.

The oddly contorted meaning is 'I am added to this list of Oxford memories for you, just as you are added to the list for me.' The parenthetic sequence of lumpy noun phrases creates a grammatical suspension, delaying the completion of the sentence until the verb: 'You're added'. This makes the monosyllabic: 'I am for you' into a coda with a simpler, more intimate meaning.

The final stanza contrasts the new Oxford of 'thirty years' on, a place of breakthroughs in labs and student sit-ins, with their own 'shared' blacked out and butterless Oxford, which 'holds us, like that *Fleae* we read about / In the depths of the Second World War.' The reference is opaque and private, but Andrew Motion's interpretation is presumably correct: 'It is a reference to Donne's "flea", in which the blood of a lover and his mistress are mingled to form a "marriage-bed, and marriage temple"' (406). Donne's intellectualized eroticism makes a suitable private language for the intimacy of two Oxford Firsts in English.

The poem of warm fellow-feeling addressed to a spouse or long-term sexual partner is a notoriously problematic genre. It is difficult to make uxoriousness poetic; easy to make it embarrassing. The problem is neatly formulated by T. S. Eliot in 'A Dedication to my Wife': 'These are private words addressed to you in public.'[1] Seamus Heaney in 'The Skunk' boldly dares the reader to take his poem the wrong way when his wife searching a bedroom drawer reminds him of a skunk he saw 'tail up' on his veranda:

> It all came back to me last night, stirred
> By the sootfall of your things at bedtime,
> Your head-down, tail-up hunt in a bottom drawer
> For the black plunge-line nightdress.[7]

Heaney's deliberate ignoring of the smell associations of the skunk, and his braving of the implications of 'tail' are intended to outface the reader's sniggers. But the hints at the married couple's bedroom games may still sound uncomfortably coy. Eliot's strategy is different from Heaney's. He begins with stiltedly elevated religious language: 'the leaping delight / That quickens my senses in our wakingtime', modulating abruptly to the physical intimacy of 'lovers whose bodies smell of each other'.[8] In 'Poem about Oxford' Larkin takes a more reticent approach than either, adopting a resolutely 'public' tone, establishing intimacy through familiar Oxford images: Bodley, the Boat Race, dark blue. The private feelings of the poem are distilled into the reticent monosyllables 'me' and 'you'.

In contrast, 'The little lives of earth and form', like 'Scratch on the scratch pad', consists of private words addressed in private. In this poem, written seven years later than 'Poem about Oxford', Larkin again risks sentimentality by employing their intimate animal language. 'We hanker for the homeliness / Of den, and hole, and set.' Its ingenuous philosophizing does, however, achieve a surprising gravity:

> The little lives of earth and form,
> Of finding food, and keeping warm,
> Are not like ours, and yet...

It is not so much a sentimental poem as an evocation of the pathos of the sentimental fictions through which we keep hard reality at bay.

It is possible to trace Monica Jones's impact throughout Larkin's work: in the emotion of 'An Arundel Tomb', the cynicism of 'Toads', and the celebration of tradition in 'Show Saturday', which was inspired by their visits to Bellingham Show in Northumberland. But the three major poems related to Monica, written at ten-year intervals: 'If, My Darling' in 1950, 'Talking in Bed' in 1960 and 'Poem about Oxford' in 1970, summarize their life-long partnership in distilled form: from first wary engagement, through the tensions of intimacy, to the relaxed mutuality of a shared past. During the final years it seems Larkin came as close as he ever did to marriage. As he became certain that his muse was not simply asleep, but dead, he returned to the marriage debate of his twenties. A few months before composing 'The little lives of earth and form', after Monica had accompanied him to Hamburg to receive a literary prize, he wrote in a letter to Winifred Dawson: 'I suppose, if I really have stopped writing, I might risk it [marriage]' (*SL* 539). At the end of his life it seems he acknowledged what the poems indicate, and what he finally confirmed by bringing Monica to live with him when she contracted shingles in 1983: in all but name their relationship had been a marriage. As he put it in a letter of 1966: 'When I am most myself, then you are there' (Motion 369).

The long courtship

On the 'Listen' recording of *The Whitsun Weddings* Larkin commented that 'Broadcast' 'seems to be about as near as I get in this collection to a love poem. It's not, I'm afraid, very near'.[9] His repeated stress on distance ('about as near', 'not very near') oddly echoes the distance within the poem between the lover and his beloved. The poem is structured around two precisely evoked visual images: the poet sitting between the illuminated wavebands of his radio-set and the winter darkness outside his window; the woman in the concert audience, her face 'among all those faces'. He is isolated, alone; she is lost in the crowd, picked out only by his imagination. This latest face does not arrive at his eyes; it forms itself in his mind. She is no 'darling', invading his head with her own assumptions. She is simply inside his head. The vignette of her face, unnoticed glove and 'new, slightly-outmoded shoes', is the poet's own image. She embodies the commonplace life he loves, but she is also out of reach, 'devout', unaware of him: a muse in a muse. The tone of courtly reserve implies, with the subtlest of sexual politics, both uncrossable distance and intimate possession.

The visual and the aural merge into each other, catching the exact 'feel' of their different situations. There is a sense of preciousness about their separation, each engrossed in his or her own world of the senses. She sits 'Beautiful and devout before / Cascades of monumental slithering', as though the music were a huge fountain or waterfall. His consciousness hovers between sight and sound:

> Here it goes quickly dark. I lose
> All but the outline of the still and withering
>
> Leaves on half-emptied trees.

Is the 'it' here the sound of the orchestra, which goes synaesthetically 'dark' in a quiet passage, or is it the poet's sight, as his eyes lose focus on the glowing wavebands? Are the withered leaves in the half-emptied trees an aural image evoked by the music, or are they real leaves visible through his darkened window? As the concert ends he is left 'desperate to pick out / Your hands, tiny in all that air, applauding.' The air is the space in the concert hall, engulfing her tiny hands. But her applause is also 'on air', in the imagined aural space evoked by the disembodied music. In this version of the Pygmalion myth the created statue has begun to walk. This woman is empirically true. But the air in which she is situated is not 'real untidy air'. It is elevated through its transmission across the radio waves onto a poetic, 'useless level'. The music over-powers his mind precisely 'By being distant'.

The context for this poem was Maeve Brennan's attendance at a con-cert in November 1961 at the City Hall, Hull, which opened with the stormy chording of Elgar's 'Introduction and Allegro for Strings'. When Larkin had arrived in Hull six years earlier, Maeve had been one of a number of younger staff members in whose engagements and 'disen-gagements' he took a detached interest. 'I myself experienced both states twice in his first three years!' she relates.[10] Then in early 1960, when Maeve passed her librarianship examinations, their relationship deepened. Partly to escape the crisis in his affections Larkin at once applied for a new post in Reading University, but he returned to Hull in a state of emotional turmoil without attending the interview (Motion 302). When, the following year, he suffered his unexplained collapse, he joked to Maeve: 'Do you think this ailment I am undergoing is God's way of putting a stop to something He thought might be getting out of hand?'[11] In 1961, without telling Maeve, he bought and read a copy of the Catholic marriage service. Three years later in 1964 he wrote dis-missively to Monica: 'I wonder if there *is* a "situation" – do I *really* want an RC wedding with Maeve and a "reception somewhere in Hull" etc. – I don't, of course, not really or even unreally' (Motion 350). It is rel-evant here that his mother, from whom he had learnt his earliest les-sons about marriage, saw Maeve as a woman of her own sort (Motion 310). Astonishingly, however, as late as 1975 he could still write to Maeve: 'I am very close to Monica and very fond of her... But it's you I *love*; you're the one I want' (Motion 453). The uneasy triangular rela-tionship remained unresolved over a period of nearly two decades, until 1979: 'There is one woman I ought to marry, and one I want to marry' (Motion 315).

Maeve Brennan played a key role in Larkin's poetry as his muse at the time of the writing of *The Whitsun Weddings*. He called it 'her book', and her copy is inscribed: 'To Maeve, who can read between the lines'.[12] Several factors contributed to the delicate flowering of Larkin's poetry at this time. He felt increasing satisfaction with his job, as work pro-gressed on the new Library Building. He was more settled in Hull, where 'only salesmen and relations come', and in whose 'urban yet

simple' inhabitants and surrounding landscape of 'neutral distance'
he found poetic inspiration. Love for Maeve focused these feelings
into a specific happiness. She was a local girl who lived with her parents and was, to use the word most often invoked by her friends, innocent. The poems of *The Whitsun Weddings* express widely diverse
aspects of Larkin's imagination; but the transfigured commonplaces
and warm humanity of such poems as 'The Whitsun Weddings' (1958),
'Afternoons' (1959), 'Here' (1961) and 'Essential Beauty' (1962), suggest
the emotional context of his relationship with Maeve; 'you have taught
me more about my emotions than anyone', he told her (Motion 443).
It is such poems which for a large faction of Larkin's readers, including
Maeve herself, constitute his most satisfying poetic achievement.

In the long perspective of her memoir, *The Philip Larkin I Knew*, published in 2002, Maeve rises above the dismay she felt immediately
following his death at learning for the first time of his 'bad' language,
his addiction to pornography, and his affair with Betty Mackereth. Her
conclusion is that their relationship had been one of close spiritual
affinity. When in 1989 she first read a letter which he had written to his
friend Jim Sutton at the age of twenty-one in 1943, she rediscovered a
Larkin whose 'idealistic views on love and marriage' seemed 'to make
explicit so much which had been implicit in our relationship.'[13] The
young poet had written:

> Once man, like the elephant, was 'slow to mate'. There were address-
> es to be paid, gloves to be picked up, dances to be requested... Now
> there is nothing but a desire to get on to the moment of ecstasy,
> whether it is the 'security' of marriage, or the sexual consummation.
> And so the ritual has been cut out... And birth-control, sex doesn't
> mean children, families, living, growing, lives twisting more and
> more richly together... – sex means nothing – just the moment of
> ecstasy, that flares and dies in a few minutes.[14]

Maeve agrees in deploring:

> the modern trend... to cut out the preliminaries in order to reach the
> moment of ecstasy as soon as possible... In the context of love, for
> instance, the ritual of wooing and courtship, he explains, has been
> abandoned.[15]

Significantly, she fails to register that the young poet has severely
qualified what she sees as his 'idealism about... marriage' by citing 'the

"security" of marriage' as a culprit in the headlong rush 'to get on to the moment of ecstasy'. She is also deaf to the contradictory yearning in Larkin's final cadence: 'the moment of ecstasy, that flares and dies'.

Their own relationship was never to develop beyond the rituals of wooing and courtship. The ecstatic moment never flared, or it flared too late; consequently it never quite died. Though their feelings for each other were 'very sensual' it was not until 1974 or 1975, two decades after their first meeting that, as she told Andrew Motion she finally 'yielded to temptation', adding: 'but only on *very* rare and isolated occasions, and at a cost of grave violation to my conscience, since I never, in principle, abandoned my stand on pre-marital sex' (447). In her view it was Larkin's spiritual idealism which dispelled any difficulty over her religious views:

> Paradoxically, it created a singular affinity between us... he may at times have found my strict adherence to the Church's teaching on sexual ethics disconcerting. However, he understood and respected my principles with a facility which struck me as remarkable.[16]

Father Anthony Storey, former chaplain to the University, believes that Maeve hoped to the end that she would bring Philip to the Church.[17] But it is clear that, despite his emotional attachment to the 'vast moth-eaten musical brocade' of Christianity, he never took its doctrines seriously. On rereading the Bible towards the end of his life he commented: 'Really, it's absolute balls. Beautiful, of course, but balls' (Motion 486).

It is a key to Larkin's distinctive artistic personality that this relationship with someone whose beliefs were so alien to his own should have been central to his imaginative world. His profoundest interest was not in belief, nor in principles. Indeed, he deferred his desire for Maeve less because he 'understood' her principles than because of the delicate intensity which this deferral gave to the relationship. He had no wish to change her, any more than he had wished to change Winifred. He feared the empty attic of fulfilment. Also, as long as their relationship remained unconsummated he could represent it to Monica as not fully serious, and to himself as not 'really' unfaithful.

Shortly before Maeve died she told Father Storey 'how she'd often asked Larkin about Monica and he would never tell her anything. But she knew that Larkin would tell Monica everything about *her*.' She was hurt and puzzled as to why this should have been so. Storey comments: 'that was an indication that Larkin's relationship to Maeve was one he didn't want to be damaged.'[18] In a strange modern version of the medieval reverence for virginity, Maeve's religious celibacy preserved the unattainable, 'unfingermarked' quality which Larkin so valued. While Winifred, his earlier muse, could not have taken seriously a man who rejected marriage and children, Maeve enjoyed their courtship rituals for their own sake, and was willing to see them indefinitely prolonged. Of the description of her face in 'Broadcast', she wrote:

> I was deeply moved that Philip commemorated it in this way. For some years afterwards, Philip would add one of the following notes to Christmas cards, depending on the nature of the illustration: 'Devout but not beautiful'; 'Beautiful but not devout' or, more rarely, 'Beautiful *and* devout'.[19]

She does not read between the lines of these witty permutations to their dialectic between religious and secular, and, as far as she is concerned, 'Broadcast' expresses 'the transcendental quality that marked our relationship from the beginning.'

For Larkin she was the ideal muse: 'very dull and ordinary', as he told Monica (Motion 364), inaccessibly 'devout', but above all beautiful. It helped also that she bore the name of a Queen from Irish myth, and that her father, though a Hull dentist, had in his youth joined the Republican Irish Volunteers in Dublin and had passed Yeats and Maud Gonne in the street. Maeve comments: 'when Philip Larkin likened me to Maud Gonne, my father retorted: "*You* like Maud Gonne? Don't be ridiculous. *She* was very beautiful, even in middle age!"'[20] Maeve was highly flattered to be compared with Yeats's muse, and unlike Winifred, she rose eagerly to the role. Flattered to be elevated on a pedestal, she made a slightly puzzled audience for the poet's self-dramatized plight of courtly lover. The phrase 'new, slightly outmoded shoes' in 'Broadcast', she explains, was a private joke between them, concerning a pair of 'winkle-pickers' with stiletto heels, which she writes, with exquisitely chosen adjectives, were of 'an unusual colour of pearlized bronze':

> Philip raved about the shoes. He used to take them off my feet, hold them up, stroke them, put them down on the sofa and continue to admire them; not just once, but every time I wore them. He thought they were the last word in fashion, until one day, slightly exasperated, I teased: 'I don't know why you go on so about these shoes. They're almost out of fashion now. You know how I haven't the nerve to wear anything until it's been in vogue for six months.' He

laughed and said: 'Well. I still adore them even if they are slightly outmoded!'[21]

She interprets Philip's pantomime of sexual fetishism as the clumsy attempt of a mere male to appreciate the finer points of female fashion. His admiration puzzles her, but she is also excited by it. As Motion says, she was 'capable of being coquettish' (298).

Her account of 'The Large Cool Store', which, as she says, she 'unsuspectingly inspired', shows a more complex version of the same pattern. After shopping in Hull on her 'split day', she returned for the evening shift at the Library:

> He was very taken with a smart summer handbag I had bought at Marks and Spencer's. He found it hard to believe that I had found anything quite so stylish there: in 1961 their merchandise was generally less well designed than in later years. The following Saturday Philip went along to 'the large cool store' which he saw through the eyes of working-class women whose humdrum existence was far removed from the tantalizing world represented by the store's 'Modes for Night'. Caressing the 'Bri-Nylon Baby-Dolls and Shorties', ethereal in colour, texture and design, the women imagine how possession of such a garment might transform their lives, showing: 'How separate and unearthly love is, / Or women are, or what they do'.[22]

She misreads Larkin's text revealingly. The poem's culminating vision of a Platonic world, like Yeats's Byzantium, 'out of nature', is not, in fact, in the women's minds. It is a projection of male dreams of what women are:

> or what they do,
> Or in our young unreal wishes
> Seem to be: synthetic, new,
> And natureless in ecstasies.

Maeve, the muse who inspired the poem, rewrites Larkin's masculine fantasy in terms of female narcissism, imagining the women escaping from their 'humdrum existence' into the 'tantalizing world' created by the clothes. On reflection, however, this is less a simple mistake than a mirror image of the poem's male obsession with mysterious, self-absorbed femaleness. Maeve remains necessarily unconscious of the full implications of her reading of the poem, and her interpretation in terms of social-realist observation of working-class culture cannot but

dissatisfy her. 'Although in some degree flattered', she says, 'the treatment of love in the poem did not strike me as commensurate with *our*
deepening feelings for one another.'[23]

Maeve's 'unsuspecting' misreading of this poem is itself a key to the
intensity of their mutual attraction. The copy of the *Listener* in which
'Broadcast' first appeared is annotated: 'To Maeve, who wd. sooner
listen to music than listen to me'. A muse, by definition, must be self-
involved and disdainful. The poet requires this of her, even imposes
it on her. It is necessary to his poetic plight. In the case of Philip
and Maeve, however, unlike that of William and Maud, the muse
responded, in terms which perfectly answered the poet's imaginative
needs. While the relationship with Monica was one of familiarity and
mutual understanding, the relationship with Maeve was one of inexhaustible unfamiliarity: the most intimate of cross-purposes. In an
unreal but compulsive dynamic of the imagination, the feminine narcissism of the muse and the masculine narcissism of the poet present
mirrors to each other, reflecting their parallel separate worlds. As Larkin
said in 'Latest Face': 'I contain your current grace, / You my judgement'.
It is scarcely surprising that Larkin's first heady realisation of what their
relationship promised sent him into the panic and collapse of April 1961.

In Larkin's imagination Maeve Brennan and Monica Jones occupy
the rôles of virginal muse and sexual companion. But this is no simple
antithesis of illusion and reality. As Philip explained to Monica, his perverse preference for 'art' over 'life', for the 'unreal' over the 'real', is a
problem for him in both relationships:

> When you talk about hair under the arms and bare breasts and nip-
> ples and the like it makes me think of *you* in these respects and I get
> *colossally* excited, almost unreally really – well, really unreally, I sup-
> pose ... It's this mood that prompted the talk of Polaroid cameras –
> in one sense there's nothing I'd like more than photographs of you
> in your private clothes, or in no clothes at all, but I can't feel it's
> right when it seems more exciting than the reality.
>
> (Motion 339)

Monica fed the poet's unreal pornographic fantasies; Maeve fed his
unreal poetic fantasies. In both cases fantasy was more exciting than
reality:

> I don't mind your allegations about Maeve, though I don't think
> they are true – they are your hated image of this 'real girl'... I think

there's something unreal about my relation with her, as indeed there is with ours and mine with Ruth – in that it isn't 'serious' in the world sense of the word, i.e. leading to marriage and children. I don't say this is particularly comforting, but I think it's my fault.

(Motion 357)

To represent these 'unreal' imaginative relations in terms of banal sexism is not adequate. Alan Bennett in his review of Motion's biography, 'Alas! Deceived', saw Maeve in caricature terms (which she greatly resented) as a northern 'lass deceived', under the sway of a sophisticated southern seducer. All Larkin 'really wants', Bennett declared, 'is just to get his end away on a regular basis and without obligation'.[24] More recently James Fenton has depicted the poet as a cynical manipulator:

His problem seems to have been that he didn't want a sexual partner near enough to be a bother. But he arranged a solution to that problem in the form of a sexual partner at a distance, a non-sexual partner close by, and a magazine collection to bridge the gap. Women ministered to him. He had no reason to feel neglected.[25]

Though more complex than Bennett's version this grossly mistakes the direction and mutuality of the 'ministering'. Monica could rely on Philip's regular visits, their shared rituals, their annual holidays. This stability enabled her to follow an independent career as a popular university lecturer in Leicester. Given their temperaments, marriage between them would have been a catastrophe. Equally, Maeve's position as the muse of a famous poet gave her greater fulfilment than most of us can expect in a lifetime. She also pursued a successful career and, more adventurous than Philip, frequently visited friends abroad. Marriage between them would have been positively dangerous. To read Philip's letters to both women is to see at once the extent to which he 'ministered' to them. What he denied was a wedding-ring, a mortgage and children. It is not self-evident that either would have led a more fulfilled life with these things. Moreover, after 1960, to have chosen either woman would have been to cause suffering to the other, which he could not do.

The fragile triangle of Philip, Monica and Maeve has by now taken its place in popular literary mythology, alongside Byron's tangled love life, the romance of Elizabeth Barrett and Robert Browning, and the marriage of Sylvia Plath and Ted Hughes. There is, indeed, an archetypal quality about the two women's responses to the poet. Following the revelations which emerged on Larkin's death Maeve Brennan felt moral disillusion: 'He had feet of clay, didn't he? Huge feet of clay' (Motion 307). Monica Jones's reaction was more simply emotional: 'He lied to me, the bugger, but I loved him' (Motion 310-11). Maeve subsequently softened her view and, like Winifred, enjoyed a late legacy from the poet in the form of her rôle as Vice-Chairman of the Philip Larkin Society, and the success of her memoir, *The Philip Larkin I Knew*. Monica remained a sad recluse until her death in 2001, not because her illusions had been shattered, but because, whatever Philip's faults, she could not bear to be without him. Early in his life he had laid his claim to be 'more deceived' than the women in his life. Opinion will remain divided as to which was the more deceived by him: the unsuspecting muse, or the tragic 'wife'.

For the male artist the roles of muse and of wife are in tension. In *A Portrait of the Artist as a Young Man* an ordinary girl paddling in the sea with her skirt tucked up, showing her drawers, strikes the young aesthete, Stephen Dedalus, as a visitation from the 'angel of mortal youth and beauty'. But, as muse the girl must be kept at a distance. In the novel Stephen 'turned away from her suddenly and set off across the strand.'[26] In real life, of course, Joyce did not turn away. He approached the girl and they married, turning impersonal vision into personal reality. If Joyce's next novel, *Ulysses*, can be said to have a muse, it takes a more irrevocably distant form of 'mortal beauty' in the person of the advertising salesman, Leopold Bloom. Nora Barnacle ceased to be Joyce's muse when she married him: Maud Gonne, it has been said, remained Yeats's muse because she refused him. Sylvia Plath became Ted Hughes's inaccessible muse upon her death.

'Broadcast' offers a vision of 'mortal youth and beauty' parallel to that of Joyce. But Larkin was a man as well as a poet, and knew as well as Joyce that real women are not muses. Maeve Brennan wanted to be his wife. He wrote grumpily to Judy Egerton in 1963: 'There's a campaign afoot to make me *more like other people*, which involves much social effort' (Motion 341). His response to this attempt to rescue him from his poetic plight was 'The Dance', which he at first hoped to include in *The Whitsun Weddings*. However, though he worked on the poem single-mindedly for ten months, it was never completed, or to be more exact, it never reached a conclusion. This poem marks the second watershed in Larkin's poetic career. He told Maeve: 'I am beginning to think this is a great obstacle in my creative life: shan't write anything till it's out of the way.'[27] His choice of words is revealing: 'a

great obstacle', and 'out of the way' suggest not a fruitful creative challenge but an immovable block. It was now ten years since, in 'Reasons
for Attendance', he had dramatized his refusal to attend the dance of
social convention. Rejecting the idea that 'the lion's share / Of happiness is found by couples' he had 'attended' instead to the 'rough-
tongued bell' of his art. Now, a decade later he finally attends the
dance, crossing the threshold between unreal and real, and attempting
to translate muse into wife in the world of 'Bargains, suffering, and
love'.

The text of the poem thus eschews the language of his 'life *vs* art'
debate. The speaker allows himself no other excuse for his reluctance to
attend the dance than simple antisocial selfishness:

> 'Drink, sex and jazz – all sweet things, brother: far
> Too sweet to be diluted to "a dance",
> That muddled middle-class pretence at each
> No one who really...' But contemptuous speech
> Fades at my equally-contemptuous glance,
> That in the darkening mirror sees
> The shame of evening trousers, evening-tie.

He depicts himself with social realism, as what in 'reality' he was, a
forty-one-year-old man simply too immature and selfish to grapple
with normal social intercourse. As the poem develops the speaker
finds himself unable to respond to his beloved's willingness, despite
his yearning to satisfy her demands, and his intense physical desire
for her. He does not even have the excuse of divided affections; there
is no equivalent of Monica Jones in the text to explain the speaker's
hesitancy.

Larkin's poetry has finally arrived at the point he reached in his
fiction in the late 1940s when he attempted to go beyond the dreams
of Kemp and Katherine and to write social-realist novels about unliterary people without transcendences. There is a close correspondence
between this poem and the rugby-club dance scene in *No For An Answer*
where Sam Wagstaff similarly eels his way from bar to toilet to dance
floor, confronting his girlfriend Sheila in erotic or obscurely distasteful
encounters. The writing in the novel was careful and accurate, but
lacked the imaginative conviction of the unreal dreams of Kemp and
Katherine in *Jill* and *A Girl in Winter*.[28] In 1950 Larkin's solution was to
abandon novel-writing in favour of the flexible 'I' of lyric poetry: 'if
you tell a novelist "Life's not like that"', he declared, 'he has to do

something about it. The poet simply replies, "No, but I am"' (*RW* 96). Or, more simply: 'novels are about other people and poems are about yourself' (*RW* 49). But now, in 1963 no such escape is possible. Other people, or rather one other person has taken a central place in his imaginative world. The statue is walking, and, wading behind her, the poet finds himself choking on 'real untidy air'. His irresponsible lyric 'I' is being held accountable by life.

The poet's arrival at the dance dispels the safe distance of 'Broadcast', and he meets a real girl on her own territory, where couples are the norm, 'with some people at some table, you.' The syntax isolates 'you' at the end of the line, and, as it were, screens the woman from him behind the abstraction of society ('some people at some table'). Overcome by emotion he asks himself 'Why gulp? The scene is normal and allowed.' But he is unable to behave normally, standing outside himself, seeing himself in a 'scene', rather than simply, like the woman and her companions, being there. As he dances with her, her look 'challenging / And not especially friendly', he tries to second-guess her emotions. He feels:

> The impact, open, raw,
> Of a tremendous answer banging back
>
> As if I'd asked a question.

But the 'consenting' language of her body in which, in a deliberately inept, archaic word, he finds himself 'descrying love', fails to prompt the question she demands. 'Why not snatch it?' he asks. But his question fails to meet her answer. For some reason he cannot 'snatch' her love, and thereby 'deflect' the acutely 'local' and 'transitory' into 'how / We act eternally.' He struggles with doubts about 'what you meant', though this is surely not at all mysterious.

A note of frustrated humour now points up the absurdity of his plight as he is cornered by a 'shoptalking shit' and his 'bearded wife'. The work shows signs of modulating to a more 'objective' artistic level of fictional comedy; less *Lucky Jim* perhaps than a 'Love Song of P. Arthur Larkin', spoken by a self-mocking persona, at a loss in society, and unable to ask the overwhelming question. But the comic tone is intermittent and insecure. We are soon returned to the speaker's raw sexual jealousy as from the bar he watches the woman dancing with 'a weed from Plant Psychology' and imagines that her body language is

giving this man the same message it gave earlier to him. Miserably he
stops watching her and souses his throat with gin:

> How right
> I should have been to keep away, and let
> You have your innocent-guilty-innocent night
> Of switching partners in your own sad set:
> How useless to invite
> The sickened breathlessness of being young
>
> Into my life again! I ought to go,
> If going would do any good...

Is the problem his contempt for her 'sad set', or does he perhaps envy
their innocent guilt? Or is it, more simply, that he is now too old for
the courtship intensities which are consuming him? Visiting the cloak-
room, and noticing his coat hanging there, he resolves to call a taxi at
once. But then, making for the bar to seek change for the telephone he
sees that 'your lot are waving' and once again finds himself drawn in:

> I sit and beam
> At everyone, even the weed, and he
> Unfolds some crazy scheme
> He's got for making wine from beetroot...

As the poem builds to its climax his gin-soaked mood begins to soften.
   In the closing stanzas he again dances with the woman. Her 'silent
beckoning' is now weaker, but nevertheless 'Something in me starts
toppling.' Surely the poem cannot be building up, after all, to a decla-
ration of love or a proposal of marriage? Some revelation seems in sight
as the poet, staring at her half-shut hazel eyes, senses 'Endless receding
Saturdays, their dense / And spot-light-fingered glut / Of never-resting
hair-dos'. Then a characteristic anacrusis introduces what must surely
be the final epiphanic stanza. Understanding dawns:

> [I...] understand
>
> How the flash palaces fill up like caves
> With tidal hush of dresses, and the sharp
> And secretive excitement running through

Their open ritual that can alter to
Anguish so easily against the carp
Of too-explicit music...

Oddly, however, instead of a revelation, what the poem 'understands'
has turned back into description, thwarting the promised climax. We
have, it appears, still one stage further to go in order to reach enlight-
enment. So the poet begins again on his epiphany, with yet another
anacrusis:

till
I see for the first time as something whole
What earlier seemed safely divisible[29]

At this point on 12 May 1964, eight lines into an eleven-line stanza, on
two characteristically euphemistic noun phrases ('something whole',
'What earlier seemed safely divisible'), and without a punctuation
mark, he abandoned the poem. What exactly the epiphanic 'something
whole' is, which he now sees for the first time, remains unwritten.

His poetic vision of the whole of society as a vast provincial dance
could conceivably promise a conclusion of reconciled submission. But,
after the poem's earlier sour comments on the repetitive rituals of the
woman's sad set, this promise is quite unconvincing. From the formal
point of view it would have been easy enough to supply the final three
rhymes, but the imaginative conviction is lacking. The poet attempts to
persuade himself to submit to 'life' in the form of the woman's 'beckoning', and to accept marriage as a satisfying epiphany. But the imagery
of 'never-resting hair-dos' and 'the carp / Of too-explicit music' fails to
leave the ground and attain the requisite level of transcendence. His art
remains unpersuaded.

'The Dance' is, as Larkin's editor indicates, 'unfinished', though in a
carefully crafted way which could be seen as placing it in the genre of
the deliberate 'fragment'. The ending is an elaborately teasing cliff-
hanger, a self-mocking, tragi-comic joke. It is Larkin's way of getting the
'obstacle', however unsatisfactorily, 'out of the way'. Had 'The Dance'
been completed, it would have taken its place at the centre of *The
Whitsun Wedding* as Larkin's personal 'Epithalamium'. By plighting
himself in marriage to the muse of the volume he would have escaped
his liminal plight between the glittering isolation of art and the social
dance of life. On one level this was his dearest wish. He gave a copy
to Maeve, and made a tape-recording of himself reading it to a background of dance music. But his 'life' and 'art' remained stubbornly

unreconciled. His poetry could only take him so far and he could not force it further. In the event his second mature volume did take its title from an epithalamium, but in 'The Whitsun Weddings' the poet remains a marginalized onlooker.

The unconcluded conclusion of 'The Dance' leaves the poet exactly where he was to stay for the rest of his life, a late attender at the dance of social community, but still refusing the commitment which would make his presence there comfortable. Though he continued to tell Maeve that he loved her, and she continued to hope for marriage, the 'wrangle for a ring' ceased to be a live issue in his poetry at this point, and this is the final poem in the long marriage debate begun with 'Deep Analysis' in 1946. At this time also, the figure of woman as inspirational other, or muse, disappears from his work, to reappear briefly in 1975–6 in the poems addressed to Betty Mackereth. From now on his major theme is the different, more universal plight of age and ageing. No longer will he make a fool of himself by inviting 'The sickened breathlessness of being young' into his life. Only four years later than 'The Dance', in 'Sad Steps' he views 'the strength and pain / Of being young' from an infinite distance: 'it can't come again, / But is for others undiminished somewhere.' We have left the world of *The Whitsun Weddings* for that of *High Windows*.

It was not until six months after he had sidestepped the obstacle of 'The Dance' that Larkin completed his next poem, 'Solar' (4 November 1964). Not surprisingly, it is the most rigorously objective poem in his *oeuvre*: a pagan hymn to the life-giving force of the sun:

> Coined there among
> Lonely horizontals
> You exist openly.
> Our needs hourly
> Climb and return like angels.
> Unclosing like a hand,
> You give for ever.

Here is a poem whose text is fully 'expressed', requiring no subtextual disentangling. Here also is a relationship which makes no emotional demands. Without recompense the sun satisfies 'Our needs', the existential basics of life, on a level where society and sentiment are sublimely irrelevant.

It was not until the late sexual intensification of their love ten years later, in 1974, which ushered in, in Maeve's words, 'the most serene phase of our relationship', that it again becomes visible in Larkin's poetry. The anything-but-serene 'Love Again' offers an object-lesson in the autonomy of art and the limitations of biographical interpretation. On 7 August 1975, after Maeve had left for a holiday in Ireland with her sister, Philip wrote:

> I wish you hadn't gone away just when you did: I miss you. A fearful boiling night was diversified by two dreams about you, both 'losing dreams' – you going off with someone else – wch was all very silly, for how can one lose what one does not possess?[30]

Hours after posting this letter, he began the poem (Motion 454). Its nightmarish anger and anxiety, it seems, were initially excited by an imagined situation, rather than a real event. The poem remained unfinished until 1979, at a time when Maeve, having lost patience with their nineteen years of courtship, had formed a new relationship with David Bassett of the University's South East Asian Studies Department (whose grave she now shares, within sight of Philip's). The fifty-three-year-old poet completed the earlier poem after seeing Maeve and David together at a party. She comments, 'Knowing Philip as I did, pure jealousy, it seems to me provoked the speculation "why it [love] never worked for me".'[31]

In 'Love Again', as in 'Broadcast', the woman is elsewhere, in other company, and the poem presents the isolated poet's imagined picture of her. In the earlier poem the vision was unique and fresh. Here, as the title suggests, the poet is at the end of a repeating sequence of wankings and tomorrows. There is cruel irony in the title, from the jazz lyric, 'I'm Falling in Love Again'. The phrase may possibly also open up a long, personal perspective deep in the poem's subtext. In a letter of 8 January 1946 the young Larkin had made arrangements to introduce Kingsley Amis for the first time to his girlfriend Ruth Bowman. He ended the letter: 'love / philip footwarmer.' Then, anxious about this potentially disastrous meeting between the representatives of the abrasive masculine and soft feminine poles of his own sensibility, he added an anxious postscript concerning times of trains and connections, concluding: 'Love again (Don't look like that.)'[32] In view of his highly developed memory for words and phrases it is possible that, three and a half decades later, he recalled this traumatic first occasion when it had failed to 'work for' him.

In a final retrospect on his marriage debate, the poem moves beyond his previous verdicts on his failure of commitment: that he was too selfish and easily bored, or that his wishes were unreal. Now he delves into psychiatry for a tragic version of the comic 'They fuck you up, your mum and dad': 'Something to do with violence / A long way back, and wrong rewards.' However, Larkin's father was not physically violent, and Andrew Swarbrick points out that the draft originally read 'difference a long way back'.[33] This phrase might suggest anything from his stammer to embarrassment at his dysfunctional family, to the lonely isolation of the artist. It is possible then that the final wording is the product not of a confessional urge but of the artistic instinct for a stronger poetic effect.

This suggestion brings up the question of biographism in acute form. The brilliantly shocking opening of the second stanza is, for instance, poetically unforgettable: 'Someone else feeling her breasts and cunt, / Someone else drowned in that lash-wide stare'. But the tone seems inappropriate to the context of Larkin's courtly relationship with Maeve Brennan who, until the meaning of the word was explained to her thought that 'wanking' was a mistake for 'working' or 'waking'. We are dealing here with the slippery lyric 'I' so envied by Julian Barnes. Though this poem takes its place within the developing story of the poet's responses to a particular relationship, it is not a direct transcription of experience. As Larkin explained to Monica, in an attempt to defuse her jealousy over 'Broadcast': 'I don't really equate poems with real-life as most people do – I mean they are true in a way, but very much dolled up & censored' (*SL* 366). Poetry is, after all, not life; and however rewarding biographical contextualization may be, poems are not answerable to 'reality'. They create their own reality.

A late fling

The word 'face' haunts Larkin's poetry. 'Face' (or 'faces') occurs, as noun or verb, forty-eight times in the post-1945 section of the *Collected Poems* of 1988, always in contexts charged with emotion.[34] At the negative extreme a face may embody the prison of social convention. In 'To My Wife' the husband has exchanged 'all faces' for 'your face', and so impoverished his life. In 'Reasons for Attendance' the dancers shift 'intently, face to flushed face' in a compulsive mauling to and fro. In 'Vers de Société' the phrase 'forks and faces' sums up the meaninglessness of social intercourse. And in 'The Life with a Hole in it' the poet sulkily blames 'havings-to, fear, faces' for blighting his life. Typically the poet finds himself at a loss, outfaced by life's demands. In the early 'Guitar Piece II' the speaker laments 'What poor hands we hold, / When we face each other honestly!' In 'The Dance' he feels obscurely threatened by his beloved's emotion: 'I face you on the floor, clumsily, as / Something starts up', a 'something' more than mere music. Most chillingly, in the very late poem, 'The Winter Palace', antisocial solitude turns into lonely isolation as the ageing poet starts 'to give offence by forgetting faces'. In other poems faces, weathered by time or by events, evoke poignant sympathy. In 'Maiden Name' the five light syllables no longer 'mean your face'. In 'An Arundel Tomb' the earl's and countess's faces are, movingly, 'blurred'. More bleakly in 'Send No Money' the poet's own face, 'bent in / By the blows of what happened to happen', confronts him 'full face on dark mornings'. In 'Sunny Prestatyn' the girl is shockingly defaced. In 'The Building', the patients' faces are 'restless and resigned'.

At the opposite, positive extreme, the life-giving sun's 'Suspended lion face' gives for ever ('Solar'), while the poet ends 'Here' in the grip of light, 'Facing the sun'. In a less sublime sense, the emotional or aesthetic impact of a face may break down all defences, as in 'Wild Oats', where 'Faces… sparked / The whole shooting-match off'. Three specific women's faces in his work inspire epiphanies of excited reverence. In 'Latest Face' and 'Lines on a Young Lady's Photograph Album' the face freely offers a beauty which the poet 'salutes', and upon which photography confers candour. In 'Broadcast' a different face, 'Beautiful and devout', elicits both aesthetic and religious reverence. The third of these faces, that in 'When first we faced, and touching showed', elicits in some ways the most complex positive epiphany in Larkin's work.

The apparently casual, prosaic phrase 'When first we faced' is rendered intense and memorable by the elliptical, intransitive form of the verb: 'we faced', rather than 'we faced each other'. It is significant, in view of Larkin's careful rationing of words that this unusual grammatical usage marks the only appearance of 'faced' in his poetry after 1945. The poem strikes a note new to his work, infusing the unillusioned candour of 'Talking in Bed' with a warm mutuality lacking in the earlier poem. Here, in a new, maturer (or simply more elderly) version of 'Latest Face', the speaker is gratefully responsive rather than euphoric. In the earlier poem the poet celebrated his imaginative control over the new face. With the ebullient egotism of youth he declared that its beauty 'had no home' until it arrived at his eyes. Now the utter intimacy of her 'inch-close eyes' is contradicted by the decades of a different life which lie behind them, which 'Belonged to others, lavished, lost'. Like the young lady with the photograph album she has a past that nobody can share, but it has now lengthened into decades. Both beloved and poet are fingermarked and laden with luggage. But, though the poet can no longer claim Pygmalion's imaginative control over the vision (visage) before him, the creative imagination still insists on its preroga- tive. This face is still a great arrival at his eyes:

> But when did love not try to change
> The world back to itself – no cost,
> No past, no people else at all – ?

All love aspires to the condition of first love. The polarities of Larkin's poems relating to women are here united with a new poignancy. The woman is both a real woman in untidy air, and also a muse, an other who takes the poet beyond himself. Their meeting is 'new, and gentle-sharp, and strange'.

This is a unique relationship in Larkin's poetry, resignedly accepting that 'the pain' of the long perspective 'is real', but also achieving a muted transfiguration of experience. Maeve Brennan speculated that the poem could relate to Larkin's memories of their first intimacy in 1960–1, a decade before the poem was written.[35] But this cannot be so. Though it clearly calls on memories of earlier encounters, the specific context of the poem is Larkin's new and different relationship with his secretary, Betty Mackereth, to whom he gave a copy of the poem in December 1975. The crisis of Larkin's newly physical relationship with Maeve in 1974-6 disorientated him, but also reawakened his emotions. Afraid of the incalculable effects of this two-decade delayed consum- mation on his precariously balanced responsibilities towards Monica and Maeve, the poet set out deliberately to rebalance himself by initi- ating an intimacy with a familiar and utterly reliable colleague. At the time of 'When first we faced', Philip Larkin and Betty Mackereth were both in their early fifties. She had been his secretary since 1957, and the poem gathers an intriguing nuance if we know that its speaker had seen this face every working day for more than eighteen years before this moment when they finally 'faced'. Moreover Betty is considerably taller than Monica Jones or Maeve Brennan, nearer to the height of the poet himself, so she could 'face' him in a way which they could not.

Among the women in his life she already occupied a unique position. As Larkin told his mother, his secretary had become his 'mainstay' at work. He praised her for her 'boundless energy'. She was, he said, 'always cheerful and tolerant, and if she doesn't do half my work she sort of chews it up to make it easier for me to swallow. I'd be lost without her.' Betty herself comments: 'I was like a wife, really. I knew everything a wife knows, more than some wives know, probably'

(Motion 282). Her phrasing indicates a crucial difference. By definition a husband keeps secrets from his wife; Larkin needed to keep no secrets from Betty. She knew about his pornography, and was unfazed by it. By the early 1970s he had infected her with his habit of casual obscenity, and she would say 'Well, *fuck you!*' to him when he had particularly irritated her (adding exasperatedly: 'there, you've got *me* saying it now!') After acquiescing in the seduction (which took her quite by surprise) she told him: 'Don't worry, Philip. I will never, ever say a word to anybody.'[36] Betty was self-sufficient, understanding, with a straightforward zest for life. She would not be overly disturbed by this affair. He relished her sense of fun, telling his mother, with an echo of the Brunette Coleman fantasies of his youth: 'under, or alongside her stern secretary manner [she] is a completely frivolous, almost skittish person, a kind of schoolgirl that giggles at the back of the class' (Motion 282).

'Morning at last: there in the snow', like 'Love Again', offers an object lesson in the limits of the biographical approach to poetry. When she was first shown it in 1985, Maeve Brennan concluded that it must have been prompted by 'my winter boots one snowy night in January 1976':

> As I was pulling them on in front of the fire at 105 Newland Park prior to going home, Philip observed how the boots distorted my feet. 'How short and stubby they look' he said (not unkindly) when in fact my feet are long and narrow. The following day he told me how, first thing, he had looked out of an upstairs window and been mesmerized by 'your small blunt footprints' imperceptibly dissolving in the melting snow. He said nothing about the deeper thoughts this scene gave rise to.[37]

In view of Maeve's very exact recollection of the incident it seems surprising that Philip did not give her a copy of the poem, since he had given her copies of 'Broadcast' and 'The Dance'. He did, however, give a typed copy to Betty Mackereth, whose small blunt shoes he had noticed during one of her evening visits following badminton in January 1976. She still possesses the copy, and also the shoes, which she uses for gardening.[38] The fact that Larkin drafted this work in a separate workbook from the main sequence alongside two poems which are definitely addressed to Betty ('Be my Valentine this Monday' and 'We met at the end of the party') seems to make the attribution conclusive. The phrase 'your life walking into mine' fits better with the new relationship with Betty than the newly-revived relationship with Maeve, though both women would, of course, have left 'small blunt footprints' outside his house around this time.

However, in the case of so pure a lyric these biographical speculations seem particularly malapropos. Intimate as it is, this is a perfectly objective, fully 'expressed' work. Its refined artifice is aimed at ensuring that its protagonists are the generic lovers of lyric, not people with names or any particular history. For all this beautifully poised text tells us, its speaker could be a young woman experiencing her first love. Its conventional, unobtrusive form and metre ensure a tone of quiet sincerity. The stanzas are tetrameter triplets rhyming perfectly on long, euphonious diphthongs, which follow a musical sequence from a long back 'oh', to a high front 'i', then down to a low front 'ai' ('snow, wine, rain'). Snow is a universal image of transience (*'où sont les neiges d'antan?'*) The footprints, coming and going, by a rhetorical leap bring one 'life walking into' another. The collocation makes even the preposition 'into' subtly expressive. And once these footprints have vanished with the rain the lovers will be left, in a noun phrase clumsy with pensiveness, with 'What morning woke to'.

Two further poems inspired by the relationship with Betty only came to light in 2002. 'Be my Valentine this Monday' is deceptively simple light verse. Its two stanzas are written in a Valentine's Day card showing a grinning alligator, and the legend, 'See you later alligator!' continuing inside, 'You tasty morsel!' The poem, however, complicates this ingenuous lasciviousness:

> Be my Valentine this Monday,
>   Even though we're miles apart!
> Time will separate us one day
>   Till then, hyphen with my heart.
>
> You are fine as summer weather,
>   May to August all in one,
> And the clocks, when we're together,
>   Count no shadows, only sun.[39]

No other relationship in Larkin's poetry elicits this tone of gratitude for undemanding companionship. The words, however, go beyond conventional Valentine's Day sentiment. The bold use of 'hyphen' as a verb is perhaps appropriate in a poem addressed to the poet's secretary. Moreover the image of a hyphen, which bridges two separate words, tempers the card's possessive lasciviousness ('You tasty morsel'). The poet does not ask the woman to 'give' her heart, nor to 'take' his. Rather he invites her, delicately, to 'hyphen with' it. There is also, perhaps, a hint of respectful wariness of the woman's unremitting optimism in the second stanza's surreal image of sundials, in the grip of light, putting a halt to the passage of time by casting sun rather than shadow.

'We met at the end of the party' gives a more extended version of this complex, mature relationship.[40] Many of Larkin's earlier poems of intimacy take the form of a dramatized debate between gendered types. Here, however, the genders of the speaker and addressee are left open. Instead of the dirty young man and 'young lady', or antisocial bloke and 'my darling', the projected archetypes are an ageing lover who feels that life is over, and an ageing beloved who feels that life is still all ahead:

> We met at the end of the party,
> When most of the drinks were dead
> And all the glasses dirty:
> 'Have this that's left,' you said.
>
> We walked through the last of summer,
> When shadows reached long and blue
> Across days that were growing shorter:
> You said: 'There's autumn too.'

The brutality of the image of the belated lover offering 'dead' wine in a 'dirty' glass shows a frankness beyond that which Larkin adopts in poems addressed to any other woman.[41] The trimeter lines are curt and nervous, and the rhymes reinforce the different inflections of the protagonists' voices. His opening double-syllable half-rhymes create an uneasy dissonance ('party/dirty; summer/shorter') resolved only in the final line, which in the first two stanzas contains the woman's brisk answer to his gloom. It is as though he is unable to rhyme successfully, so she helps him out with her perfect rhymes ('dead/said'; 'blue/too'). Her tone subtly softens between the stanzas, from the brusque monosyllables of 'Have this that's left', to the quietly consoling: 'There's autumn too', as though she has now realized just how depressed he is.

The anapaestic metre implies an unceremonious domestic familiarity, as in 'Poem about Oxford'. But this is a harder, more 'objective', symbolic poem. Though the opening scene sounds like flat realism, it emerges that the party, the 'dead' drinks and the dirty glasses are bold symbols of the humiliations of ageing. Life has been imaged as a party or festivity ever since the famous Greek grave-painting at Paestum, two and a half millennia ago. It recurs several times in Larkin's work: in 'Reasons for Attendance', for instance, and in 'Skin', with its comic apology to his 'Obedient daily dress' for not finding a suitable 'brash festivity' at which to 'wear' it. It appears also in 'The Dance', 'Vers de Société', and, most bleakly, in his final poem, 'Party Politics', where the level of his drink in the glass (never full) symbolizes the unsatisfactory tail-end of life, without a beckoning future.

The second stanza again combines realism with archetype in a simple scene, this time focused on the changing season. The shadows are 'blue' in colour and 'blue' in mood. In the third stanza the poet puzzles over the woman's instinctive anticipation of continuance:

> Always for you what's finished
> Is nothing, and what survives
> Cancels the failed, the famished...

'Famished' might seem forced as a half-rhyme for 'finished', but the awkwardness mirrors the speaker's failure to make rhyme or reason of life. The syntax also is contorted: There is a nagging reproachful whine in 'Always for you...'. The poet feels intimidated by his lover's unfailing sense of meaning and purpose.

> and what survives
> Cancels the failed, the famished,
> As if we had fresh lives
>
> From that night on, and just living
> Could make me unaware
> Of June, and the guests arriving,
> And I not there.

The smooth metre of mixed iambs and anapaests suddenly stumbles on the phrase, 'just living'. 'Just' falls in the unaccented position but bears disproportionate stress, making 'living' die away, underlining how 'mere' it is. The word 'living' depresses the optimistic solidity of 'lives' into a more tenuous and abstract gerund, whose short 'i' is the more fleeting for coming between the long 'i's of the rhyme-words 'lives' and 'arriving'. The poem concludes in abrupt curtailment, with a line of two stresses instead of the three of the foregoing stanzas: 'And I not there.'

The opening image of the party returns in the final stanza as the speaker looks backward to the June of his life, when new people were still arriving as 'guests' to share its festivity. He simply cannot bear not to be there. As in 'Reference Back' time and space are confused in a 'long perspective'. When the guests in his life arrived at his party he was of course there to greet them. What he regrets is the passing of time which means that he is no longer 'there', no longer his younger self. The imaging of time in terms of space, however, makes it seem, by a witty sleight, as though the guests are still 'there'. They arrive at a party whose host is poignantly no longer there to welcome them.

By blending an unillusioned imagery of ageing with the transcendent rhetoric of the inspirational muse, this poem recapitulates in a new form the contradictions of the poet's earlier intimacies. In 'Latest Face' and 'Broadcast' he contemplates beauty across an unbridgeable distance. Now the older poet stands in awe, not of beauty, but of vitality. His optimistic lover stands at an uncrossable distance from him, as before. Now, however, the muse has an articulate, commonsense voice of her own, inviting the poet to leap across the distance to join her. He cannot do so, yearning stubbornly after the unreal June of his memory, while she enjoys the real shadows of autumn.

To return to the contextual level: as we might expect, Betty Mackereth was, like Winifred and Maeve, 'unsuspecting'. When asked if she had ever thought of herself as Larkin's muse, she replied: 'I was his *dogsbody*!' However, she well recalls the debate which is poetically distilled in the poem:

> He said to me one day: 'I can't understand why you, on waking in the morning, don't think of death.' And I just looked at him and I said: 'I cannot understand why you, on waking in the morning, *think* of death.'

She felt that his apprehension of mortality was morbid:

> he said to me: 'My father died when he was sixty-three,' (I mean, he was *miserable*), 'and I expect I shall die when I'm sixty-three.' And I said: 'Yes you will, because you are programming yourself to die at sixty-three.'[42]

Her prediction was accurate. Larkin died ten years after writing 'We met at the end of the party', in 1985 at the age of sixty-three. Readers may speculate on cause and effect. Was Betty right, and the poet had, as it were already written his death into his life's script in poems such as this? Or was it his genetically determined plight to die early, as he himself assumed? Betty Mackereth, in contrast, still plays golf at least twice a week and is active in a Victim Support group. In 2003 in her eightieth year she joined the Larkin Society Birthday Walk and clambered down the precipitous path to Cayton Bay, Scarborough to paddle in the sea where the eleven-year-old Philip had paddled seventy years earlier, in 1933.

Larkin's love-life appears at first sight a miscellaneous *bricolage*: a traumatic broken engagement, routine life-long monogamy, a prolonged mutual narcissism, two brief affairs twenty years apart. His 'nothing if not personal' work presents perhaps the widest spectrum of different intimacies in twentieth-century poetry. Each of the seven women who appear in his work focuses a distinct personal relationship with a 'real girl'. There is a mutuality in Larkin's work rare in conventional love poetry. He submits with humility to the different women in his life. He resigns himself to inheriting his mother's 'unsatisfactoriness'; he 'learns' the limits of his selfishness from Ruth Bowman; Patsy Strang obscurely subverts him; Winifred Arnott's marriage makes him feel 'out-invented'; with Monica Jones he is 'most [him]self'; Maeve Brennan has 'taught' him about his emotions; Betty Mackereth's life walks into his, 'gentle-sharp, and strange'. In this openness and vulnerability to others Larkin approaches the sacramental submission to Life of his idol D. H. Lawrence.

But Larkin's writing is not like Lawrence's. His poetry stands clear from 'the scrimmage'. His poetry may be full of other lives, but he is also the poet of the inviolable artistic self: 'My life is for me'; 'How will I be able to write when I have to be thinking about you?' (Motion 180). Like Pygmalion, Larkin creates his own objects of desire. He makes his partners into muses: of mortal beauty like Winifred and Maeve, or of insouciant ageing, like Betty. He turns his personal plight as a man into impersonal art; his loves become grist to the poet's mill. His relationships are artistically crafted into original and memorable verbal devices, in order to project a spectrum of emotional shades: the aesthetic euphoria of 'Latest Face', the sweetness of 'Broadcast', the self-disgust of 'Reference Back', the defeated exhaustion of 'No Road', the disconsolate loyalty of 'Talking in Bed'. He may write from deeply-felt emotion, as in 'Long roots moor summer', and 'When first we faced'; he may allegorize his situation, as in 'Deceptions' and 'Whatever Happened'; or he may fictionalize a dramatic context as in 'Lines on a Young Lady's Photograph Album' and 'Love Again'. But even the poems with the most personal and private of inspirations, are 'expressed completely'; they are impersonal works of art. Poems are never transcriptions of life. The deepest lesson that lyric poetry teaches is that experience cannot be transcribed. It can only, ever, be 'freshly created'.

5
Poetic Histories

Time and history

In 1957 Larkin was among writers asked by the *London Magazine* to reflect on the contemporary relevance of their work. 'During the Thirties', the questionnaire began, 'it was a widely-held view that poets, novelists and playwrights should be closely concerned *in their writing* with the fundamental political and social issues of their time.' It went on to ask whether, 'today, in 1957' it was a valid criticism that a writer was indifferent to 'the immediate problems of human freedom involved in, say, the Rosenberg case and the Hungarian revolution', or that his work showed no awareness of the threats posed by 'the development of atomic weapons and the levelling down of classes through discriminatory taxation' (*sic*), or 'recent discoveries in such sciences as biology, astronomy and psychology' (*FR* 4–5). Larkin was nettled by the implication that what matters about poetry is its topical relevance. In his view the duty of writers 'today, in 1957', was no different from what it had always been: 'My only criticism of a writer today, or any other day, is that he writes (as I think) badly, and that means a great many things much more certainly than it means "non-engagement": being boring, for instance' (*FR* 3).

The *London Magazine*'s culminating question was whether a novel, play or poem should be criticized if it 'could, *judged on internal evidence only*, have been written at any time during the last fifty years.' Larkin responded with the rhetoric of Ben Jonson's tribute to the timeless Shakespeare:

I was brought up to think that the better a work was, the less you thought about its period: the highest praise you could give was to say that it was not of an age, but for all time. Perhaps I was brought up wrongly. But if I were shown a work written 'today' that could be placed only somewhere within the last fifty years, I should wonder if I were not in the presence of a considerable talent.

(FR 3)

In a BBC broadcast of the following year he expressed the time-honoured aspiration of the poet to transcend the limitations of period and nationality:

I suppose the kind of response I am seeking from the reader is, Yes, I know what you mean, life *is* like that; and for readers to say it not only now but in the future, and not only in England but anywhere in the world.

(FR 78)

Others, through the ages, have taken a similar view, ever since Aristotle insisted that the statements of poetry 'are of the nature rather of universals, whereas those of history are singulars.'[1] Imlac in Samuel Johnson's *Rasselas* proclaimed that the arbiter of poetic worth is posterity; the writer 'must divest himself of the prejudices of his age or country... and rise to general and transcendental truths, which will always be the same.'[2] Though Virginia Woolf welcomes novelty, she also requires 'timeless' writing: 'We want something... hard as gem or rock with the seal of human experience in it... We want what is time-less and contemporary.'[3] In their *Survey of Modernist Poetry* Laura Riding and Robert Graves wrote: 'the most intelligent attitude toward history is not to take one's own date too seriously.'[4] Wallace Stevens resolved not to 'spend my time in being modern when there are so many more important things to be.'[5] It is the poet's plight to live in history, but to be always, as it were, across the topical flow of events, attending to something more important.

Poets cannot, of course, ignore politics. In the Thirties W. H. Auden had written: 'in a critical period such as ours, I do believe that the poet must have direct knowledge of the major political events.' But this was a concession, qualifying the assertion 'I am not one of those who believe that poetry need or even should be directly political.'[6] Indeed Auden took Johnson's submission to the verdict of posterity to a new extreme. 'Time', he wrote, 'worships language and forgives / Everyone by whom it lives.'[7] Writing well, Auden believed at this stage in his career, redeems the author's ideological and political faults. Though his poetry reflects the political turmoil of the 1930s, Auden was as hostile to the demand for 'engagement' as was Larkin in the following generation. One of his recurrent themes in *Another Time* (1940) is the deadening of life by 'history':

> So many have forgotten how
> To say I Am, and would be
> Lost if they could in history.
>
> Bowing, for instance, with such old-world grace
> To a proper flag in a proper place...[8]

Lyric poetry is concerned with the 'I Am' of living, and in an age of urgent ideologies and competing nationalisms the plight of the poet is an uncomfortable one. Auden struggles against the tide of his politicized age not to be lost in history. His preferred register is one of lyric universality. He celebrates, for instance, Nature's defiance of Time, which, however deep its chimes, or fast its torrent, 'Has never put the lion off his leap / Nor shaken the assurance of the rose'.[9] Humanity, he laments, has muddied this pure existential antithesis by entangling Time in History. We have lost the innocence of lion and rose. Instead of defying time by living, we appropriate and sophisticate time for devious purposes:

> And Time with us was always popular.
> When have we not preferred some going round
> To going straight to where we are?[10]

Time, in becoming 'popular', shifts into the indirect 'going round' of history. The assurance of the rose is replaced by the wary insecurity of flags and nationalities, treaties and wars. It is the poet's task to remind us that we need not waste time on 'some going round'. We can go straight to where we are:

> Follow, poet, follow right
> To the bottom of the night,
> With your unconstraining voice
> Still persuade us to rejoice...[11]

The poet's voice is 'unconstraining'. It refuses to make or to respect the ideological demands of a 'proper flag in a proper place'. In the words of another poem, it finds 'the mortal world enough'.[12] The poet, attentive to the fundamentals of the human plight, ignores the 'popular' time of ideology, and cuts out the noise of history.

Three years after the publication of *Another Time* the twenty-year-old Larkin followed Auden's advice by emphatically rejecting political engagement in his first distinctively Larkinesque fictions and poems, rejoicing in the unconstraining voice of the pseudonymous girl's-school story writer, Brunette Coleman. In her preface to the 'Sugar and Spice' poem sequence, Brunette writes provocatively: 'I feel that now more than ever a firm grasp on the essentials of life is needed',[13] these essentials, in wartime Britain in 1943, being the dust in a deserted August classroom, bicycles, tennis racquets, cricket scores and hockey-sticks:

> How many crushes, chums, and cliques
> Recall in this sad roundelay
> Those many golden, golden weeks,
> So many summer terms away!
>
> Now the ponies all are dead,
> The summer frocks have been outgrown,
> The books are changed, beside the bed,
> And all the stitches that were sewn
> Have been unpicked...[14]

In a review of T. S. Eliot, published in *Poetry* the previous year, 1942, George Orwell had declared: 'All art is to some extent propaganda.'[15] The critic's task, in Orwell's view, was to detect and evaluate the artist's ideology, as he himself had done in his celebrated essay on boy's-school stories of 1940.[16] Three years later Brunette responded, on behalf of the girl's-school story writer, dismissing Orwell's philistinism with an airy appeal to posterity:

> I am too familiar with Mr Orwell, and others of his kidney, to pay any attention to their ephemeral chatter; it seems to me to be a self-evident fact that Art cannot be explained away – or even explained – by foreign policy or trade cycles or youthful traumas, and that these disappointed artists whose soured creative instinct finds an outlet in insisting that it can are better ignored until Time has smoothed away all that they have scribbled on the sand.[17]

Brunette's blithe confidence in Time was not, however, borne out by the succeeding decades. Though Orwell's formulation still allows some space for the purely aesthetic (*'to some extent* propaganda'), later academic theorists have increasingly denied even this partial exemption. Unsurprisingly, however, no successful artist has embraced this subjection of creativity to cultural analysis.

In 1957 Larkin was tetchy and defensive in the face of the *London Magazine's* inquisition ('Perhaps I was brought up wrongly'). Taking Orwell's Marxist lead, the dominant voices of intellectual authority were increasingly arguing that, far from transcending history, as Johnson and Woolf believed, art is the product of, and even answerable to, history. Most persuasive and elegant among the demystifiers was Roland Barthes, whose essay 'The Great Family of Man', written in 1955, two years before the *London Magazine's* questionnaire, ridiculed a current exhibition of photographs from around the world, designed to show the common concerns of humanity: Birth, Death, Work etc. The idea was to take the visitor beyond or beneath the superficial differences of race and culture to 'human nature'. For Barthes this aim betrayed a sentimental false consciousness, the ideological illusion of 'a human essence... a class of assertions which escape History'. It offered an 'alibi for our humanism', presenting 'injustices' as 'differences'. Barthes concluded:

This myth of the human 'condition' rests on a very old mystification, which always consists in placing Nature at the bottom of History. Progressive humanism, on the contrary, must always remember to reverse the terms of this very old imposition in order to... establish Nature itself as historical.[18]

The 'eternal lyricism of birth' is a mystification and the death experienced by a white bourgeois is quite different from the death of a black lynch-mob victim. Time is a 'universalist' illusion; there is only History. Later analysts such as Terry Eagleton (*The Ideology of the Aesthetic*, 1990), John Carey (*The Intellectuals and the Masses*, 1992) and Valentine Cunningham (*In the Reading Gaol*, 1994) all defer to 'History' as the touchstone by which art is to be judged. Terry Eagleton, indeed, insists that Larkin is a minor figure because his poetry 'is not really, for all its undoubted virtues, an historically answerable medium.'[19] As Barthes said, divorced from History, Birth and Death are useless concepts: 'there is nothing more to be said about them; any comment about them becomes purely tautological.'[20]

'Nothing To Be Said' (1961) could have been written as a response to Barthes and Eagleton. Its self-cancelling title denies useful history, and its casual list of disparate cultural and social contexts points to a common primitive Nature beneath cultural and ideological difference: 'nomads among stones', 'families / In mill-towns', 'hunting pig', 'holding a garden-party'. Unlike the idealistic photographic exhibition of Barthes' essay, however, Larkin's aim is not a sentimental 'eternal lyricism', but a reductively existential vision of birth, copulation and death. For everyone, the poem grimly asserts, 'Life is slow dying':

> Hours giving evidence
> Or birth, advance
> On death equally slowly.
> And saying so to some
> Means nothing; others it leaves
> Nothing to be said.

The casual zeugma which equates 'giving' evidence with 'giving' birth, crudely denies any warmth or affirmation. Our common plight is mortality, overshadowing all our activities, biological or social, primitive or civilized. The poet concedes that to some his purely tautological vision of ahistorical Time advancing upon death will mean nothing. As Barthes complained, there is 'nothing more to be said' about such things. Larkin's response to this uselessness is not, however, irritation, but bitter submission to the inevitable: 'others it leaves / Nothing to be said.'

Larkin was careful to use the charged word 'history' only once in his *oeuvre*, in 'An Arundel Tomb', written in 1956:

> Now, helpless in the hollow of
> An unarmorial age, a trough
> Of smoke in slow suspended skeins
> Above their scrap of history,
> Only an attitude remains...

History is central to the poem. On one level, indeed, it is an Ode to History. The phrase 'Such plainness of the pre-baroque' places the couple in their medieval context, and skeins of smoke deftly symbolize the industrialization which has transformed the world they knew. This history, however, is poetic rather than political. 'An Arundel Tomb' is not an 'historically answerable' poem. The plight of the couple offers no lessons in injustice or feudalism or industrialization. Socio-politics are lost in the personal intimacy of '*their* scrap of history'. As the young Karl Marx put it: 'the man is greater than the citizen, and human life than political life.'[21] The reader may explore the context of the monument in Chichester Cathedral to discover what is known about the earls of Arundel and the conditions of life in the fourteenth century. But this will not help in understanding the poem. Some readers may be disconcerted to discover that the clasped hands at its centre are historically inaccurate, being almost certainly the invention of a Victorian restorer. Indeed it is not even certain that the figures originally lay together.[22] Larkin ruefully acknowledged these inaccuracies when they were brought to his attention, and also the fact that 'it should be "right-hand gauntlet", not left-hand' (*SL* 523). He need not have been concerned. Far from spoiling the poem, such contextual dislocations beautifully reinforce the contingent dubiousness of the couple's scrap of history.

History in the poem is imagined rather than chronicled or analysed. It is reduced, or rather expanded, to the elemental passage of time, seen in metaphors of space ('lengths and breadths'), and of seasonal recurrence:

> Snow fell, undated. Light
> Each summer thronged the glass. A bright
> Litter of birdcalls strewed the same
> Bone-riddled ground. And up the paths
> The endless altered people came...

The unnumbered seasons flash by in no particular order: the 'dateless' snow of winter followed by the light of summer and the bright birdcalls of spring. Rich Keatsian synaesthesia makes the passing of time into a sensuous bustle, 'Light...thronged the glass. A bright / Litter of birdcalls strewed...'. Against this vivid medley of transience the fixed effigies seem colourless and strained: 'Rigidly they // Persisted'. There is no easy nostalgia, no sense that the poet regrets the historical changes intervening between the dead couple and our unarmorial age. Moreover, our almost-instinct about love was as questionable in the earl's and countess's age as it is in ours. What the poem evokes is the universal truth of change and transience: 'Only an attitude remains'. 'An Arundel Tomb' ignores the 'going round' of sociology and politics. Rather than holding poetry answerable to history, it holds history answerable to poetry.

Distances

It is neatly appropriate for the annals of literary history that Larkin wrote his first great extended elegy, 'At Grass', in January 1950. The work was prompted by a visit to the cinema early in the new year, when he saw a short film concerning 'Brown Jack', a racehorse famous in the 1930s, now in retirement. The horse, 'for some reason', Larkin said, impressed him 'very strongly' (Motion 188). In this period of post-war austerity, as the half-century turned and the first full post-war decade began, 'Brown Jack' evoked for the young poet a past, lost world. Though the horses in his poem are anonymous, their racing success is dated precisely 'fifteen years ago', and the poem could be read as marking the distance between ideological Thirties hubbub and apolitical Fifties quietism. But this is history at an oblique angle, refracting the 'funda-mental political and social issues' of the age through the perspective of uncomprehending animals. Its nostalgia contains a core of subversive scepticism. At the deepest level, indeed, it presents a radical antithesis between History and Being. The primitive animal 'I Am' of the horses places them quite out of reach of 'history'.

The poet is respectful, attentive, unwilling to force meanings on these indistinct creatures: 'The eye can hardly pick them out / From the cold shade they shelter in...' On the simplest level the retired horses are elegiac symbols; Larkin was writing in the numb aftermath of his father's death less than two years earlier. But these elusive animals are not mere anthropomorphic allegories. There is something mysterious about the distance between them and the poet. They are, strangely, 'sheltering' from warmth and light, effaced, physically fading from view as their fame recedes:

> Then one crops grass, and moves about
> – The other seeming to look on –
> And stands anonymous again.

This horse's world is not ours. The animal only 'seems' to look on, in a parody of the race spectators of previous days. It is not only the eye which can hardly 'pick them out'; it is also the mind.

In the lines which follow, the poet strains to make the horses out across a breadth of time rather than space:

> Yet fifteen years ago, perhaps
> Two dozen distances sufficed
> To fable them...

The choice of the exact verbs, 'sufficed' and 'fable', allows their racing careers to be summarized in the elliptical noun phrase 'Two dozen

distances', an insubstantial abstraction whose technical racing signi-
fication ('over the distance') acts as a focus for other echoing connota-
tions of 'distance'. The poet is at a distance from the horses, physically
and metaphysically, and the horses are at a distance from their former
racing careers, in time, and also existentially. The horses' history in the
human world was not one of 'fundamental issues'. There is no mention
of Fascism, Stalinism or the Spanish Civil War. These horses 'made the
news', but only in terms of almanacs, the calendar of racing 'classics',
'faint afternoons' and the beautiful diminuendo of:

> the long cry
> Hanging unhushed till it subside
> To stop-press columns on the street.

In any case the human world had always been alien to them, with its
competitiveness ('Cups and Stakes and Handicaps'), fashions ('para-
sols'), and wars (hinted at in 'Squadrons of empty cars').

Now their scrap of history is done with, the horses have returned to
their animal world: 'Do memories plague their ears like flies? / They
shake their heads.' The feebleness of the poet's wit in detecting in the
shaking heads a human gesture of negation only serves to heighten
the reader's awareness that such gestures have no such meaning for the
animals themselves:

> Almanacked, their names live; they
>
> Have slipped their names, and stand at ease,
> Or gallop for what must be joy,
> And not a fieldglass sees them home,
> Or curious stop-watch prophesies...

Their names have a place in the history of the turf, so ironically are less
mortal than the horses themselves. But the poet tactfully leaves implicit the expected antithesis: 'their names live; they // [Die]'. The anacrusis created by the enjambement of the trailing rhyme-word 'they' into
the last stanza isolates the word dramatically. At last 'they' can be themselves, as horses, having 'slipped' not only their bridles but also their
human names. The field in which they now gallop for 'what must be
joy', is more secure than the 'home' to which they were previously
'seen' by racegoers. The word 'prophesies' trails to a stop, revealing
itself, unexpectedly, to be intransitive. We are no longer curious as to

what the stop-watch prophesied; it is of historical interest only. After this eloquent pause, the voice is compelled to drop almost to a whisper for the final lines: 'Only the groom, and the groom's boy, / With bridles in the evening come.' This picture of the men bridling the horses in the dusk, the assonances in their curiously formal titles, imitating their soothing voices, is mysteriously dignified. The horses were legends of the turf, but to the poet the legend seems genuinely mythic with a gravity beyond the cliché.

Such poetry is highly resistant to demystification. There have not, however, lacked critics eager to demystify it. Alvarez, for instance, blind to the poem's careful distances, crudely elides human and animal worlds, describing the horses as '*social* creatures of fashionable race meetings and high style.' He patronizes the poem as an old-fashioned 'genteel', Georgian work, 'elegant and unpretentious and rather beautiful in its gentle way'.[23] Tom Paulin's interpretation shows an even more extreme historicism. Determined, against the grain of the poem's subtleties, to find the poem mere propaganda, he detects in it a manifesto of literary conservatism and imperialist nostalgia. The words 'cold shade' and 'distresses', he alleges, betray Larkin's affectation of 'classical' literariness. The horses, he says are 'emblems of the heroic', 'heroic ancestors – famous generals, perhaps', and, perversely misreading Larkin's 'pick out' as 'pick off' he fancies that they are 'observed almost by a sniper's eye'. He concludes inventively that the phrases 'Only the groom, and the groom's boy' show 'the last vestiges of traditional hierarchy'.[24] This reading imports a national, specifically British nuance into the poem's imagery. In fact, a reader unaware of the author's identity could not possibly tell that it had not been written by an Irish or (apart from the language) a French poet. Paulin's 'historicism' reduces literary analysis to political polemic, abolishing the simply 'historical' in favour of ideology. Such historicism bears a similar relation to history as spiritualism bears to spirituality, or Scientology to science.

Blake Morrison's historicism is altogether more persuasive and illuminating. He argues that its imagery of past glory and achievement makes 'At Grass' in some sense 'a post-imperial poem': '"At Grass" taps and expresses feelings of loss and regret that might, for a certain section of the British populace at least, have been unusually pronounced around 1950 (when the poem was written).'[25] Morrison places the poem in its context of contemporary readership, but at the same time he respects its imaginative autonomy. Alert to Larkin's poetry, he recognizes that the plight of these passive, nameless horses cannot really stand as an effective symbol of national decline. Such post-imperial nostalgia, he nicely suggests, is not intrinsic to the poem, but is part of its context, an extrinsic element in the response of some early readers. The poem concerns 'loss and regret', rather than a specific, dated political loss.

A reader bent on ideological demystification would find it easier to interpret the poem in terms of animal welfare issues. In more explicit poems such as 'Take One Home for the Kiddies' and 'Ape Experiment Room' Larkin shows a highly emotional self-identification with the plight of dumb animals. Moreover, in his will he left half his estate, ultimately, to the RSPCA. But, just as 'At Grass' marginalizes politics, it also refuses to make animal rights propaganda. The workbook shows the poet consistently refining away or rejecting his initial very explicit moralizings over the perverse relationship between the horses and the human world: 'They lived in terms of men, hedged in / By bet and bid', 'But money rode them, led them in', 'Guiltlessly they galloped, yet / Broke three people in one day.'[26] Such didacticism would trivialize the poem's effect, and is excluded from the final version in the interest of a more universal appeal. The horses are irreducible: neither allegories of history, nor victims of human perversity.

'The Movement'

In 1954 a *Spectator* article defined a new post-war spirit in literature:

> bored by the despair of the Forties, not much interested in suffering, and extremely impatient of poetic sensibility, especially poetic sensibility about 'the writer and society'... The Movement, as well as being anti-phoney, is anti-wet; sceptical, robust, ironic...[27]

Two years later, in 1956, Robert Conquest's *New Lines* anthology was published, including work by Conquest himself, Larkin, Kingsley Amis, Donald Davie, D. J. Enright, Thom Gunn, John Holloway, Elizabeth Jennings and John Wain. Larkin's 'If, My Darling', 'I Remember, I Remember' and 'Church Going' rapidly came to be regarded as key 'Movement' works. David Lodge later gave a more theorized account of 'Movement' poetics: 'They... aimed to communicate clearly and honestly their perceptions of the world as it was. They were empiricists, influenced by logical positivism and "ordinary language" philosophy.'[28] Already by 1962, however, the climate had changed, and Alvarez's Introduction to *The New Poetry*, subtitled 'beyond the Gentility

Principle', focused a reaction against what he saw as 'the Movement's' conservative failure of nerve. Later Charles Tomlinson attacked Larkin's 'Movement' aesthetic as offering a 'stepped-down version of human possibilities'.[29]

Larkin himself was wary of the label:

> Then there was an article in *The Spectator* actually using the term 'Movement' and Bob Conquest's *New Lines* in 1956 put us all between the same covers. But it certainly never occurred to me that I had anything in common with Thom Gunn, or Donald Davie, for instance, or they with each other and in fact I wasn't mentioned at the beginning.
>
> (*FR* 20)

He resisted the implication that what was most essential to his poetry was anything shared with a group. His apprehension was justified. Essential though they are to the writing of literary history, such labels risk imposing the headlines of cultural history on the fine print of unique individual writers. Today 'The Movement' is something of a literary-historical footnote, retaining currency mainly as a useful focus for students approaching *The Less Deceived*. Though Gunn and Jennings later developed significant poetic careers in different contexts, and Amis achieved success as a novelist, no 'Movement' poetry of the 1950s, with the partial exception of that of Davie, has survived the test of posterity. Moreover, any reading of these writers' work reveals that, despite a superficial similarity of tone and idiom, the 'Movement' poets were, as Larkin insists, quite disparate. Though Larkin shares a demotic brusqueness with Amis, and a thoughtful candour of tone with Davie, the greater verbal complexity and emotional range of his work makes further comparisons either embarrassing or pointless. A consistent 'Movement' reading of his work is limiting and inadequate.

'Spring' (1950), for example, set in a local park and in traditional sonnet form, might seem to fit exactly *The Spectator's* definition of 'Movement' poetry. At the time its self-conscious antisocial pose of 'indigestible sterility' would also have suggested to the reader another fashionable category: the 'angry young man'. It is notable, however, that, though its empirical directness and ironic tone are very much of its period, 'Spring' lacks specific 1950s sociological colour. As Larkin said, 'I was brought up to think that the better a work was, the less you

thought about its period.' There is nothing here to suggest any particular date, nor to locate this park in Leicester, nor even England:

> flashing like a dangled looking-glass,
> Sun lights the balls that bounce, the dogs that bark,
> The branch-arrested mist of leaf, and me,
> Threading my pursed-up way across the park,
> An indigestible sterility.

The focus is exclusively on the immediate stimuli of the poet's surroundings. The images do not suggest the Welfare State, nor post-war
reconstruction. Moreover, the speaker's alienation is quite unexplained.
There is no hint in the text as to whether his self-disgust might owe
something, say, to post-war austerity or to the recent death of his
father. The poem speaks only of children, birds, sun, barking dogs and
leaves.

This decontextualization concentrates the reader's attention on the
emotion evoked, for its own sake: a piquant mix of elation and extravagant melancholy. The speaker relishes his skill in catching the exact
empirical 'feel' of the busy sunlit scene. 'The branch-arrested mist of
leaf', with its rich alliterations reminiscent of Hopkins, is sensuously
elaborate and faintly precious, throwing into stark contrast the two
meagre syllables 'and me'. Internal rhyme reinforces the sense of isolation by clashing a satisfyingly end-stopped 'leaf' against an unsatisfy-
ing open-ended 'me'. The final line of the octave insidiously parodies
the rich poeticism of this rhyme-line, repeating the 'st' alliteration and
also the vowel-sequence (a, eh, i, ee), with an effect of heavy irony: 'An
indigestible sterility.' All five accents of this pentameter are crammed
into just two Latinate polysyllables, forcing the voice to stretch out the
words with an insinuating aggressiveness. Paradoxically, however, the
poet's sourness of tone intensifies the sweetness of the season, and for
all its sulkiness the poem is essentially a celebration:

> Spring, of all seasons most gratuitous,
> Is fold of untaught flower, is race of water,
> Is earth's most multiple, excited daughter...

Much of the poem's excitement lies in the young poet's virtuoso command of verbal artifice. Jean Hartley, who was to be Larkin's publisher,
still remembers the grateful excitement she felt on receiving this poem,
with others, in 1953.[30] As T. S. Eliot commented on reading *The Less
Deceived*, Larkin 'often makes words do what he wants' (Motion 291).

A synchronic reading of 'Spring' in the context of the 'Movement' needs to be complemented by a diachronic reading in terms of its literary topos. Dissonance between the joys of spring and the poet's despair is a familiar theme in art, and from the late Middle Ages onward malcontent melancholy has been a poetic plight self-consciously affected by young male artists. John Dowland specialized in extravagant motiveless melancholy: 'Semper Dowland; Semper Dolens.' Nicholas Hilliard's famous miniature shows a love-lorn youth surrounded by vivid spring flowers. In a later century spring fails to move the bereaved Thomas Gray from his grief:

> The birds in vain their amorous descant join;
> Or cheerful fields resume their green attire:
> These ears, alas! for other notes repine.[31]

At the beginning of 'The Burial of the Dead' section of *The Waste Land*, T. S. Eliot gives an original turn to the motif, orchestrating his lonely isolation in Marburg at the beginning of the Great War into a universalized chorus of spiritual aridity. Each of these artists gives a unique individual turn to the familiar plight. The cheerful sounds and sights of spring fail to console Gray for his loss; the stirrings of April present Eliot with a threatening spiritual challenge; Larkin's zestful negativity gives a sharper edge to his sensuous celebration of the season.

'Church Going' presents a more complex lesson in the distortions of topical reading. Ever since its publication in *The Less Deceived* in 1955 the poem has suffered from its status as, in a sense, *the* 'Movement' poem. As Larkin's reputation established itself this work became the focus for polemicized ideological readings, and it is still difficult to disentangle it from the debates which surrounded its reception in the 1950s and 1960s. A self-ironic meditation on the place of spirituality in a world without God was reduced to the trivial posturings of post-war moodiness, or alternatively, to a hesitant quest for English religious renewal.

On the one hand A. Alvarez cited the poem's 'predictable... pieties' in his 1962 attack on 'the Movement'. Larkin's speaker, he alleges, is a typical post-war Welfare State Englishman: 'shabby and not concerned with his appearance; poor – he has a bike not a car; gauche but full of agnostic piety; underfed, underpaid, overtaxed, hopeless, bored, wry.'[32] In projecting this generic cultural type, Alvarez embroiders freely on Larkin's text; there is no indication in 'Church Going', for instance, that the speaker is underfed, or underpaid, nor is the taxation system of the slightest relevance to its theme. Having thus over-historicized

Larkin's persona, Alvarez finds it easy to convict the poet of a 'common sense' which is too 'common', and worst of all, of 'gentility'.[33] On the other side, with a similar disregard for Larkin's text, some Christian readers detect in it a deep sympathy with Anglicanism. One early commentator concluded 'The whole tone of the poem expresses doubts about the validity of atheism'.[34] J. R. Watson went further, finding Larkin a fundamentally religious sensibility: 'under the pose he is *homo religiosus*, with an awareness of sacred time and sacred place'.[35] Thus reduced, the poem became a weapon in a kind of class war between the literary avant garde seeking a 'new seriousness' in poetry, and a cultural establishment who claimed it on behalf of traditional spirituality.

Once again, as in the case of 'Spring' attention to the poetry itself yields a quite different, and far more interesting picture. Rather than a statement of beliefs it presents an emotional process. Its structure, a three-part, shifting meditation, is as far removed as possible from Alvarez's and Watson's context of ideological assertion. More specifically the speaker's display of 'gauche' clowning in the first two stanzas has a harder edge than Alvarez allows. It is more a matter of calculated impertinence than respectful embarrassment. The speaker removes his cycle clips with a 'reverence', the awkwardness of which betrays a lack of sincerity as much as respect. He idly runs his hand around the font, speculates ignorantly on the newness of the roof ('Someone would know'), and apes the tones of the lesson-reader from the lectern. As in 'Spring', the speaker refuses to toe the line. Though his truculent philistinism, reminiscent of Amis, has very much the flavour of its period, it becomes clear as his meditation develops that his rejection of religion is philosophically serious. His attitude is more considered than mere shallow impudence. He reflects that the church's silence has been 'Brewed God knows how long', using 'God' as an idiomatic expletive, with a casual slight to the notion of God in the theological sense. God is in fact notably absent from the poem. As he donates an Irish sixpence on his way out, he feels a distinct sense of release from oppression. Outside he is no longer called upon to show a deference he does not feel.

The central three stanzas give a more resonant emotional depth to this scepticism in a mock-heroic futurist panorama of the Decline of Faith, with perhaps a faint hint of the rationalist prophecies of H. G. Wells behind it. The poet looks beyond the stage at which churches become museums, 'chronically on show', and beyond the incoherent residual superstitions of 'dubious women' picking 'simples for a cancer', to the point where not only religious belief, but also even its answering

scepticism will have faded from memory. It is a strange, elusive speculation: 'And what remains when disbelief has gone? / Grass, weedy pavement, brambles, buttress, sky...'. Larkin may be 'an Anglican agnostic'
(Motion 485). He may feel that the modern replacements for church
ritual, 'the registry office and the crematorium chapel', have made life
'thinner' (*FR* 22). But there is no sign anywhere in the poem of a genuine feeling for the beliefs or rituals of the church. Its interior, with its
holy stuff and flowers, vaguely repels him; he is more moved by the
idea of the ruin it will become and by the graveyard outside. Nor,
significantly, are any of the four hypothetical visitors whom he projects
in his poem as 'the very last to seek / This place for what it was', in any
sense religious: an enthusiast for architecture, a romantic 'ruin-bibber,
randy for antique', a superstitious 'Christmas-addict, counting on
a whiff / ... of myrrh', and 'my representative, / Bored, uninformed,
knowing the ghostly silt / Dispersed'. The brilliantly irreverent phrase
'ghostly silt' derides nostalgia for a lost Age of Faith, such as one finds
in T. S. Eliot.

Recently Raphaël Ingelbien has sought to place the poem in its historical context by drawing the parallel with Eliot's church-going poem
'Little Gidding', published at the height of the war in 1942. 'Church
Going', written just over a decade later, echoes, particularly in its final
two stanzas, the discursive manner and tone of Eliot's poem, to which
it is clearly in some sense an answer:

> A serious house on serious earth it is,
> In whose blent air all our compulsions meet,
> Are recognised, and robed as destinies.
> And that much never can be obsolete...

As Ingelbien says, Larkin's 'serious earth could easily turn into Eliot's
"significant soil".'[36] However, Eliot's confident sense of shared history,
'You are here to kneel / Where prayer has been valid', is attenuated in
Larkin to the prediction that when religion is dead 'someone' will continue to seek wisdom here, if for no better reason than that 'so many
dead lie round'. Ingelbien concludes that 'Church Going' 'eventually
confirms the unavailability of the values that Eliot embraced':

> that 'never obsolete' sense of community is regained through a
> rhetoric which, in the context of Larkin's new poetics, looks suspi-
> ciously obsolete (witness the inversion..., the rare 'blent' and the
> hackneyed 'robe of destiny' image).[37]

Larkin's half-hearted rhetoric fails, in Ingelbien's view, 'to find a poetically convincing way of endowing England with transcendental
significance'.[38]

But this is to read Larkin's poem too much on Eliot's terms. Larkin
has no interest in endowing England with transcendental significance,
and lacks the naturalized American's wartime concern for the Anglican
community. Such religious nationalism was as dated and obsolete for
Larkin as it had earlier been for Hardy and Housman. While Eliot's
wartime image of timeless English community was the national church
of traditional faith, Larkin's was the girls' school of secular fiction.
'Church Going' is not merely a weaker, 'less significant' 'Little Gidding',
nor is Larkin a failed Anglican. He is an unhesitant atheist. As he said
in an interview:

> It isn't religious at all. Religion surely means that the affairs of this
> world are under divine superveillance, and so on, and I go to some
> pains to point out that I don't bother about that kind of thing, that
> I'm deliberately ignorant of it – 'Up at the holy end', for instance.
>
> (*FR* 22)

His scepticism is urgently explicit: 'I go to some pains to point out', 'I
don't bother', 'I'm deliberately ignorant'.

Key to the misreading of the poem is the ambiguous register of emotion and scepticism in the final two stanzas. As in many Larkin poems
the speaker is dramatized and self-ironic, but his lyric 'I' is not clearly
distinguished from the author himself. This is a dangerous strategy to
employ when writing on a subject to which readers bring such strong
prejudices. What Alvarez reads as 'genteel' half-hearted 'piety', Watson
reads as sincere pensiveness. It seems certain, however, on careful
reading, that the gaucheness of these stanzas is carefully staged, as it
were in heavy inverted commas. Their idiom hints at a prosy Reverend
Flannel intoning vacuities in a pious Anglican sing-song. The speaker,
for instance, is drawn to the church because it 'held unspilt / So long...
marriage and birth / And death, and thoughts of these'. The loose fervour of 'and thoughts of these' betrays the speaker's reverential muddle. It is perhaps possible to detect an uncomfortably inept joke in his
cosy use of the far-fetched word 'frowsty' in 'this accoutred frowsty
barn', while the 'pi' tone of the grammatical inversion in 'A serious
house on serious earth it is' is unmistakable. The word 'house' reminds
us that this is a 'house of God', but this second-hand reverence is
subject to crushing irony. The house is, we have seen, unambiguously

unoccupied. The self-mockery becomes painful in the embarrassingly vacuous phrases 'blent air', and 'robed as destinies'.

Were Larkin a satirist these lines would foreground a heavy irony against the speaker's half-baked emotionalism. But Larkin was not concerned to score points in a debate about religion. His quarrel was not that of a polemicist, with others, but that of a poet, with himself; so the tone remains inextricably mixed. The mechanical rhetoric of Anglican religiosity is the more moving for being so manifestly inadequate. The final line returns to a prose plainness, infusing sombre meditation with offhand dismissiveness: 'If only that so many dead lie round.' Scathing reduction becomes paradoxical elevation. The poet concedes that his consolatory phrases are mere wishfulness. Far from this being a poem of 'predictable... pieties', its effect depends on a subversion of conventional piety. It generates an emotionally complicated, unillusioned transcendence, ironizing the bad faith which Alvarez detects in it, and, on the other hand, rejecting the theology which Anglican readers import into it. It is not surprising that Larkin should have been so irritated by readers who warmed to the carefully-placed sentimentalism of his peroration, while sliding over the irony. When Brenda Moon, his long-time Assistant Librarian in Hull, told him that she found the poem 'wonderful', he 'looked surprised and said: "If I'd known how popular it would be, I would have taken more trouble over it."'[39] One insistent American reader reduced him to weary sarcasm: 'Ah no, it's a great religious poem; he knows better than me – trust the tale and not the teller, and all that stuff' (*FR* 22).

Dates

The plight of the lyric poet, in history yet also outside and across it, is sharply focused in the handful of Larkin's poems which feature the precise reference of a date. 'Midsummer Night, 1940', written when Larkin was only seventeen, presents an Audenesque panorama of England, now: 'The sun falls behind Wales; the towns and hills / Sculptured on England, wait again for night...' Wartime anxiety pervades a landscape of elemental simplicity (sun, hills, night) and national identities (Wales, England). His mature date poems are, however, rather different from this. The three dates which figure explicitly within his mature *oeuvre* convey a more overtly mediated, even fictionalized history: 1914 ('MCMXIV'), 1929 ('Livings I') and 1963 ('Annus Mirabilis'). These are dates whose socio-political significance is public property, and immediately recognizable to the reader. The first two are among the most familiar dates of the era, while 1963 now has a similar status, partly because of Larkin's poem. Their heavily culturally mediated implications are evident in their distinctive form: the first in Latin, the other two spelled out in words and in the voice of particular dramatized speakers. The history these dates embody is not one of objective event, but of shared mythography or folk-memory. Other dates of similar wide currency might have been expected to appear in Larkin's work. The year 1939, however, will have seemed unusable so soon after Auden's 'September 1, 1939', while 1945 perhaps bears too public an historical significance for this poet of personal emotion.

In 'Remembering the "Thirties"', first published in *New Lines*, and included by Larkin in *The Oxford Book of Twentieth Century English Verse*, Donald Davie meditates on changing perceptions of historical events, distinguishing between the lived experience of the older generation and the mediated version learned at school by their children and grandchildren. What for our parents were 'agonies':

> for us
> Are high-brow thrillers, though historical;
> And all their feats quite strictly fabulous.

Great events which were immediate and real to Auden, Spender and Day Lewis are reduced to a story:

> The Anschluss, Guernica – all the names
> At which those poets thrilled or were afraid
> For me mean schools and schoolmasters and games...[40]

Davie worries over the poet's responsibility to this fading history. Every twenty or thirty years, he reflects, we need to relearn history's lessons; otherwise it become mere dead knowledge:

> The Devil for a joke
> Might carve his own initials on our desk,
> And yet we'd miss the point because he spoke
> An idiom too dated, Audenesque.

Perhaps, he sadly muses, the fact that style so swiftly becomes outdated means that we will never be able truly to learn our lesson.

Larkin, in contrast, has no desire to inform or instruct, nor does he find lessons in history. In 1982 he wrote to Amis: 'I reckon Heaney and Co. are like where we came in... Boring too-clever stuff, litty and "historical"' (*SL* 682). He lists his Oxford contemporaries of the early 1940s, including Sidney Keyes and John Heath-Stubbs. Larkin may write about history, but he is not concerned to claim historical insight. 'MCMXIV' (1960), for instance, casts the date in its outdated, archaic Latin form, familiar from monuments 'For the Fallen' in town squares and on village greens across the country. It recalls not the didactic historical interpretations of school textbooks, but the ritual emotion at the Cenotaph each year, intimate family memories, jerky old film footage, the battered scraps of history left behind by our parents or our parents' parents.

The poem's opening image, a group of young men queuing up to enlist 'as if it were all / An August Bank Holiday lark', seems fixed, as in a faded photograph: dated in both senses of the word. One critic detects in the poem a 'somewhat Betjemanesque... conservative Larkin'.[41] But intense though the poem's emotion is, its history is ironically placed in a way in which the older poet's glowing visions of a bygone age are not. Larkin cherishes no naïve longing for an Edwardian past he never experienced, nor does he conservatively celebrate the pre-war social order. The 'differently-dressed servants' have 'tiny rooms in huge houses', while the 'innocence' of the grinning young men queuing to die in the trenches is viewed with bitter irony. The dim historical vistas of 'fields / Shadowing Domesday lines' has been read as showing Larkin's 'deeply patriotic... feeling for his native country'.[42] But any patriotism is heavily qualified by the poem's lament over the unprecedented waste of human life of the Great War. Larkin's imagination finds no security in national or class identity, and the poem implicitly acknowledges Barthes' 'injustices'. It is not, however, concerned with history as injustice. Its subject is history as shared tragedy. The repetition in 'Never such innocence, / Never before or since', shows an awareness of its own hyperbole. The words assert an emotional attitude rather than an objective historical fact:

> Never such innocence,
> Never before or since,
> As changed itself to past
> Without a word – the men
> Leaving the gardens tidy,
> The thousands of marriages
> Lasting a little while longer:
> Never such innocence again.

The absence of a main verb ('As changed itself' rather than 'Has changed itself') denies this 'change' the status of an event. It is instead a reified myth. The loss of innocence and beauty which it enacts is a universal plight.

The most poetically intense elements of the poem are contingent. No socio-political lesson can be drawn from advertisements made out of tin, the quaint domestic vocabulary of 'cocoa and twist', the bleached sunblinds over the shops, the fact that the place-names are 'all hazed over / With flowering grasses', or most gratuitously evocative of all, 'The dust behind limousines'. At the end of the poem an ahistorical plainness of language strips away any hint of ideological rhetoric. The innocence the poem mourns may be 'quite strictly fabulous', but it is no mystified construct of sentimental nationalism. 'MCMXIV' leaves the reader not with an historical event, but surprisingly, with a tenuous and primitive breadth of time: the space between the farewells of wives and husbands, and the moment, days, weeks or months later when the husband is killed. The marriages remain technically intact during this time; the gardens tidy. To the socio-political historian, concerned with 'fundamental political and social issues', this space of time, like the 'attitude' which is all that remains of the earl and countess, 'means nothing'. To the poet it is the whole point.

Similarly, in 'Livings I', instead of Davie's purposeful interrogation of history, we find a meditative juxtaposition of private and public similar to those in Hardy's 'In Time of "The Breaking of Nations"' and Auden's 'Musée des Beaux Arts'. The ominous date 1929, the year of the Great Crash and prelude to the 'low dishonest decade' of the 1930s, appears casually, in the final words of the poem, like an afterthought or postscript. The speaker is a modernized, Larkinesque version of Hardy's 'maid and her wight' whose story will outlast 'War's annals',[43] or of Auden's 'Children who did not specially want it to happen, skating / On a pond' during the miraculous birth of Christ. Like them, Larkin's protagonist is at the margin of great events, in 'a corner, some untidy spot'.[44] In a prosy, dispirited tone he informs us how he makes a living as a travelling salesman in agricultural goods:

> I deal with farmers, things like dips and feed.
> Every third month I book myself in at
> The —— Hotel in —— ton for three days.

His masculine routine has a strong genre feel about it, as though he were a character in a short story by Kipling or Somerset Maugham:

> Afterwards, whisky in the Smoke Room: Clough,
> Margetts, the Captain, Dr. Watterson;
> Who makes ends meet, who's taking the knock...

The formal surnames and the slang are both heavily dated. Though he presents himself in the present tense, this character's language places him already deep in the past. His is an 'historical present' in more than the grammatical sense. But then, in the third stanza, the poem modulates from sociological detail and literary echoes to a purer level of living, in a brief epiphany:

> Later, the square is empty: a big sky
> Drains down the estuary like the bed
> Of a gold river, and the Customs House
> Still has its office lit.

In this moment of beauty his world becomes briefly exotic, the sky over the estuary is the bed of another river, the world, by implication turned upside down.

Though the geographical situation of the town is unspecified, the poem is situated at an exact historical moment, between the wars. The speaker stays at a hotel whose walls bear 'comic' pictures, of hunting scenes and the trenches of the Great War (presumably magazine caricatures). Both are equally uninteresting to the present customers: 'stuff / Nobody minds or notices'.

> I drowse
> Between ex-Army sheets, wondering why
> I think it's worth while coming. Father's dead:
> He used to, but the business now is mine.
> It's time for change, in nineteen twenty-nine.

The facile rhyme ('mine/nineteen twenty-nine') emphasizes the speaker's ignorance of the significance of the date. There is, however, no heavy Sophoclean irony. Though mention of the date makes us aware that events beyond this character's knowledge will soon overtake his desultory reflections on 'Government tariffs, wages, price of stock', there is no relishing of our superior vantage point. This is not a matter of 'injustice'. There is no satire or moral judgement. The effect of the date is simply to render more intense the fragility of this particular moment in the speaker's life. This character is 'lost in

history' in a more poignant sense than Auden's. Or perhaps he is lost
to history.

Elizabeth Bishop, in her poem 'Questions of Travel', ponders
'blurr'dly and inconclusively' on the inconsequential, contingent connections between local styles of craftsmanship as manifested in domestic artefacts:

> what connection can exist for centuries
> between the crudest wooden footwear
> and, careful and finicky,
> the whittled fantasies of wooden cages.[45]

In a tone of mixed whimsy and seriousness she reflects that her life
would have been diminished had she never 'studied history in / the
weak calligraphy of songbirds' cages.' It seems likely that Bishop would
have appreciated Brunette Coleman's firm grasp on the essentials of
life. Larkin also celebrates history in 'weak' contingencies: the rituals of
an old-fashioned hotel, the sky draining down the estuary, the lights
burning late in the Customs House.

Larkin's third mature date-poem is, in contrast, topical and light in
tone:

> Sexual intercourse began
> In nineteen sixty-three
> (Which was rather late for me) –
> Between the end of the *Chatterley* ban
> And the Beatles' first LP.

'Annus Mirabilis', however, is more similar to 'MCMXIV' than is at first
apparent. It too resorts in its title to Latin, the founding language of
Western Europe, and the implication of portentous history is only
partly ironic. Not surprisingly, in view of Larkin's attitude towards 'historical' poetry, the speaker presents his own (slightly misplaced) place
in history, as a ruefully comic plight. But, though the tone is lighter
than that in 'MCMXIV' the reification of the date creates the same kind
of mythic resonance. It is presented as the focus for what Barthes would
term a 'modern mythology', a euphoric ideological product of popular
culture. Larkin is perfectly aware of this constructed, ideological
quality. The assertion that 'sexual intercourse' began in 1963 is as manifestly questionable as the proposition that 'innocence' ended in 1914.
There is no subtext here for an Orwell or Barthes to demystify. 'Annus

Mirabilis' openly and explicitly constructs its mystification in the text, before the reader's eyes, as it were. The poem both celebrates the myth of Sixties permissiveness, and also mocks such mystification.

Politics

Larkin was a man of vivid prejudices. However his politics, though strident, were shallow, and his diffidence about the right-wing extremism which he inherited from his father was deep and genuine. A recurrent pattern in his letters and interviews is a self-consciously performative provocation, followed immediately by an offhand self-deprecation:

> I've always been right-wing. It's difficult to say why, but not being a political thinker, I suppose I identify the Right with certain virtues and the Left with certain vices. All very unfair, no doubt.
>
> (*RW* 52)

In 1976 I canvassed colleagues to sign a petition addressed to the Council of the University of Hull requesting that the university disinvest in companies which, as had been revealed by the *Guardian*, paid black workers in their South African subsidiaries below the official UN poverty wage. One lunchtime in the staff bar Larkin was asked what he thought of this enterprise. He is reported as replying: 'He's performing a valuable function. It will be handy to have a complete list of all the pricks in the University.' My colleague John Howarth, who was present at this exchange, had the presence of mind to interpose: 'There's one thing to be said about a prick. It usually has a pair of balls associated with it.' With a characteristic fair-mindedness Larkin gave an appreciative *moue*, as if to say '*touché*'.

The contradictions of his attitudes have frequently been remarked. He could declare 'Kick out the niggers', but his admiration for black jazz musicians was unbounded. He groused about his 'Paki' neighbours, but attempted to help the young Vikram Seth into print, and was on excellent terms with R. K. Biswas, Monica Jones's Indian colleague in Leicester University's English Department. Similarly, though he termed himself 'one of Nature's Orangemen', and possessed a Red Hand Defenders tie, his long love affair with a devout Catholic of Irish descent was never troubled in the slightest by his Loyalist sympathies.

Wary of trusting his political instincts, Larkin generally confined politics to private letters addressed to sympathetic correspondents. Almost none of his poems can be forced to yield a political meaning, despite the ingenious contortions of critics who believe all poetry to be politics in disguise. There are, however, one or two poems, written in the late 1960s and early 1970s in which he broke his otherwise firm principle never to be didactic, never to make poetry '*do* things' (*RW* 74), and attempted to answer the demands of history by intervening in topical politics. These works later embarrassed him, and remain distinct from his main *oeuvre*.

In 1969, when the radical ferment of the decade seemed to have carried all before it, he was encouraged by his right-wing colleagues to publish, in a 'Black Paper' on education, an ephemeral couplet of trochaic doggerel attacking left-wing academics and students.[46] A more serious attempt at a political poem, 'Homage to a Government', written in the same year, was included in *High Windows*. Larkin deplored the government's decision to close its base in Aden:

> Next year we are to bring the soldiers home
> For lack of money, and it is all right.
> Places they guarded, or kept orderly,
> Must guard themselves, and keep themselves orderly.
> We want the money for ourselves at home
> Instead of working. And this is all right.

The repetition that it 'is all right' has a wan, ironic eloquence. But the implication that Britain maintained overseas military bases out of an altruistic desire to keep order in the world is naïve. As Blake Morrison points out, 'financial motives are as involved in the posting of troops to colonies as they are in the withdrawal of them.'[47] And the implication that the money saved by this decision is intended to line the pockets of the work-shy is merely a party-political jibe at the Labour government of the day.

Larkin showed an uneasy awareness that the poem had taken him out of his depth:

> Well, that's really history rather than politics. That poem has been quoted in several books as a kind of symbol of the British withdrawal from a world role. I don't mind troops being brought home if we'd decided this was the best thing all round, but to bring them home simply because we couldn't afford to keep them there seemed a dreadful humiliation.
>
> (*RW* 52)

The incoherence of his position is betrayed by his use of the word 'history' in an almost opposite sense to that which informs his rejection of 'historical', politically-engaged poetry. Here the word slides into the meaning 'safely in the past', in antithesis to urgent 'politics'. Moreover, he is clearly casting about for plausible verbiage in the phrase 'the best thing all round', which yields no meaning at all. For all his protestations the poem is clearly political; worse still it is crudely topical. His uncomfortable excuses merely compound his embarrassment at having forced his art. Larkin was a great poet but, as he himself admitted in an early letter, when it came to politics or world affairs, 'I don't know anything at all about anything, and it's no use pretending I do' (*SL* 115).

Place and nation

Larkin's complex attitude towards history is mirrored by his attitude towards geography. In 'I Remember, I Remember' the poet finds his train passing through Coventry, and exclaims 'I was born here':

'Was that', my friend smiled, 'where you "have your roots"?'
No, only where my childhood was unspent,
I wanted to retort, just where I started...

Though the poem was written in 1954, barely a decade after its city centre had been destroyed by bombing, the poet ignores Coventry's public history, focusing entirely on his own private recollections, or lack of them. His attitude towards the place is couched in terms of a universal plight: 'Nothing, like something, happens anywhere.' Similarly, though he spent his last three decades in Hull, Larkin refused to identify himself with the city: 'I don't really notice where I live: as long as a few simple wants are satisfied – peace, quiet, warmth – I don't mind where I am. As for Hull, I like it because it's so far away from everywhere else' (*RW* 54). Larkin's 'here' is wherever or whenever he happens to find himself:

No, I have never found
The place where I could say
This is my proper ground,
Here I shall stay...
('Places, Loved Ones')

For Larkin place is contingent.

The proper noun 'England' occurs four times in the post-1945 section of the 1988 *Collected Poems*; only once with any charge of emotional commitment, in the commissioned poem 'Going, Going'. The adjective 'English' occurs only once after 1945. When specific locations are named in the mature work they are characteristically stereotyped (Frinton, Stoke, Prestatyn, Dublin) or given a uniquely personal meaning without any claim to general application (Coventry, Oxford). 'Hull' never appears. On the other hand the noun 'home' occurs twenty-two times after 1945. The adverb 'here', which takes us closest to the existential core of the human condition, occurs thirty-nine times, often in resonant contexts. Few of Larkin's readers will share his association with Coventry, many will not share his Englishness. All will share a notion of home, with vases and pictures; and all, without any exception, are 'here'. Larkin's lyric idiom is sparing of culturally-specific vocabulary, but rich in words denoting subjective states of being. His comment that 'poets write for people with the same background and experiences as themselves' (*RW* 69), might seem to set a barrier between himself and non-English, non-male, non-middle-class readers. However, in practice, his lyric vocabulary ensures that almost everyone is 'like' himself. As he said in his 1958 BBC broadcast:

> I suppose the kind of response I am seeking from the reader is, Yes, I know what you mean, life *is* like that; and for readers to say it not only now but in the future, and not only in England but anywhere in the world.
>
> (*FR* 78)

Seamus Heaney, for whom geography is located political history, and whose poetry is inextricably 'rooted' in a particular community, has always found Larkin's indifference to nation and province baffling. His influential essay 'Englands of the Mind' (1976) struggles to interpret Larkin's work in terms of communalist ideology, grouping him with Hughes and Hill in a group of post-imperial poets who share a 'new sense of the shires, a new valuing of the native English experience'.[48]

> The poets of the mother culture, I feel, are now possessed of that defensive love of their territory which was once shared only by those poets whom we might call colonial – Yeats, MacDiarmid, Carlos Williams.[49]

Eager to find in other poets his own defensive nationalism, he reads Hughes, Hill and Larkin as 'little Englanders', in a new benign sense, celebrating their nationality not in triumphalist images of the imperial city, but in images of the local parish. 'All three are hoarders and shorers of what they take to be the real England. All three treat England as a region – or rather treat their region as England.'[50]

However, though this conceptual context may suit Hill's and Hughes's 'historical' versions of Englishness, Heaney is forced to concede that Larkin is rather different:

> What we hear is a stripped standard English voice... that leads back neither to the thumping beat of Anglo-Saxon nor to the Gregorian chant of the Middle Ages. Its ancestry begins, in fact, when the Middle Ages are turning secular...[51]

Despite his polite tone, Heaney cannot conceal his bristling hostility to what he sees as Larkin's secular, shallow-rooted metropolitanism:

> Larkin's tones are mannerly but not exquisite, well-bred but not mealy-mouthed. If his England and his English are not as deep as Hughes's or as solemn as Hill's, they are nevertheless dearly beloved.[52]

Heaney's analysis comprehensively mistakes the spirit of the English poet. A Larkin who holds forth proprietorially on 'My England and my English', or asserts how much he 'dearly loves' them, is simply not plausible. The phrase 'in a pig's arse, friend' springs irresistibly to mind. Larkin is no hoarder and shorer of Englishness. His nationality is not a matter of provincial ideology, but of what Patrick Kavanagh calls 'parochial' identity: 'Provincial worries over what others think / Parochial doesn't care.'[53] The Englishness of Larkin's personae – Mr Bleaney, the lighthouse-keeper, the old fools – is of no consequence compared with their common humanity. Larkin's England is not, like Heaney's Ireland, an ideological territory. His poetry digs deep, but not beneath a proper flag in a proper place.

Though famous for his 'hatred of abroad' in one sense, Larkin is perpetually 'abroad' in the other. Being abroad in the world is for him the human condition. In 'The Importance of Elsewhere', for instance, the poet feels his existence affirmed by the elsewhere of Northern Ireland. It 'underwrites' his existence:

> the faint
> Archaic smell of dockland, like a stable,
> The herring-hawker's cry, dwindling, went
> To prove me separate, not unworkable.

His return to his own 'home' makes him anxious. Without the excuse of difference which Belfast gave him, he is open to the threat of being proved 'unworkable'. In Ireland the 'insisting so on difference' paradoxically 'made me welcome'. England is not so welcoming: 'These are my customs and establishments / It would be much more serious to refuse.' He will be forced to toe the line. Heaney comprehensively misreads this poem: 'during his sojourn in Belfast in the late (*sic*) fifties, he gave thanks, by implication, for the nurture that he receives by living among his own'.[54] But Larkin's plight, as a lyric poet, was precisely to have nowhere where he felt 'nurtured' by being among 'his own'. He was nurtured, indeed, by being 'abroad'.

In 'Dublinesque', the only mature poem deriving from Larkin's experience outside Britain, he finds an even richer and more welcoming Irish elsewhere. There is a hint of phantasmagoria about the poem, and the poet told Maeve Brennan that its origin was 'a dream – I just woke up and described it' (Motion 395). Characteristically, however, the poem, though written in 1970 at a time when 'the Troubles' were again flaring up, is free of political or historical specifics. Like many of his later works its inspiration, as the form of the title suggests, is mediated through literature, recalling the Yeats of 'Down by the Salley Gardens', or the Joyce of *Dubliners*. It paints Dublin as an evocative vignette, woven from the musings of a well-read tourist, and close to stereotype: the 'pewter' light, the afternoon mist bringing on the early lights in the shops, above 'race-guides and rosaries'.

The poem evokes a sense of euphoric gratification at being a spectator at a beautiful, exotic, yet also unaccountably familiar, event:

> A troop of streetwalkers
> In wide flowered hats,
> Leg-of-mutton sleeves,
> And ankle-length dresses.
>
> There is an air of great friendliness,
> As if they were honouring
> One they were fond of...

One critic wishfully converts this visionary nostalgia into a socially specific theme, detecting in the funeral procession a 'tremendous communal endeavour' expressing the 'resourcefulness and vitality' of 'working-class communities'.[55] Edna Longley is more responsive to the poem's fragile literary artifice and its emotional yearning. She detects in the poem Larkin's sad sense of the attenuation of his inspiration, and the loss of the Romantic transcendence which he had attained in his earlier work. In 'Dublinesque', she writes 'Romanticism itself becomes an object of desire.'[56]

The growing appeal of Larkin's work across the English-speaking, and non-English-speaking, world is sufficient evidence that his poetry is not narrowly English. He writes about universals with an English inflection. 'Show Saturday', for instance, his least ironic celebration of English provincial life, though based on a specific show in Northumberland, is not concerned with the Englishness of the event as such. Similar social events, combining agricultural show with craft-market and fun-fair will be familiar, with local variations, to readers all over the world, from Ireland to Russia, from Belgium to the United States. Moreover, as a celebration it is oddly muted and detached. The poet seems listless and bemused, even a little surprised by it all, not quite sure whether to find the whole desultory ritual absurd:

> Bead-stalls, balloon-men, a Bank; a beer-marquee that
> Half-screens a canvas Gents; a tent selling tweed,
> And another, jackets. Folk sit about on bales
> Like great straw dice. For each scene is linked by spaces
> Not given to anything much, where kids scrap, freed,
> While their owners stare different ways with incurious faces.

The imagery makes the scene enigmatic and meaningless: 'great straw dice' and 'spaces / Not given to anything much', across which depersonalized 'owners' of children stare 'with incurious faces'. The poet is at a loss. But then, apparently, so is everybody else: a familiar enough response to such fairs, perhaps. What affirmation there is here is distinctly concessive in tone: 'Needlework, knitted caps, baskets, all worthy, all well done'.

As the poem builds to its climax in the description of the packing-up and dispersal of the show, the reason for this weary tone emerges. This autumn ritual looms in the poet's imagination as a metaphor for Ending: 'Back now, all of them... / To winter coming'. The closing of the year, marked by this recurrent show, is an implicit metaphor for mortality. Larkin, having just reached fifty at this time, was increasingly beset by the dread of endless extinction and depressed by the hardening of his inspiration. 'Show Saturday' is a thinly-disguised elegy, celebrating, in its desultory way, human persistence in the face of approaching oblivion:

> Let it stay hidden there like strength, below
> Sale-bills and swindling; something people do,
> Not noticing how time's rolling smithy-smoke
> Shadows much greater gestures; something they share
> That breaks ancestrally each year into
> Regenerate union. Let it always be there.

The poet's fervent tone ('ancestrally', 'Regenerate union') fails quite to convince, and 'Let it always be there' sounds distinctly valedictory; he fears he will not be there to see it. It is very difficult to agree with the view that the final lines 'witness to a genuine religious feeling' attached to 'an enduring Englishness'.[57] Larkin celebrates the show not as a spiritual event with which he feels cultural self-identification, but as a distraction from the 'larger gestures' of Time. Heaney again mistakes Larkin's tone, misquoting him in the process:

> 'Show Saturday' remains encumbered in naturalistic data, and while its conclusion beautifully expresses a nostalgic patriotism which is also an important part of this poet's make-up, the note achieved is less one of plangent vision, more a matter of liturgical wishfulness: 'Let it always be so'.[58]

He reads the poem's elegiac poignancy as evidence of a lamentable faltering of patriotic conviction, the mistranscription, 'Let it always be so', supplying a hint of Heaneyesque ideological affirmativeness which Larkin's 'Let it always be there' lacks.

Whatever the ostensible subject, the lyric poet always has his or her attention focused on intangible processes of being. Consequently it is the poet's plight constantly to be misread by an audience which prefers something more immediately relevant. A. E. Housman wrote that 'most readers, when they think that they are admiring poetry... are really admiring, not the poetry of the passage before them, but something else in it, which they like better than poetry.'[59] In the later twentieth century this 'something else' has frequently gone under the name of 'history'. Poetry, however, is not an adjunct to history, and the value of a poem is not dependent on whether it accurately registers any particular socio-political moment. It is a matter only of how beautifully and memorably it embodies thought and feeling in words. Larkin is a poet; what will remain permanently interesting about his work is its poetry. To confound poetry with history, or with sociology or politics, to hold poetry 'answerable' to history is perversely to read for a preferred 'something else', rather than the poetry itself.

6
Living Rooms

Metaphor

Before there are rooms there is room in the sense of 'space' ('make more room'; 'is there enough room?'), or in the precise definition of the *Oxford English Dictionary*, 'dimensional extent'. The ultimate 'room' in which we live is our own dimensional extent: our body. Larkin's book-plate depicted a star enclosed within a circle, with the quotation from Blake: *'How do you know but ev'ry Bird that cuts the airy way, / Is an immense world of delight clos'd by your senses five?'*[1] We live always within the enclosure of our senses. The immense delight of the world 'out there' is 'clos'd by your senses five'. We are only ever here and it is only ever now: 'always is always now'; 'Days are where we live.'[2] It is such elementary intersections of place with time which are the underlying theme of all Larkin's poems: 'Going', 'Coming', 'Absences', 'Days', 'Continuing to Live', 'First Sight', 'Far Out', 'Here', 'How Distant', 'Livings'. His poems concern the existential plight of 'being here'. They are about being at grass as much as horses, the sudden shut of loss as much as ambulances, beginning afresh as much as trees. His subjects are wants, long perspectives, absences, attendance, the view.

Blake's aphorism is a paradigm of metaphor (from the Greek 'to transfer'): the translation of outer to inner, the intercourse between objective and subjective. As a 'thing in itself' the flying bird embodies a reality beyond our knowledge; the same bird, enclosed by our senses five, cutting the airy way of our mind, provides us with our world and its delights. The bird is real because it is imagined. Living itself is a process of continual metaphorical transfer between concrete and abstract, literal and figurative. As T. S. Eliot writes: 'you can hardly say where the metaphorical and the literal meet'.[3] Language, itself, indeed, is transferred reality, a metaphor for reality. As Christopher Ricks writes: 'the concept of the literal is itself stubbornly resistant to clarification'. 'Does imagination "embrace reality, or is there a turn, with reality embracing imagination?"[4] It is Larkin's distinction as a poet that his 'literal' descriptions are frequently more 'figurative' than his explicit metaphors.

'The Whitsun Weddings' (1958) is a masterly 'literal' description, but the world it creates is also a metaphorical figure for the world of delight within the poet's senses five. An intimate kinetic subtext counterpoints the literal description, just as in a figurative painting an abstract pattern of colour and shapes underpins the depiction of how things look. The poem begins with an exact evocation of the 'feel' of the travelling room of the train-compartment into which the poet settles: 'All windows down, all cushions hot, all sense / Of being in a hurry gone.' The poet's drowsiness transfers itself to the landscape as his train moves through the heat 'that slept / For miles inland'. The exactness of the visual description becomes strangely meaningful. 'A hothouse flashed uniquely: hedges dipped / And rose'. The emotive adverb 'uniquely' goes beyond the literal, while the enjambement over the end of the line, 'dipped / And rose', transfers the rhythmic visual lurches of the poet's subjective windowscape into metre. Such technical effects of diction and rhythm are themselves metaphorical images, and make this more than description.

The weddings offer a medley of recognizable social types and postures: the girls, metonymically reduced to 'heels and veils', and 'unreally' prominent in their 'lemons, mauves and olive-ochres', the frowning children, the fathers who have 'never known // Success so huge and wholly farcical', the women sharing the secret 'like a happy funeral'. However, these framed glimpses, caught through the window, are transferred into the poet's detached consciousness, where, disentangled from the prose narratives to which they belong, they become poetic epiphanies. The girls are:

> All posed irresolutely, watching us go,
>
> As if out on the end of an event
>> Waving goodbye
> To something that survived it.

It is the transient 'event' which matters. What survives it (the marriage) is a vague, vestigial 'something'. Similarly the train is loaded not with a cargo of people, but more intangibly, with 'the sum of all they saw'. Precise and real though Larkin's description is, it is also fragile and tenuous, a matter of 'wedding-days... coming to an end' rather than of weddings, of 'poses', 'events' and 'all they saw', of 'travelling coincidence' and 'the power / That being changed can give'.

> – An Odeon went past, a cooling tower,
> And someone running up to bowl –'

The bowler is transfigured by being snatched from sight before the action is completed.

> – and none
> Thought of the others they would never meet
> Or how their lives would all contain this hour.

In this Ode to Incipience what matters is the contingent shared 'hour', unnoticed except by the poet, and 'contained' like something precious. Whether the bowler takes the wicket or is knocked for six, whether the newly-weds find happiness or tragedy in their new lives, are issues of equal irrelevance. What matters is the moment in and for itself.

As the train races towards its destination the poet's imagination boldly encloses the city in its egotistical embrace: 'I thought of London spread out in the sun, / Its postal districts packed like squares of wheat'. Like Wordsworth, in his sonnet 'Composed Upon Westminster Bridge', Larkin lyrically transforms the human community in its most artificial and impersonal aspect ('postal districts') into densely 'packed', abundant nature ('squares of wheat'). With the sacramental context of the weddings in mind he perhaps recalls the biblical phrase 'all flesh is grass'.[5] In the final stanza this imaginative enclosure becomes even more intimate:

> as the tightened brakes took hold, there swelled
> A sense of falling, like an arrow-shower
> Sent out of sight, somewhere becoming rain.

The real becomes the imagined in a delicately blurred figure that follows the poet's reverie from objective stimulus (the feel of the brakes), to inner sensation (falling), to remembered image (arrow-shower), and back to 'reality' (rain). The train's trajectory ('There we were aimed') together with the brakes' rushing sound and the 'sense of falling', combine to conjure up an arrow shower, specifically that in Laurence Olivier's film of Shakespeare's *Henry V* (Motion 288). This simile, however, is inappropriately aggressive, so, in his reverie, the sound is transferred, by means of a buried pun, from death-dealing arrow shower to shower of life-giving rain. The arrows are sent 'out of sight, somewhere becoming rain.' In an even more intimately physical figure of grammar he writes not 'I felt a sense of falling', nor 'It felt as though I was falling'. Rather he is caught up in a larger movement: 'there swelled / A sense of falling'. The clash of associations (swell, fall) enacts the metaphorical ambiguity of the sensation, which, like the journey itself, is both a gathering and a relinquishing.

Some readers cling to the notion, dating from his 'Movement' beginnings, that Larkin is somehow less figurative than other poets. David Lodge describes 'The Whitsun Weddings' as largely devoid of metaphor. The scenery, he says, 'is evoked by metonymic and synecdochic detail ("drifting breadth", "blinding windscreens", etc.)', and in the description of the weddings themselves 'appearance, clothing, behaviour, are observed with the eye of a novelist or documentary writer and allowed to stand, untransformed by metaphor.'[6] The poem, Lodge feels, becomes fully metaphorical only in the final simile, 'with its mythical, magical and archaic resonances... so different from anything else in the poem.'[7] In Lodge's version Larkin's poem skilfully and surprisingly shifts at the end from the literal or 'metonymic' to 'transcendent' metaphor. 'Again and again', he says, Larkin 'surprises us, especially in the closing lines of his poems, by his ability to transcend – or turn ironically upon – the severe restraints he seems to have placed upon authentic expression of feeling in poetry.'[8]

Lodge accurately registers Larkin's movement from casual description to elevated meditation. However, in his preoccupation with metaphor as rhetorical trope, he fails to register the figurative unity of the poem. The journey is clearly, even in the simplest sense, a metaphor: a 'figure of speech in which a name or descriptive term is transferred to some object to which it is not strictly applicable' (*OED*). The *Oxford English Dictionary* cites Joseph Addison's reference to 'those beautiful Metaphors in Scripture where Life is termed a Pilgrimage'. Larkin's train, gathering its load of newly-weds, is just such a traditional metaphor; though in this twentieth-century context the journey is less a spiritual progress than the secular sum of all he saw.

More profoundly, Lodge's distinction between metaphor and metonymy is too mechanical. The literal and the metaphoric are not the well-defined antithetical alternatives which Lodge's version makes them. Metaphors are not cherries studding the plain cake of the literal.

Metaphor is the poetic element itself. Though we speak loosely of 'a metaphor for' or 'a metaphor of', metaphor properly means the entire 'figure', comprising a relationship between literal and non-literal elements.[9] Metaphor is liminal between the literal and the imagined, continually translating between the two. In the sense of explicit tropes, simile and metaphor are, in A. E. Housman's words, 'things inessential to poetry'.[10] The phrase 'someone running up to bowl', for instance, though not '*a* metaphor', is more figurative than the dead metaphor 'ships ploughed the sea', which Lodge cites in his definition of the term. Lodge says that in 'The Whitsun Weddings' and 'Here' the journey 'provides the poem with its basic structure, a sequence of spatio-temporal contiguities'.[11] He fails to see that these 'spatio-temporal contiguities' are, precisely, Larkin's metaphor of 'frail / Travelling coincidence'. Larkin's close attention to the literal is not a prosaic 'restraint' on 'authentic' poetry; it is a discipline designed to generate the purest metaphorical intensity. Far from being unmetaphorical, Larkin is one of the great masters of metaphor.

Larkin's warmest celebration of living appropriately takes as its title an existential adverb, 'Here'. The original projected title in the workbook, however, was the more overtly metaphorical 'Withdrawing Room', the archaic form of 'drawing room' (Motion 317). This title, with its heavy pun on the abstract sense of 'room', foregrounds the poem's peculiarly intimate interplay between outer and inner space. Its opening lines perfectly illustrate Housman's aphorism: 'Poetry is not the thing said but a way of saying it',[12] conjuring up a sustained expectancy by the grammatical device of delaying the main verb ('Gathers') until the beginning of the second stanza. An even stranger metaphorical effect is the absence of any explicit centre of consciousness. There is no 'I' or 'we', no poet or reader. Instead it is 'Swerving', a present participle used as a noun, which is the grammatical subject. Moreover, the destination of this swerving is grammatically not a place, but a subjective emotion: 'the surprise of a large town'. In Larkin's elaborately distinctive wording 'Swerving (swerving, swerving...')' 'Gathers' to a 'surprise'. We may not be quite sure what, but we are aware that there is something more exciting, more elevated about this process than a poet, literally, looking out of a train window.

It might seem, at first sight that the vivid descriptive vignette at the centre of 'Here' is untransfigured social observation. Though unnamed this city has the quirky specificity of a unique real place, with its estuary, ships up streets, slave museum, consulates and tattoo shops. Its inhabitants, a 'cut-price crowd', are precisely observed, as they push through plate-glass doors to their desires: 'Cheap suits, red kitchen-ware, sharp shoes, iced lollies'. Trevor Tolley comments that such poetry shows 'the interplay of evoked detail rather than... an orches-tration of imagery or verbal effects.'[13] But this is to miss the musical sequence of monosyllabic adjectives: 'Cheap, red, sharp, iced' ('ee, eh, ah, eye'); and the modulations of the miscellaneous nouns: 'suits, kitchen-ware, shoes', ending with the quaint vulgarism 'lollies'. Utterly literal though they are as 'evoked detail', these words stick in the mind as words, as metaphors of reality.

Moreover a more overt metaphorical exuberance breaks the surface in the phrase 'a terminate and fishy-smelling / Pastoral'. The strange, obsolete adjective 'terminate' evokes the 'terminus' of the railway, and also a self-sufficient completion, anticipating the mysterious ending of the poem where the land terminates at the sea. The Latinate preciosity of 'terminate' is then clashed against the cosy colloquialism 'fishy-smelling', and the phrase leaps to the utterly unexpected 'Pastoral'. This little 'urban, yet simple' world, with its ships up streets and grim head-scarfed wives, apparently possesses the same idyllic innocence as Theocritus's or Virgil's fragile visions of nymphs and shepherds. The verbal orchestration of the phrase is riotously chromatic. The imagin-ative leaps between 'terminate', 'fishy-smelling' and 'Pastoral', are delightfully vertiginous.

Though no means of transport is ever named, the poem, while remaining always 'here', maintains a continuous momentum: into the city by train and out again, implicitly by car or bicycle, across country to the sea. The reader is taken deeper and deeper into a 'withdrawing room' of privacy, from traffic all night north to picturesque urban pas-toral, to isolated 'existence'. The poem ends in a mythic landscape of the elements, where, in an extraordinary simile, 'silence stands / Like heat.' Literally the wheatfields are silent and hot in high summer. But described in terms of these abstract nouns the scene becomes solemn and portentous. 'Heat' might be said, metaphorically, to 'stand' in a landscape, but to say that 'Silence stands *like* heat' pushes the metaphor to an elusive limit in a little adventure in words. In the final lines the poem reaches – or nearly reaches – its ever-withdrawing goal: an unnamed, intimate place of withdrawn self-possession, offering infinite room for living in, 'Facing the sun, untalkative, out of reach'. This wide, limitless land-, sea- and sky-scape is, by a brilliant metaphorical trans-lation, the roomiest of living rooms.

One key to the relaxed tone of 'The Whitsun Weddings' and 'Here', is their suspension of time. They short-circuit the metaphor, 'a space of time', by losing time in place. Neither implies a narrative which extends beyond the end of the poem. The train compartment in 'The Whitsun Weddings' exempts the poet from all demands: 'all sense / Of being in a hurry gone'. The literal purpose of the journey is taken as given: 'That Whitsun, I was late getting away'. The only destinations mentioned are the postal districts of London, and perhaps the future lives of the newly-weds, 'out of sight'. The poet remains detached from these. His goal is passive contemplation. For the poet to depict himself alighting from the train, anticipating the coming Test Match or a meal with friends, would be to break the figurative spell. In 'Here' self-possession is even more complete, as a disembodied centre of consciousness travels across the landscape entirely at the disposal of the spirit of place. There are no events in this timeless present, and the poem develops a cumulative feeling rather than a purposeful narrative.

Crucial here also are the spacious stanza-forms, with their harmoniously interwoven rhymes. In 'The Whitsun Weddings' the leisurely pentameters, broken by a dimeter at line 2, rhyme musically *ababcdecde*. In 'Here' four stanzas of unbroken pentameters build up a larger twofold sweep, rhyming *ababcddc* in stanzas 1 and 3, *abbacdcd* in stanzas 2 and 4. *Stanza* is the Italian for 'room' (used particularly in the plural, *stanze*: a suite of rooms), and the comfortable stanzas of 'The Whitsun Weddings' and 'Here' are metaphors for Larkin's place in the world. They are comfortable rooms of his own. Almost all of Larkin's mature poetry, with some notable exceptions, is in stanzas. The stanzas of 'The Whitsun Weddings' and 'Here' are at an extreme of rich harmoniousness, seldom achieved elsewhere. The room triangulated by the here and now of his imagery, metre and grammar, is rented, not a freehold. His varied and inventive stanza-forms create the widest expressive spectrum: from claustrophobia, through control, disorder and panic, to sublime release.

'Afternoons' for instance, written in 1959, between 'The Whitsun Weddings' and 'Here', adopts a quite different stanza to project its different perspectives of place and room. In the insecure world of this poem it is place which shifts and dissolves under the pressure of time rather than *vice versa*. Consequently the consoling stability of repeated interwoven rhyme is rejected, and the poem is rhymeless. The lines are short (dimeters or trimeters), and the rhythm is very free. The poem focuses on a metaphorical place in time. The mothers are caught in the 'hollows' of 'afternoons', among the leaves falling from the trees, and also in the 'afternoons' of their own lives. The 'new' recreation ground is no longer the place in which they themselves played. They set free their children, being, by implication, no longer 'free' themselves. The wind is, with a touch of mock-heroic exaggeration, 'ruining' their courting-places, 'That are still courting-places / (But the lovers are all in school).' Time has closed to them the locations in which their lives have been lived. They live out a 'modern mythology': husbands in skilled trades, an estateful of washing, the albums lettered *Our Wedding* near the televisions. But, with poignant wit, their very living-rooms have become metaphors for their lack of room: 'Something is pushing them / To the side of their own lives.' Time is withdrawing from them their room for living.[14]

Rooms

Larkin admired A. E. Housman for 'the narrow yet unforgettable metaphor he made of his own life' (*FR* 343). The unforgettable metaphor which Larkin made of his own life is broader than Housman's tragic pastoral of the shires, more intimate than Yeats's romantic symbols of rose, tower and Byzantium, and less spiritually anxious than Eliot's Waste Land. Larkin's favoured metaphors, the kingdom of winter, the grip of light, the face as aesthetic object or register of experience, Pygmalion at the mercy of his own creation, focus intimate blends of the physical and psychological or dramatize unstable interactions between subjective and objective. Most familiar and intimate of all, however, and most liminally ambiguous between literal and imagined, is the all-pervasive Larkinesque image of the living-room, the most intimate of figures for our existential plight of being here.

The 'literal' rooms in which Larkin lived are as important to his poetry as Yeats's more conventionally poetic Thor Ballylee. The romantic towers and attics of his apprentice work in the 1940s acquired a local habitation in the top-floor flats in Belfast and in Hull, where he found room in which to live and write. He tentatively attributed the waning of his poetic inspiration to his ejection in 1974 from his high-windowed flat in Pearson Park (*RW* 58), and his subsequent move into 'an utterly undistinguished little modern house' (Motion 440). The word 'room' (or 'rooms') occurs thirty-five times in his poetry after 1945 (in twenty-four poems); many more poems evoke rooms without using the word. Much of his *oeuvre* can be seen as a meditation on this figure, with its related images of the locked door and the windowscape. As he retires into aesthetic isolation behind closed doors ('Best Society', 'Vers de Société') or looks out from his vantage point ('High Windows', 'Sad Steps'), his own living-room becomes an intensely imagined space: an artist's garret, ivory tower, bachelor den, cave of obscene squalor, monk's cell, prison cell or waiting-room for death. At its most human and familiar the room is a 'home' ('Home is so Sad'); or it fails to be home and becomes merely a 'hired box' ('Mr Bleaney'). It may be, by implication, an old people's 'home' ('The Old Fools'). And, as there are living-rooms, so also there are dying-rooms: ambulances or hospital wards ('The Building'). A coffin is, by tradition, the narrowest of rooms ('Counting').

In a small number of poems he is denied access ('Dry-Point'), or he stands back alienated from the bustling room of society ('Reasons for Attendance', 'The Dance'). But more usually Larkin's protagonists gaze out from within their rooms, through closed windows that provide them with aesthetic epiphanies: empty skyscapes ('The piled gold clouds, the shining gull-marked mud'), or framed glimpses of the lives of others, ('someone running up to bowl'). Larkin's are not 'windows of opportunity', promising easy intercourse with the world outside. They are never open and welcoming like those of D. H. Lawrence: 'When will the scent of the dim white phlox / Creep up the wall to me, and in at my open window?'[15] Nor does Larkin's vantage-point give him a Yeatsian overview of historical cycles swirling beneath his tower. The poet keeps his distance. The metaphor he made of his own life is one of inner intensities and states of consciousness. His vistas are within.

In the remainder of this chapter I shall trace the more-or-less literal, more-or-less metaphorical rooms of Larkin's poetry in order to explore what is, in effect, an all-embracing metaphor. Each of the three stages of Larkin's mature development sees a different use of the room image. In his early *Less Deceived* period Larkin was preoccupied with the contrasted social parlours and antisocial attics of his marriage debate ('Waiting for Breakfast while she brushed her hair', 'Deceptions', 'If, My Darling'). Later the bachelor flats which became his 'home' in Belfast in 1950 and Hull in 1955 are the focus of celebration, but also, increasingly, of self-satire ('Best Society', 'Poetry of Departures', 'Mr Bleaney'). The period of *The Whitsun Weddings* sees his most positive room images, and also some of his most characteristic meditations on transience, focused on mobile rooms ('The Whitsun Weddings', 'Ambulances', 'Dockery and Son'). In his *High Windows* phase he develops a series of mannered and elliptical variations on the familiar image which answer each other in opposed pairs or longer sequences ('Friday Night in the Royal Station Hotel', 'High Windows', 'Sad Steps', 'The Card-Players', 'Vers de Société', 'Livings'). Towards the end the

enjoyable solitude of the locked room fades into the frightened loneliness of the waiting-room of death ('The Building', 'The Old Fools',
'Aubade').

Parlour and attic

The earliest rooms in Larkin's poetry are highly abstract symbols of the
tension between public and private, life and art. In the second of the
'Two Guitar Pieces' (1946) the speaker stands with an implicitly male
companion in the dusk, sharing a cigarette and gazing at a post-war
windowscape: 'A man is walking along / A path between the wreckage.'
This scene, rather than drawing the poet's thoughts out into the world,
as it would those of Auden or McNeice, appears instead as an objec-
tification of his listless mood. In the room behind them, 'our friend' is
dealing cards: 'The pack is short, / And dealing from now till morning
would not bring / The highest hands.' Life is a cheat. However, when
this shadowy 'friend' turns instead to art, strumming a guitar, the
music fills the poet with sudden euphoria. It creates a 'harmony':

> That builds within this room a second room;
> And the accustomed harnessing of grief
> Tightens, because together or alone
> We cannot trace that room; and then again
> Because it is not a room, nor a world, but only
> A figure spun on stirring of the air,
> And so, untrue.

An intangible, 'untrue', metaphorical room of sad music comes into
being within the real room of grim card-games. This 'figure', stirring the
air, grips the poet with its formal emotion, and when the music stops,
he is left 'Empty again': 'What poor hands we hold, / When we face
each other honestly!' Even as he condemns its unreality, its dishonesty,
the poet cherishes his inner room of art. In 'Waiting for breakfast, while
she brushed her hair' (1947), the poet stands similarly irresolute at
a window, caught between the woman in the hotel room of reality
behind him, and a strangely internalized courtyard beyond the window.

At this stage in his development Larkin takes refuge in this inner,
'unreal' space of aesthetic absolution, unwilling to lock himself into a
real room of responsibility. Events in his own life intensified his indecision. The two claustrophobic years between 1948 and 1950 spent

with his recently-widowed mother made an indelible mark upon his sensibility. Moreover, he was also at this time engaged to be married, and apprehensive of committing himself to yet another domestic prison. In his letters of the time he dramatizes his plight, living wretchedly in a 'remnant of a home', but reluctant to set up house elsewhere:

> Despite my fine feelings, when it really comes down to terms of furniture and loans from the bank something unmeltable and immoveable rises up in me – something infantile, cowardly, regressive. But *it won't be conquered*. I'm a romantic bastard. Remote things seem desirable. Bring them close, and I start shitting myself.[16]

Romantic coward that he is, he cannot sacrifice his imaginative freedom to 'furniture and loans from the bank'.

In the second 'Guitar Piece' and 'Waiting for breakfast' the other people who share the poet's room remain shadowy and insubstantial. 'Deceptions' and 'If, My Darling', both written in 1950, show a new dynamic. The viewpoint shifts and divides, giving a voice to the woman with whom the room is now shared. The indistinct rooms of the earlier poems become the sharply-focused bedroom, parlour and attic of a violent gendered contest. In 'Deceptions' the poet takes the woman's side. The room in which she lies offers, not 'bridal' enclosure and security, but violent exposure, 'out on that bed', flooded with light in the desolate attic of her rapist's fulfilment. In 'If, My Darling' the context is one of comic courtship rather than tragic rape. The cosy parlour of his darling's imagination is contradicted by the poet's actual inner junkroom of disorder. The poem's form ingeniously enacts the shift from her room to his, beginning with short, orderly lines, which lengthen, as his tirade finds its stride, into baggy pentameters. The tercet stanzas pararhyme ineptly only on the first and third lines: 'cosy /lazy; recital/rebuttal; knot/pivot'. If we press the analogy of stanza with room these are the most slovenly metrical rooms in Larkin's work.

'Unfinished Poem' (1951), not published during Larkin's lifetime, shows the poet playfully rearranging the imaginative counters of 'Deceptions' to create a very different attic of desolate fulfilment. Here there is no war of the sexes, though the speaker is distinctly masculine. It is now the poet himself who lies exposed on his bed awaiting his ravisher, in the form not of a rapist, but death. Hoping to be overlooked as death busily searches out victims 'down among sunlit courts', he locks himself away in his 'emaciate attic', newspapers for sheets, smoking, like a Samuel Beckett character with 'nothing to do but wait'. As the days pass he begins to anticipate death's tread on the stair, 'Climbing to cut me from his restless mind // With a sign that the air should stick in my nose like bread'. Puzzlingly, however, at the end of the poem the figure which bursts into his attic is 'Nothing like death':

> Nothing like death has such hair, arms so raised.
> Why are your feet bare? Was not death to come?
> Why is he not here? What summer have you broken from?

This sounds suspiciously like a loose equivocation, fulfilling the poem's tricksy title. What enters may, indeed, be merely 'nothing'. The poet, however, projects a person or personification (the drafts make her unambiguously female) who is nothing like death: a wish-fulfilment fantasy from the kingdom of summer willing to share the young poet's attic with him.

In 'Dry-Point', written a few months earlier in 1950, the poet is again locked away in uncomfortable confrontation with the 'room' of his own body, but here the focus reverts to sex rather than death. On one level the poem is part of his marriage debate, rejecting the discredited magic of the 'leaden' wedding ring. Beneath this, however, runs a more primitive, existential quarrel with his own body, enclosed within his senses five. Recurrent sexual arousal is imaged as a surreal expanding and collapsing cell, in an opaque metaphor suggesting also a chemical reaction and the piston of an internal combustion engine:

> Silently it inflates, till we're enclosed
> And forced to start the struggle to get out:
> Bestial, intent, real.
> The wet spark comes, the bright blown walls collapse...

The poem ends with one of the most evocative 'unreal' rooms in Larkin's poetry: the mere imagined, untested thought of a room from which sexuality with all its complications is excluded:

> And how remote that bare and sunscrubbed room,
> Intensely far, that padlocked cube of light
> We neither define nor prove,
> Where you, we dream, obtain no right of entry.

The poet can never enter this purely metaphorical withdrawing room of the mind. Its very inaccessibility, indeed, serves to guarantee its purity. This is less an anti-marriage poem than a profound meditation on the inescapable, humiliating plight of our physical compulsions.

Larkin frequently escapes the claustrophobic room of his selfhood by projecting such sublime empty rooms as this in 'Dry-Point': 'One longs for infinity and absence, the beauty of somewhere you're not' (*FR* 59). 'Absences', for instance, also completed in 1950, seems at first sight a quite uncharacteristic poem, with its limitless vista of unobserved sea, not even framed by a window. Here, where 'there are no ships and no shallows', both sea and day are 'shoreless'. The sea is constantly 'at play'; the clouds change shape, 'shift to giant ribbing' and then disperse. Paradoxically the denial of a secure vantage point fills the poet, not with panic, but with euphoric awe. By the most vertiginous of metaphorical leaps, the infinite room of this remote seascape becomes an attic of his imagination, though one which offers not selfish 'fulfilment', but selfless 'absence': 'Such attics cleared of me! Such absences!' This imagined room, like that in 'Dry-Point' is not to be withdrawn into; it sublimely excludes the poet.

The poem's ten lines enact the theme of 'clearing', or withdrawing, in a miracle of eloquent concision. The form is disguised *terza rima*. The first two tercets are run together, making an *ababcb* stanza, with the *b* rhyme sliding beautifully away on its third appearance from o to a: 'hollows/follows/shallows'. The third tercet makes a separate three-line stanza, but only half the length of the first. The final single line, required to complete the *terza rima* scheme, echoes the *d* rhyme only at the furthest distance: 'galleries/absences'. The effect is an emphatic subversion of stanzaic enclosure: three brief dramatic statements, diminishing in verbal extent and structure as they increase in emotional intensity. Such sublime roominess spurns domestic comfort and annihilates cosy self-possession.

Home

The antithesis between outer room of reality and inner room of the self runs throughout Larkin's work. However, when in 1950 the young poet took up his post in Belfast he achieved a temporary unification of the two rooms: his own version of the artist's garret, his Larkinesque ivory tower:

> The best writing conditions I ever had were in Belfast, when I was working at the University there. Another top-floor flat, by the way. I

wrote between eight and ten in the evenings, then went to the University bar till eleven, then played cards or talked with friends till one or two.

(RW 58)

In 'Best Society' (1951), written within months of his arrival, he shamelessly withdraws into privacy. In a sharper, 'vicious' version of the self-possession of 'The Whitsun Weddings' and 'Here', he symbolizes freedom as a locked door and rejects social 'virtue':

> Our virtues are all social...
>
> Viciously, then, I lock my door.
> The gas-fire breathes. The wind outside
> Ushers in evening rain. Once more
> Uncontradicting solitude
> Supports me on its giant palm;
> And like a sea-anemone
> Or simple snail, there cautiously
> Unfolds, emerges, what I am.

The poem's tetrameter octaves blend vulnerable defensiveness with subtle aesthetic satisfaction. They rhyme regularly *ababcddc*, but the *b* and *d* rhymes are edgy pararhymes with musically shifting vowels ('wrong/thing', 'get/what', 'expressed/just', 'if/chafe'). The rhyme sequence of the final lines is peculiarly haunting: 'palm/anemone/ cautiously/am'. The long vowel of 'palm' shortens to the hard 'am' in an emphatic assertion of selfhood.

Here the poet can relax his guard, free from the self-reproaches of his marriage debate, and surrender to his inner world of aesthetic delight. The snail is a traditional metaphor for self-containment, carrying its 'house' on its back. The 'simple snail' which 'emerges' here, however, is an objective correlative for a less definable psychological state. It also suggests a 'vicious' expression of 'freedom' in the form of auto-eroticism. In this hard-won sanctum the poet finds his first real version of home. In its almost embarrassing emotional defence of solitariness 'Best Society' represents a moment of epiphany in Larkin's development. It is, perhaps, not surprising that he left this extremist antisocial manifesto unpublished during his lifetime.

In the poems which follow in the mid-and later 1950s, as he enters his thirties, irony soon qualifies his brief euphoria, as he projects various stereotypical or ironic versions of 'home'. 'Poetry of Departures'

(1954), for example, begins, like 'Best Society' as a celebration of bachelor freedom, inverting the familiar platitudes ('home is where the heart is'). In a characteristic *faux naïf* gesture, the poet casually assumes a common admiration for those who have 'just cleared off'. The proverbial assurance of tone in 'We all hate home' neatly subverts 'there's no place like home'. However, in contrast with 'Best Society', this room of solitary bachelorhood reveals itself not as an escape from constricting domesticity, but as itself a version of 'home sweet home'. The bold 'we' of the opening shifts, in scathing self-satire, to a self-doubting 'I':

> We all hate home
> And having to be there:
> I detest my room,
> Its specially-chosen junk,
> The good books, the good bed,
> And my life, in perfect order:
> So to hear it said
>
> *He walked out on the whole crowd*
> Leaves me flushed and stirred...

The four neat rooms of the stanzas are wrecked from within by a spirit of comic chaos. The octave rhyme-scheme is not dissimilar to that of 'Best Society': a regular *abcbadcd* of rhymes and pararhymes. However here the pararhymes dominate, only the concluding *d* rhyme being perfect, and they create not the subtle music of similar vowels, but ingeniously blundering, often polysyllabic discords such as 'epitaph/cleared off'; 'think/junk'; 'home/room'; 'fo'c'sle/artificial'; 'if/life'. In the final stanza even the *d* rhyme which in previous stanzas offered a glimpse of harmonious closure ('bed/said'; 'stay/today') is also spoiled, the rhyme words ('object/perfect') being disyllables chiming, with an inflection of contempt, only on the second unstressed syllable:

> Such a deliberate step backwards
> To create an object:
> Books; china; a life
> Reprehensibly perfect.

The joke is that though the rhymes sound subversive and bad-mannered, the considerable technical pains that have been taken with them reveal the poet to be, as he concedes, perfectly house-trained, with a pusillanimous regard for the decorums of room and stanza.

'Mr Bleaney', which celebrates (as it were) Larkin's arrival in Hull in 1955, offers a more intimately humiliating illustration of what the poet must settle for as home. The *abab* pentameter quatrains, with perfect rhymes usually on long-vowelled monosyllables, reduce the inter-weavings of 'Best Society', and 'Poetry of Departures' to workmanlike plainness. Moreover, the diction ('My bit of garden', 'stub my fags', 'Stuffing my ears') bristles with less-deceived crudity. The poem's metaphorical implications are casually introduced through the land-lady's unintended comic pun: 'He stayed / The whole time he was at the Bodies, till / They moved him.' She means literally that Mr Bleaney worked at a factory making car-bodies.[17] In the context of the poet's moody reflections, however, the words cannot but suggest the ultimate 'powers that be' ('They'), who move people from their 'bodies' in a more radical sense than changing their job-location.

The poet's decision to take this room is jokily portentous. On one level it is a tragic defeat. He loses his poetic nerve and commits himself to a room without room for books. On another level, however, he perversely relishes this reduction to bare essentials, without room even for bags which might promise escape to roomier accommodation. This room is more satisfying than he will openly admit. It excludes, for instance, any question of 'furniture and loans from the bank', and has no room for a partner. The view from Mr Bleaney's window is also somewhat deceptive. Though it offers only the prospect of a 'strip of building land, / Tussocky, littered', it also yields a sudden muted epiphany in the sight of 'the frigid wind / Tousling the clouds'. Bleaney's plight is presented, on the poem's surface, as a metaphor for the poet's fear of failure. However, it is perhaps truer to the poem's enjoyable lugubriousness to see it as another wry celebration of his bachelor satisfactions. The euphoria of locking oneself away in a room of one's own is still audible.

Other poets satirize the modern domestic interior for its bad taste and spiritual emptiness. Eliot's Prufrock laments that he has measured out his life with coffee spoons. John Betjeman attacks bourgeois decorums: 'Oh! Chintzy, chintzy cheeriness, / / Half dead and half alive!'[18] At first reading Bleaney's room seems subject to a similar satire. Bleaney has his 'yearly frame' of sad routine: gardening, the same regular summer holiday, and 'Christmas at his sister's house in Stoke'. In a sign of his working-class lack of taste he prefers ('HP') sauce (in a bottle) to prop-erly-prepared gravy.[19] He has measured out his life with Pools coupons ('the four aways').[20] But Larkin lacks Eliot's and Betjeman's satirical superiority. Common humanity prevails. The poet accepts Bleaney's room as his own: 'I'll take it.' T. S. Eliot's 'Sweeney Erect' depicts a not dissimilar, crude, working-class post-Christian archetype. But where the gap between Larkin and Bleaney is social and aesthetic, the gap between Eliot and Sweeney is spiritual. Sweeney is defined, in the context of anthropology and theology, as an archaic 'survival' from a primitive age, a man without a soul, a portentously sinister element in the 'mind of Europe'.[21] Bleaney, in contrast, belongs in the bourgeois secular tradition of sympathy and sentiment.

> But if he...
>   ...lay on the fusty bed
> Telling himself that this was home, and grinned,
> And shivered, without shaking off the dread
>
> That how we live measures our own nature,
> And at his age having no more to show
> Than one hired box should make him pretty sure
> He warranted no better, I don't know.

The final 'I don't know' irritatedly dismisses the poet's speculations as to Mr Bleaney's feelings. But it also shows impatience with his own defeatist self-indulgence. There is an existential authenticity in Larkin's self-criticism here, beyond the easy class-based satire of Eliot and Betjeman. The poet does not judge the world; the world judges the poet.

'Best Society' cast the poet's anti-social plight in the form of a personal confession, 'Mr Bleaney' recast it in the form of dramatized social comedy. 'Counting' (1955), unpublished during the poet's lifetime, brilliantly reduces plight and room to a reductive aphorism. In an inversion of the symbolist equivocations of 'Unfinished Poem', the speaker here, brightly and perversely, celebrates his bachelor flat as the most convenient short-cut to the private locked room of the grave:

> One room, one bed, one chair,
> One person there,
> Makes perfect sense; one set
> Of wishes can be met,
> One coffin filled.

The hired box of a living-room becomes another, smaller box, satisfyingly 'filled', and it all makes 'perfect sense'. The form, with its jaunty couplets and monosyllabic rhymes, is mockingly neat. The first seven lines, describing 'one', make up a simple but satisfying stanza of alternate trimeter/dimeter lines with a climactic repeated trimeter in the penultimate lines and no rhyme (appropriately) on the final line of death. The second stanza, however, describing 'two', comes to a close after only two couplets, neatly demonstrating the problematic nature of this number: 'Two is harder to do.'

'Home is so Sad' (1958), which comes towards the end of this sequence of meditations on home, shows Larkin's earlier hard-edged, 'less deceived' tone softening into the open, emotional manner of *The Whitsun Weddings*. Here a familiar domestic interior stands as the tragic symbol of the transience of human aspiration. Answering 'home sweet home' the poet fabricates another proverb of his own, intoning lugubriously: 'Home is so Sad'. The quarrels of his marriage debate are left behind in the sombre reflection that all attempts to make our rooms into 'home', must ultimately fail, if only because we grow old and die. As if to make up for its lack of inhabitants, the room is pathetically personified:

> It stays as it was left,
> Shaped to the comfort of the last to go
> As if to win them back. Instead, bereft
> Of anyone to please, it withers so,
> Having no heart to put aside the theft
>
> And turn again to what it started as,
> A joyous shot at how things ought to be.

The rhymes of the first five-line stanza are all perfect ('left/go/bereft/so/theft'). In the second stanza, however they blur ('as/be/was/cutlery/vase') in a metaphor for the failure of the home, and to create an effect of stumbling emotionality. The phrases shorten and the poet abruptly addresses the reader, as if both were standing together in the abandoned room:

> You can see how it was:
> Look at the pictures and the cutlery.
> The music in the piano stool. That vase.

The furniture and loans from the bank that have gone into making this home are poignantly concentrated into an eloquent metonym: 'That vase'.

Travelling coincidence

In a few key works of his high maturity Larkin focuses not on the home of domestic ideology, nor the attic of bachelordom, nor the tower of aesthetic solitude. In 'The Whitsun Weddings' (1958), 'Ambulances' (1960), 'Here' (1961) and 'Dockery and Son' (1963), he turns to the purest lyrical room of travelling coincidence: a railway carriage or an ambulance. These works, more than any in his *oeuvre*, involve the reader in life as fleeting, elusive process. The 'wild white face' above red stretcher-blankets in 'Ambulances', for instance, is never allowed to become a literal individual, distinguishable from poet or reader. Instead the human centre of the poem remains a shifting assemblage of phrases. This is yet another poem of two rooms. The 'fastened doors' of the apparently secure room of the ambulance close on the insecure room of the patient's fading consciousness, which is in its turn 'shut' by the 'solving emptiness' of loss:

> For borne away in deadened air
> May go the sudden shut of loss
> Round something nearly at an end...

The grammatical subject of the sentence is an intangible state of being: 'the sudden shut of loss'. Elaborate, lingering noun phrases further attenuate life in the substantial flesh, as they postpone the verb which will only bring dissolution closer.

> And what cohered in it across
> The years, the unique random blend
> Of families and fashions, there

> At last begin to loosen.

The ominous grammatical completion delivered by the verb is suspended as long as possible, by adverbs, by the gap between the stanzas ('there // At last'), and by the verb's infinitive construction: 'begin to loosen', which puts the stress with cruel irony on 'begin', when the real action is an ending. The grammatical structure itself barely coheres. The word 'blend' is a singular noun, so the verb should correctly be 'begins'. But by the time we have reached this verb what cohered in 'it' no longer coheres, and is plural. A grammatical solecism stands as a metaphor for the moment of dissolution. Behind locked doors the young Larkin of 'Best Society' could allow 'what I am' to unfold. Here, behind doors fastened by someone else from the outside, 'unfolding' becomes a more radical 'loosening'. A locked door offers security only if one has the key.

In the first three stanzas the poet has clung to the security of an observer, viewing the scene from outside. The ambulance's windows 'absorb' our glances, its doors 'recede'. In the fourth and fifth stanzas the point of view shifts imperceptibly to the inside, and poet and reader find themselves sharing the dying patient's plight. A baroque elaboration of noun phrases reduces the patient to an infinitive intersection between time and place:

> Far
> From the exchange of love to lie
> Unreachable inside a room
> The traffic parts to let go by
> Brings closer what is left to come,
> And dulls to distance all we are.

The phrase 'to lie' relates not to any particular victim, but to all of us. The half-rhyme on 'come' ominously dulls the earlier long vowel of 'room', while what is dulled to distance, in this dying-room, is not a bravely independent end-stopped 'what I am', but an open-vowelled, defenceless 'all we are'.

In 'Dockery and Son' (1963), the moving room of vagrant existence is a railway carriage, offering the poet, as in 'The Whitsun Weddings', a passive vantage-point. The second, contrasting room is the poet's former college room of youthful promise, in which a more substantial, rooted life, such as Dockery's, was still a possibility. Reminiscing about his half-forgotten student days ('"Dockery was junior to you, / Wasn't he?" said the Dean. "His son's here now"'), the poet seeks out his former room, only to find it inaccessible to his older self. 'I try the door of where I used to live: // Locked.' Shocked resentment resonates in the phrase 'where I used to live', with the implication that he is no longer 'living' with the same intensity. He stands for a moment uncomfortably outside. Then in a brilliantly elliptical evocation of emotional confusion, he makes a scrambled movement back within himself:

> Locked. The lawn spreads dazzlingly wide.
> A known bell chimes. I catch my train, ignored.
> Canal and clouds and colleges subside
> Slowly from view.

Five brief sentences telescope his progress from dark landing, out across the exposed 'dazzling' quadrangle and back, safely 'ignored' and anonymous, to the traveling-room of his train compartment, watching the windowscape of Oxford recede.

This traveling-room of detachment, however, fails to cast its absolving spell. The fourth, climactic stanza breaks the predictable interwoven rhyme-schemes of the previous octaves, falling into disorder as the poet struggles to come to terms with this glimpse of an alternative life:

> ...To have no son, no wife,
> No house or land still seemed quite natural.
> Only a numbness registered the shock
> Of finding out how much had gone of life,
> How widely from the others. Dockery, now:
> Only nineteen, he must have taken stock
> Of what he wanted, and been capable
> Of... No, that's not the difference...

With a sly technical finesse the *b* rhyme, on the pleading, self-justificatory word 'natural', is not answered until a full five lines later, and even then only by the clumsy (unnatural) pararhyme, 'capable', dramatizing a failure of confidence in his argument. Moreover the third line, instead of repeating the *a* or *b* rhyme, as in all the other stanzas, introduces the small formal shock of a new rhyme, on 'shock'.

In contrast with the serene outward journey of 'The Whitsun Weddings', this return home is anxiously haunted by long perspectives, as he seeks to persuade himself that Dockery was wrong, and life is really a state of existential transit rather than of accumulated family and possessions. He seeks detachment in reducing the intersecting lines of life to abstract patterns of rails in moonlight.

> I changed,
> And ate an awful pie, and walked along
> The platform to its end to see the ranged
> Joining and parting lines reflect a strong
>
> Unhindered moon.

In 'The Whitsun Weddings' the promising venture of the newly-weds' journey was caught in the eloquent passive construction 'all the power that being changed can give'. Here, instead, we have a grimly intransitive offhand pun: 'I changed'. The unpromising change which now preoccupies him is caused by what something hidden from us chose: 'And age and then the only end of age.'

Death's waiting-room

By the mid-1960s Larkin was developing the mannered, self-referential versions of his familiar room images which are so prominent a feature of *High Windows*. In the late 1960s and early 1970s dens of squalor, towers of isolation, and cells of loneliness follow each other like musical variations on a theme, increasingly revealing themselves as waiting-rooms for death. 'Friday Night in the Royal Station Hotel' (1966), for instance, one of the earliest *High Windows* poems to be written, infuses the rich textures of his *Whitsun Weddings* manner with a new self-conscious symbolism. The context is again the railway, but this is very much an 'end-of-the-line' poem. The element of travel is wilfully negated in immobile stasis, and the decontextualized description teasingly denies the reader any secure point of view or sense of direction. Synaesthetic images and surreal personifications defamiliarize the commonplace fitments. 'Light spreads darkly downwards' like a viscous liquid. The chairs of different colours 'face each other' in empty confrontation. We do not 'see' the vista of the dining-room. Instead the personified room, in an extravagantly baroque noun phrase, '*declares / A larger loneliness of knives and glass*'. Rather than the floor being deeply carpeted, and the hotel silent, the silence becomes tactile and is 'laid like carpet'. Reality is subverted as words denoting material things: chairs, doors, knives, glasses, carpet, are grammatically subordinated to large abstractions: light, loneliness, silence.

The effect is to imbue the scene with portentous significance, like a description in a *nouveau roman* by Alain Robbe-Grillet, or an interior in a Magritte painting. And, as in Magritte the apparently banal and ordinary effervesces with portentous absurdist humour: 'And all the salesman have gone back to Leeds, / Leaving full ashtrays in the Conference Room.' The speaker contemplates the hotel's headed paper, 'made for writing home', and interjects in lugubrious parenthesis '(If home existed)'. This may be a hotel in Hull, but it is also a metaphorical plight, like that of Kafka or Beckett, in which we wait for our trial to begin, or for Godot to arrive. The form of the poem, a spoiled sonnet, participates in the game. The first eight lines constitute an octave in the regular Shakespearean form (*ababcdcd*). But then line 9 follows without the possibility of a pause, leaving the new *e* rhyme, 'Room', with its pompous capital, hanging. The 'sestet' which follows after the break has only five lines to make up the sonnet's required fourteen. It rhymes *fgefg*, the *e* rhyme, which answers 'Room' in the 'octave', being the heavily meaningful pararhyme: 'home'. Larkin is playing with the form.

In the absence of a windowscape the poem makes an arbitrary symbolist shift 'outside', to an italicized evocation of the Holderness coast, in a gloomy reduction of the ending of 'Here': '*Now / Night comes on. Waves fold behind villages.*' The abrupt shift of perspective is not dissimilar to that in 'Absences', though this time the move is from room to darkening sea, rather than from sea to empty room. In place of the euphoric surrender of 'Here' or 'Absences', there is melodramatic foreboding: '*Now / Night comes on*', while the strange intransitive verb 'fold' gives the final phrase '*Waves fold behind villages*' a heavy prophetic gloom. For all its melancholy, this poem brims with a strange sense of aesthetic fun. The solitude it celebrates has not yet lost its delight, despite the threatening larger loneliness which encompasses it.

However, in the poems which followed in the later 1960s this threat is not so easily turned to imaginative profit. The differently viewed windowscapes of 'High Windows' (1967) and 'Sad Steps' (1968), for instance, chart an inexorable deepening of mood and hardening of style. Time presses urgently as the poet contemplates his own ageing. In 'High Windows' he contrives to escape from his sordid, wrangling envy of the young into a version of the unproven cube of light of 'Dry-Point':

> Rather than words comes the thought of high windows:
> The sun-comprehending glass,
> And beyond it, the deep blue air, that shows
> Nothing, and is nowhere, and is endless.

But this resolution, though carefully formulated in negatives was, it seems, still too romantically self-indulgent. Larkin wrote 'and fucking piss' in one of the drafts after the last line (Motion 355), and in 'Sad Steps' he ruthlessly reverses the emotional pattern. The source of escape in 'High Windows' becomes the source of imprisonment in the later poem. It is the intensely beautiful windowscape itself which, instead of offering escape, arouses his imaginative yearnings by reminding him

> of the strength and pain
> Of being young; that it can't come again,
> But is for others undiminished somewhere.

The same basic pattern produces a contrasting emotional music and a bleaker conclusion. In 'High Windows' the young are envied in their caricature 'paradise' of plentiful sex; in 'Sad Steps' youth is seen, with more complexity, as 'strength and pain'. In 'High Windows' the thought of a daytime windowscape offers the poet an absolving 'nowhere' in which he can evade the desolate attic of his envy. In 'Sad Steps' he looks out at a night-time windowscape which speaks of an unattainable 'somewhere' where the young live their still undiminished lives. The self-possessed transcendence of the ending of 'High Windows' is replaced by selfless, irremediable loneliness.

The secure inner sanctum of Larkin's earlier work is turning into an insecure cell of existential despair. In the poems which follow in the early 1970s, raw defensive anxiety drives the poet into increasingly histrionic projections of antisocial solitude. Like 'High Windows', 'The Card-Players' depicts a transcendent escape: not, however, into the attenuated sublimity of an empty blue sky, but into a grotesque carnivalesque 'lamplit cave' of masculine squalor. Mutely uncommunicative male fellowship is celebrated in a brutal rejection of domestic refinement. All the barriers between outer and inner which usually define Larkin's self-possession are transgressed, and, uniquely in his work, this room is exposed to the elements, its door wide open on the dark, at which Jan van Hogspeuw pisses. Elemental nature, imaged in other poems as sea, clouds, moon and wind, is seen here as rain, ale and piss, gale, belch and fart, in awesome flux, personified in the obscene mythic metonyms of 'Hogspeuw', gobbing at the grate, 'Dogstoerd', pouring the ale, and 'Prijck', snoring with the gale: 'Rain, wind and fire! The secret, bestial peace!' Self-possession is transcended in an obscene carnival of bodily functions.

In what seems a deliberate formal and generic juxtaposition, 'Vers de Société', completed in the following year, 1971, returns from this symbolist intensity to the secular withdrawing-room of social sentiment. Here, in a reworking of the then unpublished 'Best Society', written exactly twenty years earlier, the ageing Larkin comes closest to accepting defeat at the hands of society:

> Just think of all the spare time that has flown

> Straight into nothingness by being filled
> With forks and faces, rather than repaid
> Under a lamp, hearing the noise of wind,
> And looking out to see the moon thinned
> To an air-sharpened blade.

The lamp, the noise of the wind outside, and the moonlit window-scape, create a room of aesthetic isolation. In death's waiting-room, however, solitude no longer seems the best society. 'The time is shorter now for company', and the alternative social room of 'forks and faces', though still contemptible, offers an escape from loneliness. Moreover, it is implied, the poet can no longer so easily write the poems which formerly 'repaid' his spare time. And as he laconically acknowledges: 'sitting by a lamp more often brings / Not peace, but other things.' With resignation the final stanza returns, after four sestets of shifting, irregular rhyme-patterns, to the simple *aabbccdd* couplets of the open-ing, as he begins to write – not a poem, but an acceptance of Warlock-Williams's invitation. It is significant, however, that the poem ends here. We do not see the poet leave the room of solitude to venture into society. Despite its defeated ending, this poem still clings to his pre-cious isolation. It offers the last more-or-less comfortable withdrawing-room in Larkin's work.

'Livings II', written later in 1971, turns back to the sublime, imper-sonal mode of 'The Card-Players', but with the obscene impulse reined back to a grim secular asceticism. It rejects both male fellowship and polite society in the most aggressive assertion of self-possession in Larkin's work. There is no reference here to the poet's vocation. This lighthouse is no ivory tower, nor is the keeper, passing the time with his divining cards, pursuing an artistic vocation. His is a sublime version of Bleaney's plight, as he does his job and keeps himself to himself. The barely furnished narrow rooms of the stanzas, in free unrhymed trimeters, express his edgily uncomfortable selfhood. We are far indeed from the relaxed roominess of the stanzas of 'The Whitsun Weddings' and 'Here':

> By day, sky builds
> Grape-dark over the salt
> Unsown stirring fields.
> Radio rubs its legs,
> Telling me of elsewhere...

The radio, like a cricket which has strayed inside from the sterile 'salt... fields' of the sea 'rubs its legs', keeping the speaker company while not burdening him with another human presence. In a starker, ungendered version of the juxtaposition of 'If, My Darling' the bare, uncomfortable lighthouse is clashed against the cosy inns of society, which keep the sea at a safe distance, their sea-pictures humorously 'kippering' in the pipe-smoke. To the lighthouse-keeper they are unbearably claustropho-bic: 'Keep it all off!' His is a deeper, less sentimental security. Gripped by light atop his tower in the sea, savagely lyrical and 'Guarded by brilliance', he seems to occupy the impenetrable padlocked cube of light of 'Dry-Point', to inhabit the uninhabited sea of 'Absences'.

In the final phase of Larkin's poetry a terminal reduction takes place, as his rooms narrow down to the existential 'room' occupied by his mortal body. The 'loosening' of the end of 'Ambulances' is painfully re-enacted over several poems. In 'The Building' the rooms are a maze of oubliettes rather than places to inhabit:

> For past these doors are rooms, and rooms past those,
> And more rooms yet, each one further off
>
> And harder to return from...

Like the remote sun-scrubbed room of 'Dry-Point', these rooms offer escape from the flesh, but now in a terrifyingly literal sense.

This poem adopts a complicatedly ingenious structure (paralleled in Larkin's work only in 'I Remember, I Remember') in which rhyme-scheme and stanza-form, though both perfectly regular, fail to coincide. An eight-line rhyme-scheme is observed throughout. The stanzas, how-ever, are only seven lines long, with a final isolated line at the end to complete the scheme. Since mid-sentence enjambements between stan-zas are the rule in the poem, it might be felt that Larkin is merely indulging in perverse typography. Regrouping the lines into eight-line stanzas destroys some felicities (the emotive anacrusis in the last quot-ed passage, for instance), but this more normal arrangement would not seem obviously wrong had Larkin adopted it. As it is, the layout he has chosen gives each stanza a different pattern, creating an underlying feeling of anxious insecurity, of firm ground slipping subtly away. Or perhaps, reading more allegorically, the reader is led through similar rooms, none quite the same, each with confusingly rearranged furni-ture. It must be conceded that the reader can scarcely hear this effect with any precision. Larkin seems to be encoding a deep structure in his form without concern for its audibility, playing a private formal game with himself, just as some Renaissance poets bury numerological patterns or acrostics in their work.

The reduction from rooms to primitive existential 'room' is taken a stage further in 'The Old Fools' (1973). Here, the metaphorical tension between inner and outer is cruelly lost, and Blake's aphorism is given a sinister spin. The old fools no longer live inside real rooms; the imagined rooms in which they live are inside them. The 'untrue', 'unreal' inner world which was the unfailing source of delight in Larkin's earlier work, becomes now their only world.

> Perhaps being old is having lighted rooms
> Inside your head, and people in them...
>   or sometimes only
> The rooms themselves, chairs and a fire burning,
> The blown bush at the window, or the sun's
> Faint friendliness on the wall some lonely
> Rain-ceased midsummer evening.

Larkin writes 'Inside your head' not 'Inside your mind'; at this extreme of physical being it is 'dimensional extent' which matters. These waiting-rooms of the mind achingly parody the consoling aesthetic solitude of 'Best Society' and 'Vers de Société'. More crudely, in the blackest of popular clichés, all the lights are on, but there's nobody at home.

In 'Aubade' the familiar Larkinesque contrast of rooms recurs in muted form. On the one hand there is the room which 'takes shape' in his senses as light strengthens, a room in which he confronts the plain-as-a-wardrobe fact of death. On the other hand there is the longed-for room of 'infinity and absence, the beauty of somewhere you're not'. In this poem, however, the beautiful room of escape takes not the figurative form of a remote cube of light or a symbolist attic, but the banally literal form of 'locked-up offices' in which telephones crouch, getting ready to ring, as 'all the uncaring / Intricate rented world begins to rouse.' In the face of death life at its most prosaic and ordinary is charged with unattainable beauty. The tension between real and figurative rooms is lost as his tenancy of both nears its end.

The room image recurs to the very end of Larkin's work, in the sad coda of poems written following the faltering of his inspiration after 'Aubade'. The 'palace' in 'The Winter Palace' (1978) is, with the flattest of ironies, a wide landscape inside his head, an image of blanking out the damage of age: 'Then there will be nothing I know. / My mind will fold into itself, like fields, like snow.' In 'Love Again' the poet finds himself, as he had been in 'Dry-Point', nearly thirty years earlier, uncomfortably alone with his body in his room, still unable to escape his importunate desires. Finally in 'Party Politics' (1984) he depicts himself defeated, in the corner of a room of forks and faces, waiting for his glass to be filled. The image ostensibly offers a satire on the arbitrariness of life's rewards: 'You may get drunk, or dry half-hours may pass. / It seems to turn on where you are. Or who.' However, the limp political metaphor poignantly fails to generate interest in comparison with the literal plight of the poet, deserted by his muse, drinking himself into insensibility in death's ante-room.

7
Empty Gestures

Larkin as elegist

Mortality is our common lot, and for a lyric poet concerned with the liminal plight of 'being here', death, the ultimate threshold, is an inevitable theme. Few poets of the twentieth century are so consistently death-obsessed as Larkin. Sitting on a gravestone in Spring Bank Cemetery in 1964 he told John Betjeman: 'everything I write, I think, has the consciousness of approaching death in the background.'[1] His inner biological clock ticked loud, and he could always hear it distinctly. His poetry is fundamentally elegiac. It seems surprising, therefore, that his name scarcely features in recent theoretical treatments of elegy. This is largely because he writes the less-theorised genres of meditative elegy or self-elegy rather than mourning elegy, which has received by far the greatest attention from commentators. It is mortality as our common fate, or more immediately his own death, which concerns him.

Of the three modes of elegy – mourning elegy, meditative or reflective elegy, and self-elegy – the mourning mode is the major focus of recent theorists from Eric Smith[2] and Peter Sacks[3] to Jahan Ramazani[4] and Melissa Zeiger.[5] Freud's essay of 1915, 'Mourning and Melancholia', has provided an attractive interpretation of elegy in terms of the psychological 'work of mourning'. Apollo and Pan, Peter Sacks argues, are the archetypal 'successful mourners', working through their grief for the lost nymphs Daphne and Syrinx by sublimating their plight in art or music: 'Only when Apollo turns to the projected founding of a sign, the laurel wreath, does he appear to accept his loss, by having invented some consoling substitute for Daphne.'[6] Pan, likewise, fashions a flute from the reeds into which Syrinx has been transformed. Milton's

'Lycidas' and Tennyson's *In Memoriam* are interpreted as modern exam-ples of such 'healthy mourning', which enables the poets to move on. Milton concludes briskly: 'Tomorrow to fresh Woods and Pastures new'.[7] At the end of *In Memoriam* Tennyson sees grief as an agent of spiritual improvement:

> Regret is dead, but love is more
> Than in the summers that are flown,
> For I myself with these have grown
> To something greater than before...[8]

In the elegy of healthy mourning poetry acts as therapy for the poet's grief-stricken plight. As Sacks puts it, an elegist should close 'with a *henceforth*'.[9]

Freud's essay also describes an alternative, 'melancholy' mourning, in which the mourner remains unconsoled and despairing. Melancholy prevails, for instance, in Gray's 'Sonnet on the Death of Mr. Richard West': 'I fruitless mourn to him that cannot hear, / And weep the more, because I weep in vain.'[10] Unsurprisingly, twentieth-century, post-Freudian elegies usually adopt this melancholy mode. Wilfred Owen insisted that his 'elegies' for fellow soldiers were 'in no sense consola-tory.'[11] Ramazani comments: 'If the traditional elegy was an art of saving, the modern elegy is what Elizabeth Bishop calls an "art of losing".' He concludes that the modern elegy is usually 'an elegy for elegy – a poem that mourns the diminished efficacy and legitimacy of poetic mourning.'[12] In the elegy of melancholic mourning there is no therapy beyond the poet's expression of his or her morbid grief.

Harold Bloom offers a different literary interpretation of the sur-vivor's mourning. In order to fashion his own distinctive voice, the poet, Bloom says, must master the anxiety of influence induced by his forerunners. Elegy dramatizes this trial of strength.[13] As Melissa Zeiger explains: 'mainstream elegies have treated an admired but not inti-mately known male acquaintance or peer. Most often, too, these are fel-low poets.'[14] In this very masculine perspective the 'great tradition' of the elegy comprises poems written about a man, perhaps another poet, to whom the writer owes a debt. Examples are Milton's 'Lycidas', Shelley's 'Adonais' and Auden's 'In Memory of W. B. Yeats'. The psy-chological 'work of mourning' becomes the literary work of asserting one's unique artistic identity.

These theories are of limited relevance to the reader of Larkin. He wrote two mourning elegies concerned with animals, 'Myxomatosis' and 'The Mower', which look back to Cowper's 'On Mrs. Throckmorton's bullfinch' and Matthew Arnold's 'Poor Matthias'. However, there is only one bereavement elegy proper, 'An April Sunday brings the snow', completed in 1948 when he was twenty-five, and addressed to his father. Its depersonalized grief offers little purchase to the analyst of mourning or influence. Indeed, for all the text reveals the mourned jam-maker might be a mother or a lover. In place of a psychological drama of relationship the poem offers a delicate tissue of traditional images of mortality. The wintry snow on the spring plum-blossom will go in an 'hour or two' and the blossom will soon follow it. Last autumn's fruit is now the jam which the poet is carrying from cupboard to cupboard. The seasonal cycle is unobtrusively completed when we are told that this jam will be eaten at next summer's teas, though, poignantly, the jam-maker will not be there to enjoy it.

Compared with other twentieth-century elegies for fathers this is a markedly reticent poem. Betjeman affectionately recalls his father's deafness and his liking for 'Potatoes in their skin'. Plath conjures from her complicated grief a fictional Nazi 'Daddy'. Larkin gives no personal details. Dylan Thomas foregrounds a rejection of 'healthy' mourning by urging his father to 'rage against the dying of the light.'[15] Larkin's address to the dead man is, in comparison, restrained. He mourns merely, in simple monosyllables, that 'you will not sit and eat'. The poet's address to the dead parent generates neither a loving, picturesque portrait as in Betjeman, nor passionate pleas as in Thomas, nor grating accusations as in Plath.

Moreover, although Sydney Larkin's views on literature and culture exerted a strong and problematic influence on his son, no anxiety of influence is audible. The personality of the dead man is realized in terms of the simplest domesticity. All that 'remains' of him are jars of jam. These are not 'remains' in the sense of finger-bones sticking shockingly through finger-ends as in Betjeman's elegy; nor are they literary 'remains' incurring debts or rivalries. With subtle indirection Larkin focuses on the jam beneath the cellophane as the simplest of metonyms for 'sweet / And meaningless' life. Instead of a vivid dramatization of the bereaved poet's plight such as we find in the other poets, the identities of both mourner and mourned are effaced and the 'work of mourning' is lost in a contemplation of death as the end of everything.

Characteristically the 'work of mourning' is most evident not in a poem concerned with a relative or friend, but in 'Deceptions', concerned with a long-dead Victorian prostitute. The poem's unsuccessful attempt at sublimation offers a complicated variant of Sacks's mourning model in which the poet grieves over a long-dead woman, focusing not on his own loss, but on her loss of innocence. Much of the poem is devoted to his ineffectual attempts to console the dead girl for the destruction of her life by her rapist. Melissa Zeiger complains that elegy 'will often make use of female figures in order finally to exclude them', and cites HD's reproachful poem, 'Euridyce'.[16] The 'successful' mourning of Sacks' version, she feels, shows a patriarchal sexual politics. Roland Barthes, similarly, saw Orpheus as signifier 'condemning Euridyce (the signified) to eternal death by looking back at her'.[17] 'Deceptions' could be read as such an attempt to appropriate female suffering and relegate it to the past ('Slums, years, have buried you'). However the poet's intense guilt dooms his strenuous elegiac 'work' to failure. In this most original elegy of melancholic mourning, the poet's plight remains unresolved. The long-dead girl lies beyond his consolations, and he will never be able to lay her vividly-evoked suffering to rest.

'An April Sunday brings the snow' and 'Deceptions' are both unique pieces in Larkin's work. He is too introverted a poet for the mourning genre; moreover, after the death of his father no close relative or friend of his died for several decades. His elegies belong predominantly to the reflective or contemplative, rather than the mourning type, and need to be placed in a different theoretical context. Though the modes of mourning and meditation frequently intermingle, they pull in different rhetorical directions, and at their extremes they produce quite separate genres. Mourning, whether 'healthy' or 'melancholic', contrasts live poet with dead subject. The plight of the bereaved, mourning elegist is one of continuing life. He or she dramatizes survival: 'I weep for Adonais – he is dead!'[18] *I* am not *he*; *I* survive. The reflective elegist, in contrast, contemplates shared extinction. In reflective elegy the 'I' of dramatized mourning becomes a generalized 'we' or 'you': 'And all our yesterdays have lighted fools / The way to dusty death';[19] or it becomes impersonal, abstracted: 'all that beauty, all that wealth e'er gave, / Awaits alike th'inevitable hour.'[20] The plight of the reflective elegist is shared, universal, ruling out the survival which is central to mourning elegy.

The theoretical neglect of reflective elegy arises partly from its relatively recent recognition as a genre. Crucial here is Thomas Gray's decision to change the original title of his graveyard poem from 'Stanzas wrote in a Country Churchyard' to 'Elegy...'.[21] Both Eric Smith and Peter Sacks find Gray an 'anomalous' elegist because of his failure to answer to the mourning pattern. However, his uniquely familiar 'Elegy' serves to give focus to a different, clearly defined genre which goes back to antiquity, and includes the Anglo-Saxon 'Wanderer' and 'Seafarer', *Ecclesiastes* in the King James Bible, Jacques' Seven Ages of Man soliloquy in *As You Like It*, Edward Fitzgerald's *Rubáiyát of Omar Khayyám*, the 'O dark dark dark' section in T. S. Eliot's 'East Coker', and Carol Ann Duffy's 'And Then What'.[22] Its preoccupation with mortality as a common plight, it could be argued, makes the reflective elegy more centrally *about* death, more intrinsically elegiac, than the mourning elegy, with its focus on the grief of the living survivor.

The elegiac

Before examining Larkin's reflective elegies it will be useful to step back and consider the artistic plight of the poet who writes about death. Two factors conspire to make 'the elegiac' the most protean and self-contradictory of literary modes. Firstly death, though of the greatest import, is paradoxically also the most banal and familiar of topics. As Freud briskly put it: 'everyone owes nature a death and must expect to pay the debt.'[23] Secondly death is like no other event (except birth), in that no-one writes about dying from first-hand experience. Our own death is a signifier without a signified. As Ludwig Wittgenstein said: 'Death is not an event in life.'[24] The artistic plight of the elegist is defined by these two aporias. Samuel Johnson's comment 'Where there is leisure for fiction there is little grief' is, of course, naïve in the extreme.[25] Grief frequently prompts a plethora of ineffective 'fictions'. However Johnson does grasp the fundamental truth that mortality humbles our words to meaninglessness. Elegy readily becomes self-referential, uneasy with the artifice of its empty verbal gestures. It acknowledges that in the face of death words are always ineffective. The paradoxical plight of the elegist is to be eloquently at a loss for words.

Death's combination of banal familiarity with awesome inscrutability generates a wide spectrum of different rhetorical responses. At one extreme the elegiac impulse fosters the concision of graveyard humour, the Roman mosaic, for instance, depicting a sprawling skeleton under the philosopher's exhortation *Gnothi seauton* ('know thyself'), the gnomic epitaph, 'As I was, so are ye / And as I am, / So shall ye be,[26] or the transgressive humour of epitaphs punning on the name or profession of the dead, such as the celebrated lines on an eighteenth-century Oxford academic called Pricke: 'In a Jùly moister than December / Christ's College lost a privy member...'[27] More sombrely, A. E. Housman jokes drily in 'To an athlete dying young': 'silence sounds no worse than cheers / After earth has stopped the ears.'[28] Death is the ultimate 'farewell to the flesh', so it is not surprising that a carnivalesque disregard for decorum frequently infuses the elegiac mode. At the opposite extreme is the grandest rhetoric: 'The Flower that once has blown for ever dies.'[29] Tautologous truisms are dignified by sombre grandiloquence. But even at its most eloquent elegy is rich in subversive undertones:

> Can storied urn, or animated bust,
>> Back to its mansion call the fleeting breath?
> Can honour's voice provoke the silent dust,
>> Or flatt'ry soothe the dull cold ear of death?[30]

The polished diction, rhetorical questions, and precise personifications elaborate the simple thought with a rococo, faintly camp gusto.

Larkin can take the high literary ground of Gray's beautiful Latinisms: 'nothing contravenes / The coming dark' ('The Building'); 'Arid interrogation' ('Aubade'). But his love of cliché draws him also towards the more mixed registers of elegy. Ambiguous tones abound, from the grotesque singsong rhyme of: 'Death will be such another thing, / All we have done not mattering' ('The local snivels through the fields'), to the excruciating hidden puns of 'Ambulances', when the patient is 'borne away in deadened air'. In 'The View' the poet asks: 'Where has it gone, the lifetime?' and shrugs in answer: 'Search me.' In 'Aubade' he writes, in a tone between chirpy admonition and lugubrious despair, 'Being brave / Lets no one off the grave.' The poignant wryness of the lugubrious is at the heart of his work:

> Life is first boredom, then fear.
> Whether or not we use it, it goes,
> And leaves what something hidden from us chose,
> And age, and then the only end of age.

Gloomy though the thought is, its lugubrious relish elicits a wry smile of enjoyment. In an age of self-referential complexities the lugubrious offers perhaps the most authentic note of blithe *jouissance*. It clings to the controlling wit of high art, while at the same time subverting its own gravity, conceding the inadequacy of words.

The wan wit of the lugubrious, however, points the way deeper into the elegiac, towards the no-wit which is the ultimate rock-bottom of elegy. Confronted with death all affectation of literary mastery, all discriminations of taste fall away. However eloquent a poet may be, he or she can never be more moving than the artless mourner of the local newspaper *In Memoriam* column:

> Life without you is not the same, the memories we have will remain, so does the hurt and the pain. Sleep tight little one, till we meet again.

> No thoughts can tell, no words can say, how much I miss you every day.

> Dear Dorothy, let me call you sweetheart, I'm in love with you, let me hear you whisper, you love me too. See the love light flowing in your eyes so blue, Love you forever – your loving husband Harry xxx.

Such inept conventionality, unlineated to save money, disarms irony and is unbearably moving. It comes from the abject world of Larkin's moustached women in flowered frocks in 'Faith Healing', the widow in 'Love Songs in Age', or the neighbours in 'Ambulances' whispering 'poor soul' to themselves 'at their own distress'. The banal cliché and the flat commonplace belong at the heart of Larkin's elegiac poetics, generating either lugubrious ambiguity, or the wit-less anti-irony of the hard-core elegiac. Death is a literary as well as a social leveller, and the greatest elegists defy irony, daring the reader to mock the ingenuous, the naïve, the at-a-loss. To this extreme elegiac mode belong Lear fumbling with his button as he holds the dead Cordelia, the embarrassingly uninhibited thumps on the timpani at the beginning of Verdi's *Dies Irae*, and Flaubert's moving depiction of a dying old woman in *Un Coeur Simple*, dreaming that her stuffed parrot is welcoming her into heaven.

Memento mori

In terms of rhetorical structure the elegiac plight is characterized by a tension between life and death, hope and despair, consolation and melancholy. The *memento mori* poem focusing on an emblem of mortality offers inexhaustible variations on this binary. George Herbert's devotional poem 'Vertue', for instance, deploys familiar images of mortality with playful wit: the dew of night will 'weep' for the death of the passing day, the rose's root is 'ever in its grave'.[31] He ends with unambiguous consolation, asserting that the 'sweet and vertuous soul' never dies. Shelley, in 'Ozymandias', chooses the equally familiar image of a ruin. Ironically the legend of the boastful statue: 'Look on my works, ye Mighty, and despair!' carries a different meaning from that originally intended. It is grimly consoling to reflect that though the king's great works are lost in the desert sand, so also is his vainglorious pride.[32] Hopkins revitalizes that most commonplace image of mortality, falling leaves, by casting 'Spring and Fall' as a dramatized address to a girl, whose childlike 'fresh thoughts' are as moved by the leaves as by 'the things of man'. Her tears become an elegy for all mankind, and for herself: 'It is the blight man was born for, / It is Margaret you mourn for.'[33] In Hopkins' poem the confident theological consolation offered by Herbert is replaced by mere emotion. The admission that there is no consolation becomes itself, in the emptiest of elegiac gestures, a kind of consolation.

The young Larkin produced a large number of exercises in this flexible *memento mori* form. He is particularly inventive in his choice of topics. Some of his images are traditional: dusk ('Going'), dead butterflies in a case ('Autumn') a deserted church ('Church Going'); but other Larkin elegies concern retired racehorses ('At Grass'), a holiday poster ('Sunny Prestatyn'), old sheet music ('Love Songs in Age'), pigeons and ambulances. 'Where can we live but days?' he asks with startling ingenuousness. In 'Tops' he describes how tops, sent spinning, 'draw gravely up', then falter and lose their poise, to clatter and sprawl pathetically over:

> what most appals
> Is that tiny first shiver,
> That stumble, whereby
> We know beyond doubt
> They have almost run out
> And are starting to die.

The co-option of a child's toy to so elegiac a purpose is witty and surprising; reminders of death are, apparently, everywhere about us. In another poem the poet apologizes to his skin for not having found a suitable 'brash festivity' to wear it at, before it thickened and sagged. He foresees it soon succumbing to the change of 'fashion' of death. These *memento mori* poems recall the concentratedly epigrammatic 'emblems' of the seventeenth century, by Herbert, Vaughan and Quarles.

'Next, Please' reduces life to a queue at a check-out, while its 'sparkling armada of promises' adapts the saying: 'I'm waiting for my ship to come in'. The 'figurehead with golden tits / Arching our way', with its hint of Hollywood historical romance is a metaphor acutely conscious of its status as 'discourse'. Its mock-heroic, kitsch quality indicates that optimism is hollow from the beginning. At the end of the poem a literary, 'highbrow' metaphor of the 'ship of death' (or medieval 'ship of fools') trumps the folk-image of the ship of wealth and success:

> Only one ship is seeking us, a black-
> Sailed unfamiliar, towing at her back
> A huge and birdless silence. In her wake
> No waters breed or break.

There is a chilling sense of fun about this portentous wit.

Larkin's elegies frequently focus, as here, on images which are already mediated: a Victorian rape victim from a book ('Deceptions'), a funerary monument in a church ('An Arundel Tomb'), miners viewed through the literary lens of D. H. Lawrence ('The Explosion'), a dream of a funeral in picturesque old Ireland ('Dublinesque'). The familiar, 'second-hand', even banal nature of such images is intrinsic to the contemplative effect. 'MCMXIV' mediates its emotionally charged subject matter through two filters: the familiar Roman numerals on a First World War Memorial, and an implied faded photograph of young men queuing to enlist. The artifice of these poems is self-consciously formal. And like Keats's Odes they embody explicit abstract themes. Each of Larkin's large-scale meditative elegies could be subtitled with its own differently-nuanced binary opposition: 'Expectancy and Disappointment' ('Next, Please'); 'Fulfilment and Desolation' ('Deceptions'); 'Superstition and Doubt' ('Church Going'); 'Hope and Disillusion' ('Love Songs in Age'); 'Ideal and Reality' ('Essential Beauty'); 'Existence and Oblivion' ('The Old Fools'). Each offers a different variation on the dynamic between consolation and despair.

'An Arundel Tomb', which formulates this antithesis in the classic form of Love and Death, projects the positive side of the dynamic more vigorously than any other of his poems, and is consequently central to Larkin's contribution to the genre. The challenge is to have his cake of hope while eating his cake of irony. A resolution on the side of hope will result in banal sentimentality; a resolution on the side of despair will rob the poem of its emotional appeal. For the maximum formal tension it is essential that this sceptical poem should end, resoundingly, on the upbeat, with the word 'love'.

> Time has transfigured them into
> Untruth. The stone fidelity
> They hardly meant has come to be
> Their final blazon, and to prove
> Our almost-instinct almost true:
> What will survive of us is love.

The contradiction is as explicit as possible. 'Time has transfigured them...' the poet intones grandiloquently. The sentimental reader expects the organ tone to swell:

> Time has transfigured them into
> A blazon of the dreams and hopes
> Of love eternal...

Instead we lurch, with a distortion of metre and unexpected full-stop, into a shuddering discord: 'Untruth', the negative prefix emphatically capitalized at the beginning of the line. The word may be read as a reversed iamb (/x), or, more emphatically, as a spondee with both syllables stressed (//), enacting the freezing of the human warmth of the earl and countess's love into an oxymoronic 'stone fidelity'. Any fidelity they may have demonstrated in their lives is, in any case, quite hypothetical; their 'faithfulness in effigy' may have been a fiction from the beginning. Nevertheless, a sentimental rhetoric reasserts itself against the simple meaning of the words. The starkly unqualified noun 'Untruth' is immediately reformulated in the softer form of a hopefully concessive adjectival phrase 'almost true', and in the poem's famous last line the impulse to affirm and celebrate triumphs emotionally, if not rationally. Great poetry is conjured out of nothing more respectable – on reflection – than the 'Forever united' of the local newspaper's 'In Memoriam' column.

The imperative need to end his poem on the word 'love' places Larkin in a specific technical plight. The *Penguin Rhyming Dictionary* gives only ten perfect rhymes for 'love'.[34] Two of these are compounds containing the word itself ('truelove', 'ladylove'), and therefore useless in a serious poem. 'Dove', 'ringdove' and 'turtledove' are reminiscent of the Victorian greeting-card, while 'guv' and 'shove' could only work in a comic context. 'Foxglove' would only be possible with some very clever footwork. 'Glove' could perhaps be made to fit Larkin's purposes (the knight's 'gauntlet' has already been mentioned), but would probably sound forced. We are left with 'above', the only generally usable perfect rhyme for 'love', and consequently rather predictable and familiar.

Larkin's solution is the half-rhyme 'prove', which is less facile than 'above/love', and also beautifully isolates the final word's pathetic challenge to the reader's scepticism:

> and to prove
> Our almost-instinct almost true:
> What will survive of us is love.

The long, emphatic 'o' of 'prove', echoed by the intervening 'true', descends, with poignant bathos, to the short weak 'o' of 'love'. The rhyme is imperfect, but is sanctioned by literary convention, 'prove/ love' being a familiar rhyme in the seventeenth century, at which time it was perfect even in ordinary speech, 'love' being pronounced with a long ō. Later, when pronunciation changed, it was too useful a rhyme to abandon, since there are so few alternatives, So in the nineteenth century 'prove/love', like 'move/love', persisted as an 'eye-rhyme'. Does this hint of archaism impart a touch of historical self-consciousness to the poem, appropriate, perhaps, to its subject-matter?

To ascend to the hypertextual level for a moment, did Larkin just possibly have in mind the prominent use of this rhyme in Ben Jonson's much-anthologized *carpe diem* lyric, or erotic elegy, from *Volpone*?

> Come, my Celia, let us prove,
> While we may, the sports of love;
> Time will not be ours, for ever:
> He, at length, our good will sever.[35]

Whether he did have this poem in mind or not, Larkin's 'time' and 'love' do seem to answer Jonson's across the centuries, in a sad echo. With the vigour of youthful lust Jonson's lyric claims that 'love' is the only way to redeem 'time'. Volpone urges Celia, earthily, to seize the day and 'prove' (enjoy) love before it is too late. In Larkin's elegy, however, it is already too late for the earl and countess. Whether they 'proved' love's delights or not, their lust is now laid in earth. Nevertheless they still seem to 'prove' (with a slight shift of meaning) that love does indeed redeem time. Time was not theirs for ever; but it has now ironically 'transfigured them' into an 'Untruth' which denies Time's destructive effect. The thought is painfully contorted and Larkin's neologistic diction ('almost-instinct almost true'), jars awkwardly against the pure seventeenth-century diction of 'time' and 'love', almost spoiling the lyric effect – but not quite. The final positive resolution is, however, achieved audibly against the grain, as Larkin's own irritated gloss written in the workbook draft indicates: 'Love isn't stronger than death just because statues hold hands for 600 years' (Motion 274). Just as Keats's urn proved our almost-instinct almost-true that 'Beauty is truth, truth beauty', so the earl and the countess proclaim amid other woes than theirs the consoling but wishful message that 'What will survive of us is love'.

In 'The Trees', written a decade later, scepticism ('No, they die too'), is once again irrationally swept aside at the close of the poem by emotional optimism ('afresh, afresh, afresh'). But the effect is on a smaller scale, and the euphoric rhetoric fails to drown out the sense of strain. The opening thought seems, at first sight, forced by the need to find a rhyme for 'leaf'; otherwise why should greenness be identified with grief?

> The trees are coming into leaf
> Like something almost being said;
> The recent buds relax and spread,
> Their greenness is a kind of grief.

Responding to the apparent awkwardness of the thought James Fenton remarks sourly that Larkin's emotions 'seem to work in a different timeframe to ours in this poem, because it is the sight of the new buds which says to him: "Last year is dead." Most people, I think, would have noticed that in the autumn.'[36] Fenton's 'ours', and 'most people', are not as inclusive as he implies. Robert Frost, for instance, uses this 'leaf/grief' rhyme to draw exactly the same equation between incipience and transience:

> Nature's first green is gold,
> Her hardest hue to hold.
> Her early leaf's a flower;
> But only so an hour.
> Then leaf subsides to leaf.
> So Eden sank to grief,
> So dawn goes down to day.
> Nothing gold can stay.[37]

The shift from tight bud to full 'leaf' is seen as leading inevitably to the 'grief' of the fall to come. The difference lies in the two poets' relative degrees of explicitness. Frost's pun on the biblical meaning of 'fall' makes the leap from 'leaf' to 'grief' more immediately comprehensible than it is in Larkin's poem, which relies on the reader's familiarity with the 'spring and fall' topos to supply the tenuous elegiac connections.

The sense of strain persists in the painful tone of the succeeding *faux naïf* rhetorical question, 'Is it that they are born again...?', so easily answered: 'No, they die too.' The plight of mortality is universal, and the trees' apparent immortality is a 'trick'. And so also is the poem's hopeful rhetoric. 'Yet still', the poet says, despite having revealed his trick, 'Yet still the unresting castles thresh'. This emotional reversal, 'Yet still', is the emptiest of gestures. There is no argument behind it; only grammar. Moreover the artificial sweetness of the diction ('unresting castles', 'fullgrown thickness') might remind older readers of the refined weightless sweetness of the post-war sugar-substitute, saccharine, and also of saccharine's unpleasant chemical aftertaste, mimicked by Larkin's added manuscript note following the last line: 'Bloody awful tripe' (Motion 372). The poet is aware that he has written an irresistible anthology piece, and he is contemptuous of himself for being able to perform the trick with such facility. Also, more profoundly, he is sad that his trick does not work. In his review of *The Oxford Book of Death*, in 1983 Larkin declared that 'the only miracle worth talking about is immortality' (*FR* 345).

Larkin's afterword also makes audible an ominous undertone in the trees' insistent imperative, 'Begin afresh, afresh, afresh', which hurries life onward urgently towards the fall. In 'Next, Please', our 'expectancy' causes us to wish our lives away; in 'The Trees' we are hurried on by the cycle of nature itself. Leonardo da Vinci provides a hypertext at this point, in the form of a proleptic paraphrase of Larkin:

> the hope and the desire of returning to the first state of chaos is like the moth to the light, and... the man who with constant longing awaits with joy each new springtime, each new summer, each new month and new year – deeming that the things he longs for are ever too late in coming – does not perceive that he is longing for his own destruction. But this desire is the very quintessence, the spirit of the elements, which finding itself imprisoned with the soul is ever longing to return from the human body to its giver.[38]

Our bad habit of expectancy, which is the very 'spirit of the elements', betrays our impatient unconscious desire to return to the primal chaos of nature. Every fresh year marks the trees' mortality in 'rings of grain'.

Aware of this ambiguity Larkin famously preferred inactivity and routine to starting afresh:

> I suppose everyone tries to ignore the passing of time: some people by doing a lot, being in California one year and Japan the next; or there's my way – making every day and every year exactly the same. Probably neither works.
>
> (*RW* 57–8)

The hollow optimism of 'The Trees' strains against Larkin's deepest compulsion: to resist change, and the decay that change brings.

Orpheus and Pan

So far we have been concerned with elegies which belong in the world of humane civility. They may not provide consolation, but they still make the poignant attempt to do so. Behind such poems as 'An Arundel Tomb', 'MCMXIV', 'Ambulances' and 'The Trees' lies the archetype of Orpheus, whose lyre soothes the savage beasts and wins back his wife from the underworld. These poems are social, sentimental, human. Even after he finally loses Euridyce, Orpheus's inconsolable grief is life-affirming. What survives of them is love. But there is also a darker elegy whose model is not the mortal hero Orpheus, but the primitive god Pan. His frustrated lust at the transformation of Syrinx into reeds turns itself into an elegy of desire forever unfulfilled, played on pipes which he cuts brutally from her reed-stems. His divine death-affirming elegy transcends the sentimentalities of human, social existence, and its flute music pierces its mortal hearers with panic. Larkin's later elegies bring this hard-core Panic element into tension with humane Orphic sentiment. Larkin is the most civilized of poets, and anti-humanism never wins the rhetorical struggle, as it does in Ted Hughes's *Crow* and *Cave Birds*. However, the contest is sometimes very close.

The most problematic occurrence of this darker elegiac plight in Larkin's work occurs in his only mature Eros-Thanatos elegy, 'Sunny Prestatyn'. As in 'Deceptions' the picture is complicated by undertones of sexual anxiety which upset the composure of an apparently light poem about advertising. Larkin's elegies usually focus on sexuality only in its socially-mediated form of love or marriage. Here, however, the binary is not Love and Death but, reductively, Sex and Death. The first stanza and the last four lines preserve the humane, sentimental frame, but in a very bleak form, the two posters contrasting an image of hope in the form of 'that universal symbol of happiness, a pretty girl',[39] with an image of despair in the form of cancer:

> Come to Sunny Prestatyn
> Laughed the girl on the poster...
>
> She was too good for this life.
> Very soon, a great transverse tear
> Left only a hand and some blue.
> Now *Fight Cancer* is there.

The poet makes no attempt at the trick of transcendence, and irony wins an easy victory over hope. Like 'An Arundel Tomb', 'Sunny Prestatyn' moves the reader to empathetic sorrow, but its conclusion is one of sad despair rather than consolation.

More subversively, in the midst of the poem's elegy of sentiment there erupts the grim violence of the Freudian *id*. 'This life' is not viewed in the polite terms of 'lengths and breadths / Of time' and 'endless altered people' washing at the 'identity' of the elegiac subject. The destruction of the girl is speeded up ('Very soon'), and is brutally physical:

> A couple of weeks, and her face
> Was snaggle-toothed and boss-eyed;
> Huge tits and a fissured crotch
> Were scored well in, and the space
> Between her legs held scrawls
> That set her fairly astride
> A tuberous cock and balls...

Without too much forcing we may parallel this defaced icon with those Medieval and Renaissance depictions of buxom maidens dragged off by the hair by skeletons pointing to yawning graves, or kissing them on the lips as they struggle to cover their modesty with a winding-sheet.[40] The vandals play the same role as the skeletons in the genre-paintings. On the surface level there is didactic moralism: vanity is chastened by a reminder of mortality; the false glamour of the advertising image is gratifyingly satirized. There is grim satisfaction in bringing an apparently untouchable perfection 'down to earth'. On a second, sexual-political level however, the skeleton, the vandals, and perhaps the poet himself, show an enjoyment of power over the woman. They desire to degrade and humiliate. The skeleton is always pornographically male, though, since it is the maiden's death that is at issue, it should be female. In the Romantic poem 'Death and the Maiden', which Schubert set to music, the 'man of bone' becomes, indeed, a sinister lover: 'Be of good cheer. I am not cruel. / You shall sleep gently in my arms.'[41] The graffiti of Larkin's vandals force a more crudely grotesque intimacy on the girl's image.

However, Larkin's poem is elegiac rather than didactically moral or pornographically sexist. The vandals' defiling of their own unattainable dreams, in the form of the girl's image, can itself be seen as a perverse expression of the elegiac impulse. For the girl, just as for them, as the second poster confirms, life is really struggle and disease. The autograph on the cock and balls may even suggest that young Thomas is capable of self-mocking wit. Then, at the end of the poem her image is overlaid with the cancer poster in a stark juxtaposition of Thanatos with Eros. The ultimate agent of death is not the male vandals, but an ungendered disease, which threatens Titch Thomas as much as the girl. They will have no motive to deface this second poster.

The darker undertones are, however, not quite dispelled. The poem's comic destructive gusto, even though directed at a mere poster, is unsettling. It may be remarked that the graffiti convert the civilized satin-clad girl-on-holiday into something resembling a prehistoric clay Venus whose dehumanized face is also subordinated to 'Huge tits and a fissured crotch...scored well in'. The vandals uncover the mother goddess of prehistory beneath the sophisticated glamour-icon of modern advertising. They are not only frustrated at the girl's provocative beauty and offended by her unrealistic happiness. They are also overawed by her erotic power. If 'obscenity' is 'our name for the uneasiness which upsets the physical state associated with self-possession', then this is obscene writing.[42] Camille Paglia's heady formulation might be invoked at this point:

> Eroticism is society's soft point, through which it is invaded by chthonian nature. The femme fatale can appear as Medusan mother or as frigid nymph, masquing in the brilliant luminosity of Apollonian high glamour.[43]

In Paglia's terms Titch Thomas and his friends convert frigid Apollonian nymph into Medusan mother. Ever since Lucretius pronounced 'The universal mother is also the common grave' this has been a familiar masculine response to Venus.[44] Paglia provocatively defends the rationality of such horrified responses to female sexuality: 'disgust is reason's proper response to the grossness of procreative nature', and 'Man justifiably fears being devoured by woman, who is nature's proxy.'[45] The defacing of the poster is a manifestation of Leonardo's 'spirit of the elements', the confused expression of the vandals' headlong rush to return to the first state of chaos.

This will be uncomfortable territory for many readers of Larkin. 'Sunny Prestatyn' is not usually read as an obscene vision of Venus. Moreover, Larkin's instinct is generally to avoid this heady Eros-Thanatos, sex-and-violence version of elegy. Even in 'Sunny Prestatyn' the ultimate violence comes not from the vandals, but, more abstractly, from Nature, in the form of disease. Though Larkin's great mature set-piece elegies also focus on the obscene self-dispossession of death, they avoid the complications of sexual politics. 'The Building', 'The Old Fools' and the self-elegy 'Aubade' depict our mortal plight in starker, more reductive terms than this. They concern life not as procreation, nor as love, but simply as the 'next, please' of Nature: mere, infinitely precious, existence.

Metaphor *in extremis*

In Larkin's three last great set-piece elegies the plight of mortality is closely mirrored in the plight of the poetry which describes it. These poems are highly wrought rhetorical constructions, but much of their technique is designed paradoxically to deconstruct itself. The advance of the 'incompetent cold' of death is enacted in the flattening of verbal decorum. Larkin's registers are at their most mixed; metaphors are patently inadequate; eloquence is the more eloquent for sounding hollow. The grand opening simile of 'The Building' for instance, 'Higher than the handsomest hotel', creates an etymological short circuit. With primitive superstition the poet avoids calling the building a 'hospital'. 'Hotel', however, as Larkin was no doubt aware, derives (through 'hostel') from the same root as 'hospital', both being places of 'hospitality'. The illusory contrast between hospital and hotel painfully highlights the juxtaposition of life and death. An early rejected title for the poem was the ominous, euphemistic 'The Meeting House'.[46] The opening elevation of tone at once falters on the sighing aspirated 'h' alliterations, while the stilted inflation of 'The lucent comb shows up for miles' falls flat as the stanza descends into prosiness, concluding with a jokey zeugma: 'in the hall / As well as creepers hangs a frightening smell.' The word 'ambulances' is clumsily evaded by the euphemism 'not taxis'.

Consolation is reduced to the displacement activity of humdrum routine: 'There are paperbacks, and tea at so much a cup'. It is all apparently ordinary: harmless enough, surely. But the building refuses to be ordinary. Everything is different here. These are no longer 'people', but more chillingly 'Humans, caught / On ground curiously neutral'. The noun 'humans' occurs only twice in Larkin's mature work, while the adjective 'human' occurs only once.[47] The use of the word here marks a dramatic extension of Larkin's idiolect to indicate the patients' descent below the civil, social level which makes us 'people'. Later they are reduced further, as even age and gender become irrelevant: 'women, men; / Old, young; crude facets of the only coin // This place accepts.'

Paradoxically it is this paring away of the figurative dimension which gives the poem its metaphorical strangeness. The poem's actual metaphors are hollow and dispirited. The building's white-clothed inhabitants, for instance, climb in a secular parody of heaven, to 'their appointed levels', where they take their places among 'The unseen congregations whose white rows / Lie set apart above'. Conversely it is the least metaphorical, least 'poetic' elements which generate the most moving poetry:

> Red brick, lagged pipes, and someone walking by it
> Out to the car park, free. Then, past the gate,
> Traffic; a locked church; short terraced streets
> Where kids chalk games, and girls with hair-dos fetch
>
> Their separates from the cleaners – O world,
> Your loves, your chances, are beyond the stretch
> Of any hand from here!

The word 'someone' concentrates a knot of intense envy, as the 'loves' and 'chances' of life are distilled into the precious ability to walk 'free', past car park, traffic, kids and shops. Ordinariness glows with an elegiac poignancy beyond that of any golden Byzantium. In a revision of the usual poetic decorums it is 'separates from the cleaners' which open the stanza, relegating the grand rhetorical apostrophe 'O world' to the end of the line. The abrupt elevation of tone to a 'poetic' register raises a smile, but there is no real irony. The faint echo of the secure romantic rhetoric of Shelley's 'O world! O life! O time!' simply adds to the tone of downbeat helplessness. A flat, even-toned indicative denies all the consolations of rhetoric:

> All know they are going to die.
> Not yet, perhaps not here, but in the end,
> And somewhere like this...

By this stage the poem has succeeded in infusing the dullest of monosyllables with paradoxical eloquence: 'Each gets up and goes / At last', while the grammatical solecism of leaving the preposition to the end of the clause wrings the heart: 'each [room] further off // And harder to return from'.

In the final lines archaic Latinisms, reminiscent of Gray's great 'Elegy' ('contravenes', 'propitiatory'), combine with a faintly Dantesque vision of purgatorial crowds, to lend dignity to the hospital visitors:

> nothing contravenes
> The coming dark, though crowds each evening try
>
> With wasteful, weak, propitiatory flowers.

The isolated last line sounds almost like an afterthought, the sentence being grammatically complete at 'try'. There is a hint of exasperation in its dismissiveness. The suggestion of prudential commonsense in 'wasteful' is at once overwhelmed by the absurd pleonasm of 'weak... flowers', while the exhausted metrical stumbling of 'propitiatory' concedes the inadequacy of religion. Finally, the weight of this cruelly emphatic triad of epithets falls with crushing pathos on the soft consonants and open vowels of 'flowers'. Theological and rational consolations are reduced to the ineffectual emotional solace of flowers.

'The Old Fools' adopts a startlingly different strategy, foregrounding the poet's own emotional plight. His panicky histrionics startlingly blend civilized with atavistic impulses in an artificial *faux naïf* posture. Rational disapproval of the old fools' failure of physical control is confounded with the visceral compulsion to jeer, as a fascinated child jeers at disfigurement:

> Do they somehow suppose
> It's more grown-up when your mouth hangs open and drools,
> And you keep on pissing yourself...?

The speaker's psychology is incoherent in rational terms, though embarrassingly familiar emotionally. His sympathy for the old dears is subverted by his desire to distance himself from the appalling plight of the old fools. Hence his raucous elation, his *Schadenfreude* that it is not yet *his* turn: 'Their looks show that they're for it' he sniggers, rhyming jokily: 'How can they ignore it?'

But panic subsides and empathy quickly reasserts itself. Despite his *jouissance* at not being not yet 'for it', the poet well knows that he is not immune to the old fools' fate. In the second stanza his jeering shifts to pensiveness as the third person of the poem's opening gives way to a second person which embraces both reader and poet:

> At death, you break up: the bits that were you
> Start speeding away from each other for ever
> With no one to see.

This 'you' then becomes an intimate self-elegiac 'we' as the poet tries, rationally, to accept the inevitable: 'It's only oblivion, true: / We had it before'. But this pathetic evasion is brusquely rejected: 'then it was going to end'. The primary state of Nature is not life, but oblivion, an oblivion only briefly interrupted by the 'endeavour / To bring to bloom the million-petalled flower / Of being here'. One of his early letters wittily concludes 'Till death starts';[48] here with a plain denial of wit he acknowledges that when oblivion resumes, 'you can't pretend / There'll be anything else'. The stanza ends with hooting assonances imitating the old fools' loss of wits: 'Not knowing how, not hearing who, the power / Of choosing gone.' 'Oh, ow, eeh, oo, ow, oo'. The poet's self-possession is under obscene threat.

The consolatory impulse, however, reasserts itself in the most surprising form: the senile visions in the old fools' heads. Their disjointed maunderings modulate into unexpected beauty:

> chairs and a fire burning,
> The blown bush at the window, or the sun's
> Faint friendliness on the wall some lonely
> Rain-ceased midsummer evening.

The old fools transcend their decrepitude by living 'where all happened once.' Drooling and incontinent though they are, in their absent minds they are still dancing all night or going to their wedding. Their 'air of baffled absence' is a strange echo of the sublime oblivion of the 'attics cleared of me' in 'Absences'. They sit 'through days of thin continuous dreaming / Watching light move.' Though, literally, 'Watching light move' cruelly evokes the emptiness of their days, it is a beautiful phrase, with all the resonance of a poetic epiphany, like the frigid wind tousling the clouds outside Mr Bleaney's window, the luminously peopled air at the end of 'Here', or 'the moon's cleanliness' in 'Sad Steps'. The poem snatches the poignant shadow of consolation from the grim plight of gaga bewilderment. As in 'An Arundel Tomb' and 'The Trees', this is a rhetorical trick, but a much more subtle and complex one. The same words that convey the awesome state of witless senility also convey the poem's consolatory beauty.

Self-elegy

At the extreme of mourning the elegist has the altruism of Levinas: 'It is the other's death that is the foremost death.'[49] In contrast, the self-elegist follows the selfish Heidegger: 'By its very essence, death is in every case mine, in so far as it "is" at all.'[50] Elegy for the self forms an undercurrent in many mourning and reflective elegies, but at its extreme self-elegy comprises a distinct genre. Though neglected by theorists some of the best known poems in the language belong to the genre.[51] Its psychological dynamic lies between mourning and reflection but is distinct from both. It mourns the self, but, as in the elegy of reflection, the poet's survival is ruled out. Consequently fear, which plays little part in mourning and reflective elegies, may predominate in self-elegy. No 'healthy' 'work' of mourning is possible, and self-elegies all belong in Freud's 'melancholic' category. Freud wrote that it is 'impossible to imagine our own death; and whenever we attempt to do so we can perceive that we are in fact still present as spectators.'[52] The self-elegist imagines him or herself, irrationally, as a spectator at his or her own deathbed. Shakespeare's Richard II and Macbeth show the combination of self-pity and meditation characteristic of the genre ('I wasted time; and now doth time waste me.')[1] Tennyson insisted that his self-elegy 'Crossing the bar' be placed at the end of all editions of his poems.[54] Hardy's 'Afterwards' and Housman's 'Tell me not here, it needs not saying' are similar intimate acts of self-mourning, as are Edward Thomas's 'Rain' and 'Lights Out': 'I must enter, and leave, alone, / I know not how.'[55]

It has been suggested that the anxious egotism of the self-elegist is distinctly masculine. Jonathan Dollimore writes: 'I hazard the generalization that it is men more than women who experience the seduction of non-being',[56] It is interesting however that the women poets whom

Larkin most admired are strongly self-elegiac. Christina Rossetti's 'Song', 'When I am dead, my dearest', Emily Dickinson's 'I heard a Fly buzz – when I died' and 'Because I could not stop for Death' are among the most original works in this genre. Stevie Smith built her whole poetic persona on self-mourning, while much of Sylvia Plath's work is self-elegiac: 'The woman is perfected. / Her dead // Body wears the smile of accomplishment'.[57]

Some of Larkin's earliest poems are portentously resonant exercises in self-elegy:

> Nothing will be left to show
> Why I am standing here, twisting this cord,
> Watching your calm young eyes.[58]

The final lines of 'Going', written in 1946 focus on the poet's sudden sense of his own mortality:

> ...What is under my hands,
> That I cannot feel?
>
> What loads my hands down?

'Träumerei' (1946) expounds an ingenuous allegory, in which the poet walks with a silent crowd under a wall, as if from a football match. A second wall closes in on the right, shutting in the crowd 'Like pigs down a concrete passage'. A 'giant whitewashed D' appears too high on the wall for anyone but the poet to notice. He now awaits the E he already knows will come next, and the crowd becomes like water in a sewer. A 'striding ' A appears, then the 'decapitated cross' of a T, and finally, anticipating 'Aubade': 'The walls of my room rise, it is still night, / I have woken again before the word was spelt.' Other early self-elegies in this vein are 'At the chiming of light upon sleep' and 'Unfinished Poem'.

As Larkin matured this self-consciously literary self-elegy divided into two separate strands. On the one hand there are poems of self-criticism ('Wants', 'The Dance'), and on the other poems of self-abnegation ('Absences', 'Solar'). Early self-critical poems, such as 'On Being Twenty-six' and 'At thirty-one, when some are rich', show a dissatisfied taking stock: of his artistic development or his ageing, or both. But as he entered middle age this youthful self-analysis deepened to a darker self-elegiac tone, culminating in a sequence of poems written at five-year intervals, marking his August birthday: 'Send No Money' (1962), 'Sympathy in White Major' (1967), 'The View' (1972). 'Aubade', his final, uniquely definitive self-elegy, can perhaps also be included in the series. It was begun in 1974, taken up again after his mother's death in November 1977, and completed three months after his fifty-fifth birthday.

As often in these self-analytical poems, the central image in his forti-eth-birthday poem, 'Send No Money' (1962), is a wildly excessive pro-jection of histrionic despair. The poet views his face 'bent in by the blows of what happened to happen', and sees that his patient atten-tiveness to his art has yielded him a Truth no better than a 'truss-adver-tisement'. This is, however, not a lament over things left undone, but simply over the passing of time. The poet does not regret his refusal to have 'a bash' at real life, like his non-artist friends. If he had chosen life rather than art he would still have aged, but would not be writing exhil-arating poems such as this. Even his self-derision is a sign of his artistic superiority over the 'other lads', though it is a superiority which must be its own reward, since it offers 'sod all' else.

'Sympathy in White Major', his forty-fifth birthday poem, takes the poet back to the edge of self-elegy proper. He again couches his anti-social vocation in terms of a gauche self-ridicule which barely hides his passionate conviction of his own superior sensibility. While others led a normal social existence, wearing the people in their lives 'like clothes', he set himself:

> to bring to those
> Who thought I could the lost displays;
> It didn't work for them or me...

He concludes by writing his own epitaph as a way of taking ironic stock of his plight. Thomas Gray famously employed this device in his 'Elegy', which ends with an elaborate, and faintly absurd self-portrait delivered by an uncomprehending rustic swain:

> 'Mutt'ring his wayward fancies he would rove;
> Now drooping, woful-wan, like one forlorn,
> Or craz'd with care, or cross'd in hopeless love.'[59]

Larkin's grotesquely refracted eulogy on himself is also delivered in reported speech:

> *A decent chap, a real good sort...*
> *How many lives would have been duller*
> *Had he not been here below?*
> *Here's to the whitest man I know –*

Like Gray's bumpkin, the dramatized speaker of Larkin's epitaph is incapable of understanding the real implications of his words. The lonely, alienated artist is celebrated as the life and soul of the party. *Living for Others* was an intended title for the volume which finally became *High Windows*, in which this poem appeared; but as Larkin said in a letter 'I could never write the title-poem.'[60] 'Sympathy in White Major' would be a good, if ironic, candidate for this status. By living for others the poet has betrayed his poetic self and wasted his life. The poem is both a sentimental cry for sympathy and at the same time an irritated rejection of sympathy: 'Though white is not my favourite colour.'

Counterpointing this poetry of defensive self-analysis, however, is a series of poems showing the opposite impulse towards self-abnegation. 'Absences', for instance, seems to transcend the plight of mortality by gladly accepting the annihilation of self. After describing a sublimely impersonal seascape without ships or shallows, the poet exclaims in a tone of awe: 'Such attics cleared of me! Such absences!' This is a strangely pure metaphysical poem for Larkin. It belongs in the tradition of the 'ode to oblivion', a form which, in the nineteenth and early twentieth centuries, sought to preserve, in a new secular rhetoric, the old spiritual consolation of religion. Metaphor replaces theology, and loss of self is presented, however, tenuously, as gain. Edna St Vincent Millay in 'Elegy' sees the body returning at death to the nourishing soil:

> Sweetly through the sappy stalk
> Of the vigourous weed...
> On and on eternally
> Shall your altered fluid run.[61]

D. H. Lawrence in 'The Ship of Death' evokes biological continuity through a more tenuous metaphor of procreation. Death is a journey back into the 'womb' of Nature:

> Oh lovely last, last lapse of death, into pure oblivion
> at the end of the longest journey,
> peace, complete peace – !
> But can it be that also it is procreation?[62]

A. E. Housman's bleaker consolation calls not on biology but on ancient atomism:

> From far, from eve and morning
> And yon twelve-winded sky,

The stuff of life to knit me
Blew hither: here am I.[63]

Millay's and Lawrence's biological imagery, and Housman's imagery from physics share the characteristic pattern of this materialist embrace of oblivion. Both proclaim our re-entry into Nature at death, euphorically relinquishing selfish individual identity. Both celebrate Leonardo's 'spirit of the elements'.

Larkin's 'Absences', however, develops no metaphor from biology or physics. His 'me' is not relocated in the seascape he has described. Indeed it is his absence from this seascape which is the poem's subject. Larkin attenuates the philosophical framework of the materialist 'ode to oblivion' to vanishing point. The scientific arguments which lie behind Millay's, Housman's and Lawrence's imagery become in Larkin a mere symbolist gesture. His empty attics and sublime seascape remain unphilosophized, reductively existential. There may be awe here, but there is little sign of the consolation which, however bleakly, the earlier poets all offered.

But 'Absences' is unique in his work. Elsewhere Larkin prefers emotional self-elegy to the philosophical celebration of oblivion. When oblivion is welcomed in other works, as it frequently is, it is not in the form of metaphysical transcendence. Rather it provides a more secular emotional release from the tangled problems of his messy selfhood. Self-contempt validates exasperated gestures of self-annihilation. In 'Dry-Point' the poet escapes from the endless irritant of sexual desire into a remote 'padlocked cube of light / We neither define nor prove' where sex has no right of entry. In 'Wants', written shortly before 'Absences', the poet summarizes his social plight in a series of bitter elliptical images:

However the sky grows dark with invitation-cards
However we follow the printed directions of sex
However the family is photographed under the flagstaff –

He responds with an irritable wish to escape: 'Beyond all this, the wish to be alone.' The second stanza then repeats the pattern but replaces selfishness with a desire for an end to the self: 'Beneath it all, desire of oblivion runs.' 'High Windows' shows a more developed version of the pattern. An outburst of angry, sterile self-argument gives way, in the final lines, to a sublimity which 'shows / Nothing, and is nowhere, and is endless.' The climactic 'endless' sounds like a triumphant assertion of permanence. But its transcendence is an empty gesture created by syntax rather than the meanings of the words. Restored to its normal grammatical position as a premodifier ('endless blue air' or 'endless nothing') the word loses its resonance. The rhetorical effect is a poetic conjuring trick, and as in the case of 'The Trees' Larkin admits the subterfuge, scrawling 'and fucking piss' mockingly at the end of an early draft of the poem (Motion 355). Though oblivion may often seem a welcome release from selfhood, Larkin cannot argue himself out of his fear of physical extinction. Throughout his life he expressed ingenuous fear of death. In a review he referred to Kathleen Raine's 'almost-ethical desire for annihilation' (*FR* 74). He himself felt an almost-ethical indignation against death. After one stage of the redrafting of 'The Building' he wrote 'We must never die. No one must ever die.'[64] He sounds like a petulant child crying for the moon.

In 'Aubade', his 'in-a-funk-about-death poem' (*SL* 574), the euphoria of oblivion is totally dispelled by 'the dread / Of dying, and being dead'. There is a frightening oxymoron half hidden in the last phrase: 'being dead' is in fact not 'being'. Although he is a materialist Larkin cannot accept the extremist atheist contention that death is irrelevant to life. 'So death... is nothing to us', said Epicurus airily, 'since so long as we exist, death is not with us; but when death comes, then we do not exist. It does not then concern either the living or the dead.'[65] The poet of 'Aubade' is unpersuaded:

> And specious stuff that says *No rational being*
> *Can fear a thing it will not feel*, not seeing
> That this is what we fear – no sight, no sound,
> No touch or taste or smell...

It is significant that this ironized passage of indirect speech provides only the second occurrence in the mature poetry, of the word 'being', or 'beings', as an abstract noun ('no rational being'). On the thirty-six remaining occasions on which he uses the word, it is always a present participle. Larkin is more interested in living than in Life; in the immediate plight of being than in the abstract concept of Being. He is an extremist aesthete. *Aesthesis*, perception through the senses, is all that matters. 'To be alive, in the flesh.' The ultimate horror is to be unable to perceive: 'No touch or taste or smell, nothing to think with, / Nothing to love or link with'. Death is 'The anaesthetic from which none come round.'

The philosopher Richard Rorty disbelieves in Larkin's declared 'fear of dying':

> 'fear of extinction' is an unhelpful phrase. There is no such thing as fear of inexistence as such, but only fear of some concrete loss. 'Death' and 'nothingness' are equally resounding, equally empty terms. To say one fears either is as clumsy as Epicurus's attempt to say why one should not fear them.[2]

'Clumsy' is not a word that would occur to many readers of 'Aubade'. Rorty fails to comprehend the way words work. His analysis attempts the same kind of rhetorical trick as Larkin's in 'The Trees' or 'Absences', but without Larkin's verbal precision or eloquence. It is in fact perfectly possible to imagine the plight of being without vision, hearing, touch, taste or smell, and it is perfectly possible to fear this plight. The 'empty' term 'death', signifies 'total emptiness for ever', and it is precisely this 'inexistence as such' that Larkin fears. No sophistical rhetoric can reconcile him to the loss of his precious self to 'sure extinction'. He is afraid in a way which 'No trick', whether of religion or philosophy or rhetoric, 'dispels'.

In Larkin's youthful aubade, 'At the chiming of light upon sleep', the prospect of death was seen romantically as giving life its meaning by fostering a 'fracturing... ecstasy'. Here, on the contrary, now that it is actually in sight, it 'slows each impulse down to indecision'. Death is still the prime mover of life, but now only because his fear of death is so vivid that he simply cannot think of anything else:

> Unresting death, a whole day nearer now,
> Making all thought impossible but how
> And where and when I shall myself die.
> Arid interrogation: yet the dread
> Of dying, and being dead,
> Flashes afresh to hold and horrify.

The vocabulary recalls that of 'The Trees'. But perversely it is now death which is 'unresting', and it is the fear of death which flashes 'afresh'.

However, the most telling element in this most extreme of elegies is not the ironized poetic metaphors, but rather the failure of metaphor. In exhilarating rhetoric Auden reduced death to banal physicality: 'In headaches and in worry / Vaguely life leaks away, / And Time will have his fancy / To-morrow or to-day.'[67] Larkin's more risky rhetoric sounds as reduced and dispirited as his meaning.

> I work all day, and get half-drunk at night.
> Waking at four to soundless dark, I stare...
> ...I see what's really always there:
> Unresting death, a whole day nearer now...

Metaphor and poetry have to make their way against daunting odds. In the seventeenth century Rochester brutally declared: 'Dead, wee become the Lumber of the World.'[68] Larkin employs a similar image of domestic furniture: 'It stands plain as a wardrobe, what we know'. The denial of metaphorical elevation is oddly comic, lending a hint of lugubriousness to the line. But this failure of eloquence is paradoxically eloquent. Auden's euphoric surrealism, 'The glacier knocks in the cupboard, / The desert sighs in the bed',[69] is reduced to the prosaic witlessness of seeing a narrow wooden box as a symbol of death. Plain though Larkin's wardrobe is, it possesses a sublimity of utter reduction. The ageing poet is being forced to conjure metaphor from more and more exiguous materials, making his most original poem out of the very failure of the stuff of poetry. 'Work has to be done', the dying poet tells himself, in an ambiguous tone between irritating exhortation and resigned despair. As he said in a letter, this poem not only anticipates his own death, it also enacts the 'death-throes of a talent' (*SL* 574). The subversion of the life of poetry, metaphor, becomes itself a metaphor for death. It is inevitable that 'Aubade' is virtually the last poem of any importance that he wrote. It is not simply an elegy for life; it is an elegy for poetry.

This metaphorical subversion of metaphor in Larkin's late mature elegies is one of his most original achievements. It is an achievement, however, with which readers who require simpler consolations feel uncomfortable. Even the most perceptive commentators are unnerved and confused by it. Casting around for words to express her discomfort, Margaret Drabble preposterously accuses 'The Old Fools', of cowardice: 'He, a coward, wanted us to be cowards too.'[70] Seamus Heaney is dismayed by Larkin's 'dauntedness' in the face of death. He accuses 'Aubade' of failing to offer the 'corroborative' spiritual 'redress' required of the poet.[71] Edna Longley prefers Edward Thomas's 'active curiosity to penetrate the unknown' to Larkin's 'passive yielding to the inevitable'. 'One would rather wander with Thomas along "The green roads that end in the forest"', she writes, 'than limp with Larkin "down Cemetery Road".'[72] Well, some readers may indeed prefer Thomas's sombre, self-possessed stoicism, but others will prefer Larkin's hapless plight of black jokes and histrionic despair. John Bayley, for instance, writes:

> If I am feeling really low I often read 'Aubade', or 'The Building', and they have an immediate and bracing tonic effect: However perverse the process might seem, they at once raise my spirits.[73]

His response is no more perverse than Yeats' assertion that 'Hamlet and Lear are gay.'[74]

Last words

There remains Larkin's final contribution to the elegiac mode, the miniature elegy of his self-epitaph or 'famous last words'. This is a genre in its own right. Politicians, philosophers and poets have striven over the centuries to make their contributions to it as memorably characteristic of their genius as possible, from the wit of John Gay's 'Life is a jest; and all things show it, / I thought so once; but now I know it',[75] to the stubbornness of Samuel Johnson's 'I will be conquered; I will not capitulate',[76] the poignancy of Keats's 'Here lies one whose name was writ in water',[77] and the comic self-pity of Spike Milligan's 'I *told* you I was ill'.[78] Larkin admired W. H. Auden's valedictory exhortation to his flesh to 'pay no attention / To my piteous *Don't*s, but bugger off quickly', commenting: 'It is a Stoic aspiration', and adding: 'It is good to know it was granted' (*FR* 40). Larkin himself, however, was by temperament an Epicurean rather than a Stoic. His own self-epitaph, 'I am going to the inevitable', whispered to a nurse at the moment of his death, has none of Auden's bracing enviability (Motion 521). It does, however, present us, in little, with the quintessential Larkinesque.

On the philosophical level it is a weary acknowledgement of the strain of maintaining his selfhood. The struggle is over and he has no alternative but to surrender to oblivion. On the literary level it recalls Gray's half-personified 'inevitable hour' which 'The boast of heraldry, the pomp of pow'r, / And all that beauty, all that wealth e'er gave' awaits. But the tone is elusive and ambiguous. It is too blindingly obvious to be a precious insight or a revelation. Is it then, perhaps, like so many other famous last words, a joke: a tautology so banal as to be comic? If it is the inevitable then of course he has to go there. We may perhaps hear Larkin's glum voice whispering the sentence with an orotund wryness, helplessly aware of its inadequacy. Is the sombre 'I am going to the inevitable' really, ultimately any different from the carnivalesque jokiness of – say – 'Dunlarkin'?

On the grammatical level, however, there is something chilling about the hyperabstract noun, 'the inevitable', conjured up insecurely from a mere adjective, in an abruptly truncated revision of Gray's mellifluous classical phrase. Is it a self-pitying sob, pitting a lonely, defenceless 'I' against the grandly orotund weight of 'The Inevitable'? Or does 'inevitable', perhaps, remain a premodifying adjective awaiting the completion of a noun? 'The inevitable' what? Well, that is the question. The sentence can only be completed after death; and since death is not an event in life, the grammar must remain incomplete. This is perhaps the most distinctively Larkinesque element of the sentence: its refusal of the metaphorical development that would be entailed in any completion of the grammar. 'I am going':– i) 'to meet my maker'; ii) 'to the womb of rebirth'; iii) 'to the wind's twelve quarters'; iv) 'to the first state of chaos'; v) 'to what is plain as a wardrobe'. These formulations all fail to express his plight adequately, since each implies, grammatically, that he will still *be* where he is going. Wherever it is will be his new 'here'. 'Being' will not have ended. But he can no longer countenance this metaphorical trickery. In the empty phrase 'the inevitable' he once again, at an even more reductive extreme, conjures paradoxical sublimity out of the very refusal of sublimity. As the physical body of the man approaches dissolution, the verbal plight of the poet reaches its nadir. The time for words is over.

APPENDIX: 'Be my Valentine this Monday' and 'We met at the end of the party'

These poems came to light in 2002, as a result of a complicated sequence of events. Following Monica Jones's death on 15 February 2001, the staff of the Brynmor Jones Library, Hull, cleared 105 Newland Avenue of Larkin's remaining books and manuscripts. The Philip Larkin Society then purchased the remaining non-literary items: furniture, pictures and ornaments. These were removed in late 2001 and early 2002, and are now on long-term loan to the Hull Museums Service and the East Riding Museum Service.

Both searches missed a small dark red '©ollins Ideal 468' hard-backed manuscript notebook which had slipped behind the drawers of a bedside cabinet. This cabinet was removed by the house-clearer with the final debris, and subsequently fell into the hands of a local man, Chris Jackson, who contacted the Larkin Society. I confirmed the authenticity of the book in a brief meeting with Mr Jackson in the *Goose and Granite* public house in Hull on 17.vii.2002.

The notebook seems initially to have been intended for 'Required Writing', which Larkin wished to keep separate from the drafts in his workbooks proper. The first eleven sides are occupied by pencil drafts of 'Bridge for the Living', dated between 30 May 1975 and 27 July 1975. These are followed by notes on Thomas Hardy and other topics. Seven months later, however, Larkin used the book again, this time for more personal writing. The central pages were left blank but on the final five sides he wrote pencil drafts, dated between 7 February 1976 and 21 February 1976, of 'Morning at last: there in the snow', 'Be my Valentine this Monday' and 'We met at the end of the party'.

Mr Jackson subsequently took the notebook to Christie's Auction House, one of whose employees leaked the details to a journalist, and on 22 October 2002 the *Evening Standard* printed the first stanza each of 'We met at the end of the party' and 'Be my Valentine this Monday' in the course of a news item: '"Lost" Larkin poems found in furniture bound for tip'.

At this point Betty Mackereth was told of developments by James Orwin, a committee member of the Larkin Society who happened to be decorating her living-room. She allowed him to transcribe her own copy of 'We met at the end of the party', which was published in full in *About Larkin* 14, October 2002. Subsequently Betty allowed me to transcribe her copy of 'Be my Valentine this Monday', which appears here in full for the first time.

The texts printed here are those which Philip sent to Betty Mackereth, and differ in details from the drafts in the notebook.

The poems are reproduced by permission of the Society of Authors as the Literary Representative of the Estate of Philip Larkin. Copyright © 2005 The Estate of Philip Larkin.

'Be my Valentine this Monday'

Written in black ballpoint in a Valentine's Day card showing a grinning alligator and the legend 'See you later alligator!', continuing inside 'You mouthwatering morsel! Happy Valentine', after which Larkin has written '& love!' Philip left the card on Betty's desk on Saturday 14 February 1976 (addressed 'Personal / Secretary to the Librarian / Brynmor Jones Library'), before departing for Oxford. She found it on her arrival at work on Monday 16 February.

> Be my Valentine this Monday,
> Even though we're miles apart!
> Time will separate us one day –
> Till then, hyphen with my heart.
>
> You are fine as summer weather,
> May to August all in one,
> And the clocks, when we're together,
> Count no shadows, only sun.

'We met at the end of the party'

Written in black ink and sent from All Souls College, Oxford on 22 February 1976. In an accompanying letter Philip apologises for sending a handwritten poem, rather than a typescript: 'again apologies. I know how embarrassing it all is.'

> We met at the end of the party,
> When most of the drinks were dead
> And all the glasses dirty:
> 'Have this that's left,' you said.
>
> We walked through the last of summer,
> When shadows reached long and blue
> Across days that were growing shorter:
> You said: 'There's autumn too.'
>
> Always for you what's finished
> Is nothing, and what survives
> Cancels the failed, the famished,
> As if we had fresh lives
>
> From that night on, and just living
> Could make me unaware
> Of June, and the guests arriving,
> And I not there.

Notes

Chapter 1: The Poet's Plight

1   Thomas Gray, letter to Mason, 9.xi.1758, *Poems, with a Selection of Letters and Essays* (London: J. M. Dent and Sons), 215.
2   Gray, 'Elegy', *Poems*, 31.
3   A. E. Housman, 'The Name and Nature of Poetry', *Collected Poems and Selected Prose*, ed. Christopher Ricks (London: Penguin, 1989), 363.
4   T. S. Eliot, *Complete Poems and Plays*. London: Faber and Faber1969), 182.
5   Fleur Adcock, Introduction to *The Faber Book of 20th Century Women's Poetry*, 1987, 1.
6   Letter to James Sutton, 28.xii.1940; in James Booth, *Philip Larkin: Writer* (Hemel Hempstead: Harvester Wheatsheaf, 1992), 15.
7   Letter to James Sutton, 12.vii.1943. Brynmor Jones Library, Hull, MS DPL/174/2.
8   'The View'.
9   'Aubade'.
10 Philip Larkin, *Trouble at Willow Gables and Other Fictions*, ed James Booth (London: Faber, 2002), 241.
11 T. S. Eliot, *Collected Poems and Plays* (London: Faber, 1969), 182.
12 Letter to Sutton, 12.vii.1943.
13 'This Be The Verse', 'An Arundel Tomb'.
14 Michael Hamburger. *Philip Larkin: A Retrospect* (London: Enitharmon Press, 2002), 21–2.
15 Derek Walcott, 'The Master of the Ordinary', *New York Review of Books*, 1 June 1989, 39.
16 London: Faber and Faber, 2005.
17 R .J. C. Watt, *A Concordance to the Poetry of Philip Larkin* (Hildesheim: Olms-Weidmann, 1995).
18 'Love Songs in Age', 'Talking in Bed', 'The Old Fools', 'Aubade'.
19 Seamus Heaney, 'Englands of the Mind', *Preoccupations. Selected Prose 1968–1978* (London: Faber, 1980), 164–5.
20 Neil Powell, 'A Postcard from Pearson Park', *PN Review* 157 (2004), 6.
21 In the *oeuvre* as defined by the 1988 *Collected Poems*, counting the 'Two Guitar Pieces', 'Oils', 'Dry-Point', and the three 'Livings' poems as separate works.
22 'Dry-Point', 'First Sight', 'Triple Time', 'An Arundel Tomb', 'Broadcast', 'Solar', 'Sad Steps'.
23 'A slight relax of air where cold was', 'Home is so Sad', 'The Whitsun Weddings', 'Talking in Bed', 'Ambulances'.
24 'Love Songs in Age', 'Faith Healing', 'Ambulances'.
25 'Church Going', 'An Arundel Tomb', 'Home is so Sad', ''When first we faced, and touching showed', 'Morning at last: there in the snow'.
26 'Best Society', 'Ambulances', 'The Old Fools'.

27 'Home is so Sad', 'The Whitsun Weddings', 'Send No Money', 'Wild Oats', 'This Be The Verse', 'High Windows', 'The Building', 'The Old Fools', 'Aubade'.

28 'Going', 'And the wave sings because it is moving', 'Guitar Piece I', 'The Dedicated', 'Thaw', 'Sinking like sediment through the day', 'Coming', 'Oils', 'Dry-Point', 'The Literary World', 'Arrival', 'Days', 'Autumn', 'Water', 'Age', 'Long roots moor summer to our side of earth', 'Afternoons', 'None of the books have time', 'Nothing To Be Said', 'Solar', 'The Explosion', 'How', 'Dublinesque', 'Forget What Did', 'I have started to say', 'Livings II', 'The Mower'.

29 Some poems of the late 1940s and early 1950s, such as 'Waiting for breakfast while she brushed her hair', 'Guitar Piece II' and 'Born Yesterday' break irregularly into rhyme at points of climax or conclusion.

30 Five further sonnets remained unpublished: three early pieces in regular form, 'To Failure' (1949), 'To My Wife' (1951), 'Autobiography at an Air-Station' (1953), and two later, more inventive exercises in the form, 'And now the leaves suddenly lose strength' (1961) and ' A slight relax of air where cold was' (1962).

31 Dust-jacket of the American edition of *The Whitsun Weddings*, quoted in David Timms, *Philip Larkin* (Edinburgh: Oliver and Boyd, 1973), 62.

32 *Imagist Poetry*, ed Peter Jones (Harmondsworth: Penguin, 1972), 67.

33 Jacques Derrida, 'The Law of Genre', *Critical Inquiry* 7 (1980), 65.

34 *Strong Words: Modern Poets on Modern Poetry*, ed W. N. Herbert and Matthew Hollis (Tarset, Northumberland: Bloodaxe, 2000), 150.

35 Anthony Thwaite, Introduction to Philip Larkin, *Collected Poems* (London: Faber, 1988), xv.

36 James Booth, Introduction to *Trouble at Willow Gables and Other Fictions* (London: Faber, 2002), xliii.

37 Thwaite, xxiii.

38 Walcott, 40.

39 Oliver Marshall, 'Stories from the Doldrums', *The Irish Times*, 18.v.2002, 8.

40 Adam Kirsch, 'A Poet in Full', at www.walrusmagazine.com/article.pl?sid =04/03/10/2221215&... (accessed 22.iii.2004).

41 Kirsch, *loc.cit.*

42 Written in a Kate Greenaway Valentine's day card, sent to Betty Mackereth on 30.xii.1975 (unpublished).

43 Thwaite, xxii.

44 'The Dedicated' (carried forward from *In the Grip of Light*), 'Modesties', 'Oils', 'Who called love conquering' and ' Arrival'.

45 Thwaite, xxiii.

46 I wrote to Stephen Page, Chief Executive of Faber, on 19 December 2002, suggesting that these poems should not be withdrawn from print: 'Either you could keep the original 1988 *Collected Poems* available, alongside the new reduced version... Alternatively... you could add to the new volume, an appendix of "Poems Not Published during Larkin's Lifetime" (in small print if you need to save space).' He replied on 10 January 2003: 'We understand the concerns you raise and hope you will be pleased that we are actively investigating ways in which we can make these unpublished poems available ... I would ask you just to be a little patient.' *About Larkin* 14, April 2003, 30–1.

Chapter 2: Poetry as a Living

1. *Letters of Wallace Stevens,* sel. and ed. Holly Stevens (London: Faber, 1967), 243.
2. In James Boswell, *The Life of Samuel Johnson* (London: OUP, 1952), 731.
3. Christopher Ricks, *T. S. Eliot and Prejudice* (Berkeley and Los Angeles: University of California Press, 1988), 106.
4. Robert Crawford, *The Modern Poet: Poetry, Academia, and Knowledge since the 1750s* (Oxford: OUP, 2001).
5. T. S. Eliot, 'Tradition and the Individual Talent', *Selected Essays 1917–1932* (London: Faber, 1932), 15.
6. Crawford, 191.
7. Crawford, 183.
8. Laura Riding and Robert Graves, *A Survey of Modernist Poetry* (London: Heinemann, 1929), 260–1.
9. Riding and Graves, 199.
10. H. W. Garrod, *The Profession of Poetry and Other Lectures* (Oxford: OUP, 1929), viii.
11. Les Murray, in Crawford, 11.
12. James Fenton, 'Chapter and Verse on Reputation', *Guardian*, 26.vii.2003, 20.
13. T. S. Eliot, *The Rock* (London: Faber, 1934), 7.
14. Charles Osborne, *W.H. Auden: The Life of a Poet* (London: Michael O'Mara, 1980), 227.
15. W. H. Auden, 'On the Circuit', *About the House* (London: Faber, 1966), 61.
16. At this period the 'Third Programme' (now 'Radio Three') broadcast classical music and highbrow cultural programmes. 'Chatto' is the publisher, Chatto and Windus.
17. 'Philip Larkin reads and comments on *The Whitsun Weddings*', Listen Records (Hull: Marvell Press, 1965).
18. Auden, 'On the Circuit', 63.
19. Terry Eagleton, 'Larkin: A Left View', *About Larkin* 9, April 2000, 7.
20. *The Penguin Dictionary of Twentieth Century Quotations*, ed J. M. and M. J. Cohen (Harmondsworth: Penguin, 1995), 152.14.
21. Letter to James Sutton, 22.iii.1944. Brynmor Jones Library, Hull, DPL/174/2.
22. In Ian Hamilton, *Against Oblivion* (London: Viking, 2002), 34.
23. *The Modern Academic Library: Essays in Memory of Philip Larkin*, ed. Brian Dyson (London: Library Association, 1988).
24. Father Anthony Storey, interview with the author, 1.viii.2003.
25. John Saville, *Memoirs from the Left* (London: Merlin Press, 2003), 139, 143–4.
26. Brenda Moon, 'Working with Philip Larkin', *About Larkin* 8, October1999, 6, 8.
27. Maeve Brennan, *The Philip Larkin I Knew* (Manchester: MUP, 2002), 96.
28. Moon, 11.
29. Moon, 8.
30. Brennan, 124.
31. Betty Mackereth, interview with the author, 4.viii.2003.
32. Brennan 126.
33. A. Alvarez, 'The New Poetry, or Beyond the Gentility Principle', *The New Poetry* (Harmondsworth: Penguin, 1962), 19.

[34] Seamus Heaney, 'The Journey Back', *Seeing Things* (London: Faber, 1991), 7.

[35] Seamus Heaney, 'Joy or Night: Last Things in the Poetry of W. B. Yeats and Philip Larkin', *The Redress of Poetry: Oxford Lectures* (London: Faber, 1995), 159.

[36] Andrew Duncan, *The Failure of Conservatism in Modern British Poetry* (Cambridge: Salt, 2003), 63.

[37] Jean Hartley, *Philip Larkin, the Marvell Press, and Me* (Manchester: Carcanet, 1989), 63, 113.

[38] Crawford, 271.

[39] Crawford, 269.

[40] Graham Stroud, 'Philip Larkin: "A Sense of Duty"', *About Larkin* 9, April 2000, 10.

[41] Stroud, 9.

[42] Crawford, 268.

[43] *The Poetical Works of Wordsworth* (London: OUP, 1950), 206.

[44] *Mammon and the Black Goddess* (London: Cassell, 1965), 3.

[45] Arthur Schopenhauer, *Essays and Aphorisms*, sel. and trans. R. J. Hollingdale (Harmondsworth: Penguin, 1970), 170.

[46] 'Adagia', *Opus Posthumous*, ed. Samuel French Morse (London: Faber, 1959), 165.

[47] James Fenton, 'Philip Larkin: Wounded by Unshrapnel', *The Strength of Poetry* (Oxford: OUP, 2001), 46.

Chapter 3: Loves and Muses I

[1] T. S. Eliot, 'Tradition and the Individual Talent', *Selected Essays: 1917–1932* (London: Faber, 1932), 21.

[2] Wallace Stevens, 'Adagia', *Opus Posthumous*, ed. Samuel French Morse (London: Faber, 1959), 159.

[3] D. H. Lawrence, *Studies in Classic American Literature* (New York: Doubleday and Company Inc., 1951), 13.

[4] Virginia Woolf, *A Room of One's Own* (London: Hogarth Press, 1931), 86.

[5] W. H. Auden, 'In Memory of W. B. Yeats', *Another Time* (London: Faber Library edn, 1996), 97.

[6] Roland Barthes, 'The Death of the Author', *Image-Music-Text*, trans. Stephen Heath (London: Fontana, 1977), 143.

[7] Eliot, 'Tradition and the Individual Talent', 21.

[8] D. H. Lawrence, letter to Carlo Linati, 22.i.1925, *The Collected Letters*, ed. Harry T. Moore (London: Heinemann, 1962), II, 825.

[9] Auden, 'In Memory of W. B. Yeats', 98.

[10] Jean Hartley, *Philip Larkin, the Marvell Press, and Me* (Manchester: Carcanet, 1989), 62.

[11] Julian Barnes, *A History of the World in 10_ Chapters* (Harmondsworth: Penguin, 1989), 227.

[12] Roland Barthes, *Mythologies*, sel. and trans. Annette Lavers (London: Paladin, 1973).

[13] 'Toads Revisited', 'Wild Oats', 'This Be The Verse', 'If, My Darling', 'High Windows'.

[14] 'This Be The Verse'.

15 'Wild Oats'.
16 'Lines on a Young Lady's Photograph Album'.
17 'The little lives of earth and form'.
18 Letter to James Sutton, 12–14.iv.1943. Brynmor Jones Library, Hull, DPL/174/2.
19 'Philip Larkin reads *The Less Deceived*', Listen Records (Hull: Marvell Press, 1958).
20 Andrew Motion writes: 'Eva, more than Monica and Maeve, was his muse – not a beauty to be won like Maud Gonne, but a misery which had to be both resisted and accepted. Moaning and wringing her hands, she preceded her son through his life, loading him down with examples of the constraints he dreaded but also embraced' (468). The concept of the muse as 'a misery' to be 'resisted and accepted' is an unconventional one. I adopt here, instead, the traditional notion of the muse as an embodiment of inaccessible transcendence.
21 Hartley, 74.
22 Janice Rossen, *Philip Larkin: His Life's Work* (Hemel Hempstead: Harvester, 1989), 89.
23 Joseph Bristow, 'The Obscenity of Philip Larkin', *Critical Inquiry* 21, Autumn 1994, 176–7.
24 Suzuyo Kamitani, 'Jane Exall – "A Bosomy English Rose"', *About Larkin* 16, October 2003, 19. 'The letters do not suggest an intimate friendship; their mood is more that of old friends sharing memories ... [Ruth's] name is never mentioned.'
25 Winifred Dawson (Arnott), interview with the author, 21.x.2003. Motion misdates the engagement to July 1952.
26 Dawson, 21.x.2003.
27 Robert Herrick, *Poems from Hesperides and Noble Numbers* (Harmondsworth: Penguin, 1961), 69; Andrew Marvell, *The Poems* (London: Routledge and Kegan Paul, 1963), 22.
28 Dawson, 21.x.2003.
29 Winifred Dawson, 'Photograph Albums Revisited', *About Larkin* 13, April 2002, 4.
30 Auden, 'In Memory of W. B. Yeats', 98.
31 Dawson, 21.x.2003.
32 Dawson, 21.x.2003.
33 George Gilpin, 'Patricia Avis and Philip Larkin', *New Larkins for Old*, ed. James Booth (Basingstoke: Palgrave Macmillan, 2000), 70.
34 Gilpin, 70–1.
35 The version in *Collected Poems* (1988) is dated 6 December, earlier than the letter of 10 December). It has 'Stupefied' for 'Hypnotised' (78).
36 Patsy Strang fictionalized Larkin as Rollo Jute in her novel *Playing the Harlot: or Mostly Coffee*, eventually published under her maiden name, Patricia Avis (London: Virago, 1996).

Chapter 4: Loves and Muses II

1 Larkin considered 'unprintable', but took Amis's advice that this 'would just mean cunt, whereas unpriceable *probably* meant cunt but could mean all sorts of other things too' (*FR* 55).

2 Monica Jones' dress-sense was very independent. See for instance the photograph in *About Larkin* 12, October 2001, 17.
3 In Anthony Gardner, 'What will survive of us is love', *Sunday Times Magazine*, 21.xi.2004, 38.
4 Motion dates the first meeting to Easter 1947 (165); but Monica Jones assured me (January 1999) that she met Philip immediately upon his arrival in Leicester, in September 1946.
5 Betty Mackereth, interview with the author, 1.viii.2003.
6 T. S. Eliot, 'A Dedication to my Wife', *The Complete Poems and Plays* (London: Faber, 1969), 206.
7 Seamus Heaney, 'The Skunk', *New Selected Poems 1966–1987* (London: Faber, 1990), 122.
8 Eliot, 206.
9 'Philip Larkin reads and comments on *The Whitsun Weddings*, Listen Records (Hull: Marvell Press, 1965).
10 Maeve Brennan, *The Philip Larkin I Knew* (Manchester: MUP, Larkin Society Monograph 3, 2002), 23.
11 Brennan, 75.
12 Brennan, 7.
13 Brennan, 6.
14 Brennan, 80–1.
15 Brennan, 73.
16 Brennan, 73.
17 Father Anthony Storey, interview with the author, 1.viii.2003.
18 Storey, 1.viii.2003.
19 Brennan, 57–8.
20 Brennan, 8–10.
21 Brennan, 57.
22 Brennan, 56–7.
23 Brennan, 57.
24 Alan Bennett, 'Alas! Deceived', *Philip Larkin: Contemporary Critical Essays*, ed. Stephen Regan (Basingstoke: Macmillan New Casebooks, 1997), 243.
25 James, Fenton: 'Philip Larkin: Wounded by Unshrapnel', *The Strength of Poetry* (Oxford: OUP, 2001), 47.
26 *The Essential James Joyce*, ed. Harry Levin (Harmondsworth: Penguin, 1963), 186–7.
27 Brennan, 58.
28 See James Booth, Introduction to *Trouble at Willow Gables and Other Fictions* (London: Faber, 2002), xxxii–xxxiv.
29 The final incomplete stanza is omitted in *Collected Poems* (1988). It is discussed by A. T. Tolley in *Larkin at Work* (Hull: Hull University Press, 1997), 111.
30 Brennan, 67–8.
31 Brennan, 68.
32 Booth, Introduction to *Trouble at Willow Gables*, xix, fn.
33 Andrew Swarbrick, *Out of Reach: The Poetry of Philip Larkin* (Basingstoke: Macmillan Press, 1995), 173.
34 R. J. C. Watt, *A Concordance to the Poetry of Philip Larkin* (Hildesheim: Olms-Weidmann), 149–50.
35 Brennan, 66.

36 Mackereth , 4.viii.2003.
37 Brennan, 67.
38 Mackereth, 4.viii.2003.
39 A different version of the first stanza, taken from Larkin's notebook drafts, was printed in the *Evening Standard*, 22.x.2002, the fourth line being transcribed as 'Till then you will [be] in my heart.' The final text, as sent to Betty Mackereth, is published here for the first time. See Appendix.
40 The poem, first published in *About Larkin* 14, October 2002, 4, is reprinted in the Appendix.
41 'I didn't feel offended. It was 1975. I was fifty-something... I'm very, very practical and not a bit romantic.' Mackereth, 4.viii.2003.
42 Mackereth, 4.viii.2003.

Chapter 5: Poetic Histories

1 Aristotle, *Poetics*, trans. Ingram Bywater (New York: Random House, 1954), 235.
2 Samuel Johnson, *Rasselas, Poems and Selected Prose*, ed. Bertrand H. Bronson (New York: Holt, Rinehart and Winston, 1958), 528.
3 *The Essays of Virginia Woolf, Vol. III, 1919–1924*, ed. Andrew McNeillie (London: Hogarth Press, 1988), 153.
4 Laura Riding and Robert Graves, *A Survey of Modernist Poetry* (London: Heinemann, 1929), 179.
5 Wallace Stevens, in Samuel French Morse: *Wallace Stevens: Poetry as Life* (New York: Pegasus, 1970), 120.
6 *The English Auden*, ed. Edward Mendelson (London: Faber, 1986), xviii.
7 W. H. Auden, 'In Memory of W. B. Yeats', *Another Time* (London: Faber Library edn, 1996), 99.
8 Auden, 'For us like any other fugitive', *Another Time*, 50.
9 Auden, 'The hour-glass whispers to the lion's paw', *Another Time*, 24.
10 *Ibid.*
11 Auden, 'In Memory of W. B. Yeats', *Another Time*, 99.
12 Auden, 'Lay your sleeping head, my love', *Another Time*, 32.
13 'Brunette Coleman' (Philip Larkin), 'What Are We Writing For?', *Trouble at Willow Gables and Other Fictions*, ed. James Booth (London: Faber, 2002), 243.
14 'Coleman', 248.
15 *The Complete Works of George Orwell, Vol. 14, 1941–2*, ed. Peter Davison (London: Secker and Warburg, 1998), 65.
16 *The Complete Works of George Orwell, Vol. 12, 1940–1*, ed. Peter Davison (London: Secker and Warburg, 1998), 57–79.
17 'Coleman', 'Ballade des Dames du Temps Jadis', *Trouble at Window Gables etc.*, 256.
18 Roland Barthes, *Mythologies*, sel. and trans. Annette Lavers (London: Paladin, 1973), 101.
19 Terry Eagleton, 'Larkin: A Left View', *About Larkin* 9, April 2000, 7.
20 Barthes, 101.
21 Karl Marx, *Vorwärts* 64, 10.viii.1844. Online at www.marxists.org/archive/marx/works/1844/08/07.htm (accessed 28.vi.2004).

22 Trevor Brighton, 'An Arundel Tomb: The Monument', in Paul Foster, Trevor Brighton and Patrick Garland, *An Arundel Tomb*, Otter Memorial Paper 1, 14–22.

23 A. Alvarez, 'The New Poetry, or Beyond the Gentility Principle', *The New Poetry* (Harmondsworth: Penguin, 1962), 26.

24 Tom Paulin, 'She Did Not Change: Philip Larkin', *Minotaur: Poetry and the Nation State* (London: Faber, 1992), 236.

25 Blake Morrison, *The Movement: English Poetry and Fiction of the 1950s* (London: Methuen, 1980), 84.

26 Philip Larkin, 'Worksheets of "At Grass"', *Phoenix* 11/12, 1973/4, 93–8.

27 Morrison, 2.

28 David Lodge, 'Philip Larkin: The Metonymic Muse', *Philip Larkin: Contemporary Critical Essays*, ed. Stephen Regan (Basingstoke: Macmillan New Casebook, 1997), 72.

29 Charles Tomlinson, 'Poetry Today', *The Pelican Guide to English Literature: The Modern Age*, ed. Boris Ford (Harmondsworth: Penguin, 1973), 478.

30 *Philip Larkin, the Marvell Press, and Me* (Manchester: Carcanet, 1989), 62.

31 Thomas Gray, 'Sonnet on the Death of Mr. Richard West', *Poems* (London: J. M. Dent and Sons, 1963), 27.

32 *The New Poetry*, 20.

33 *The New Poetry*, 20.

34 R. N. Parkinson, 'To keep our metaphysics warm: A study of "Church Going" by Philip Larkin', *Critical Survey*, 5 (Winter 1971), 231, 224.

35 J. R. Watson, 'The Other Larkin', *Critical Quarterly* 17.4 (Winter 1975), 358.

36 Raphaël Ingelbien, 'The Uses of Symbolism: Larkin and Eliot', in *New Larkins for Old*, ed. James Booth (Basingstoke: Palgrave Macmillan, 2000), 138.

37 Ingelbien, 138.

38 Ingelbien, 142.

39 'Working with Philip Larkin', *About Larkin 8* (October 1999), 11.

40 Donald Davie, *Collected Poems*, ed. Neil Powell (Manchester: Carcanet, 2002), 28.

41 Terry Whalen, *Philip Larkin and English Poetry* (Basingstoke: Macmillan Press, 1990), 41.

42 Ronald Draper, 'The Positive Larkin', *Critical Essays on Philip Larkin: The Poems,* ed. Linda Cookson and Bryan Loughrey (London: Longman, 1989), 95.

43 'In Time of "The Breaking of Nations"', *The Complete Poems of Thomas Hardy*, ed. James Gibson (London: Macmillan, 1979), 545.

44 Auden, 'Musée des Beaux Arts', *Another Time*, 35.

45 Elizabeth Bishop, 'Questions of Travel', *Complete Poems* (London: Chatto and Windus, 1991), 94.

46 'When the Russian tanks roll westward', *Collected Poems* (1988), 172.

47 Morrison, 256.

48 Seamus Heaney, 'Englands of the Mind', *Preoccupations: Selected Prose 1968–1978* (London: Faber, 1980), 169.

49 Heaney, 150–1.

50 Heaney, 150.

51 Heaney, 165.

52 Heaney, 167.

53 Patrick Kavanagh, *The Complete Poems* (New York: Peter Kavanagh Hand Press, 1972), 347.
54 Heaney, 167.
55 Stephen Regan, *Philip Larkin: The Critics Debate* (Basingstoke: Macmillan Press, 1992), 138–9.
56 Edna Longley, '"Any-angled Light": Philip Larkin and Edward Thomas', *Poetry in the Wars* (Newcastle upon Tyne: Bloodaxe Books, 1986), 129.
57 Neil Corcoran, *English Poetry Since 1940* (Harlow: Longman, 1993), 93.
58 Seamus Heaney, 'The Main of Light', *The Government of the Tongue* (London: Faber, 1988), 19–20.
59 A. E. Housman, 'The Name and Nature of Poetry', *Collected Poems and Selected Prose*, ed. Christopher Ricks (London: Penguin, 1989), 363.

Chapter 6: Living Rooms

1 'Larkin's Bookplate', *About Larkin* 12, October 2001, 26.
2 'Is it for now or for always', 'Days', *Collected Poems* (1988), 296, 67.
3 In Christopher Ricks, 'The Pursuit of Metaphor', *Allusion to the Poets* (Oxford: OUP, 2002), 248.
4 Ricks, 246, 259.
5 Larkin perhaps also had in mind Auden's 'The crowds upon the pavement / Were fields of harvest wheat' in 'As I walked out one evening', *Another Time* (London: Faber Library Edition, 1996), 43.
6 David Lodge, 'Philip Larkin: The Metonymic Muse', *Philip Larkin: Contemporary Critical Essays*, ed. Stephen Regan (Basingstoke: Macmillan New Casebook, 1997), 77.
7 Lodge, 78.
8 Lodge, 79.
9 Ricks, 245.
10 A. E. Housman, 'The Name and Nature of Poetry', *Collected Poems and Selected Prose*, ed Christopher Ricks (London: Penguin, 1989), 353.
11 Lodge, 78.
12 Housman, 364.
13 A. T. Tolley, *My Proper Ground: A Study of the Work of Philip Larkin and its Development* (Ottawa: Carleton University Press, 1991), 177.
14 Bafflingly, Lodge cites 'Afternoons' as among those 'many' poems by Larkin which 'have no metaphors at all' (76). He lists also 'Myxomatosis', 'Poetry of Departures', 'Days' and 'As Bad as a Mile'. Does he imagine that Larkin actually engaged rabbits in conversation, or was concerned to perfect his aim with apple-cores?
15 'End of Another Home Holiday', *The Complete Poems of D. H. Lawrence*, ed. Vivian de Sola Pinto and Warren Roberts (London: Heinemann, 1972), I, 62.
16 Letter to James Sutton, 26.vii.1950. Brynmor Jones Library, Hull: DPL/174/2.
17 Larkin is thinking not of Hull, but Coventry or Oxford, with their car-assembly plants.
18 John Betjeman, 'Death in Leamington', *Collected Poems* (London: John Murray, enlarged edn, 1973), 2.

19 Non-British readers need to know that the flat-sided 'HP' brown-sauce bottle, with its Houses of Parliament label and encrusted rim, was a fixture of every British working-class dinner-table or café in the 1950s and 1960s.

20 Non-British readers will miss the allusion to the 'Pools', very popular in the post-war period, which, for a penny or halfpenny stake, gave punters the chance of winning hundreds of thousands of pounds by correctly guessing the draws or away wins in British Football League soccer matches.

21 Robert Crawford, *The Savage and the City in the Work of T. S. Eliot* (Oxford: OUP, 1987), 105.

Chapter 7: Empty Gestures

1 'Down Cemetery Road', 'Monitor', BBC TV, 15.xii.1964.

2 Eric Smith, *By Mourning Tongues: Studies in English Elegy* (Ipswich: Boydell Press, 1977).

3 Peter M. Sacks, *The English Elegy: Studies in the Genre from Spenser to Yeats* (Baltimore and London: Johns Hopkins University Press, 1985).

4 Jahan Ramazani, *Poetry of Mourning: The Modern Elegy from Hardy to Heaney* (University of Chicago Press, 1994).

5 Melissa Zeiger, *Beyond Consolation: Death, Sexuality, and the Changing Shapes of Elegy* (Ithaca, NY: Cornell University Press, 1997).

6 Sacks, 6, 4.

7 *Milton's Poems* (London: J. M. Dent and Sons, 1959), 46.

8 *The Poems of Tennyson*, ed. Christopher Ricks (London: Longmans, Green and Co Ltd, 1969), 982.

9 Sacks, 125.

10 Sonnet 'On the Death of Mr. Richard West', Thomas Gray, *Poems* (London: J. M. Dent and Sons, 1963), 27.

11 *The Poems of Wilfred Owen*, ed. Jon Stallworthy (London: Chatto and Windus, 1990), 192.

12 Ramazani, 4, 8.

13 Harold Bloom, *The Anxiety of Influence* (New York: OUP, 1973).

14 Zeiger, 44.

15 John Betjeman, 'On a Portrait of a Deaf Man', *Collected Poems* (London: John Murray, enlarged edn, 1973), 96; Sylvia Plath, 'Daddy', *Collected Poems* (London: Faber, 1981), 183; Dylan Thomas, 'Do not go gentle into that good night', *Collected Poems 1934–1952* (London: J. M. Dent and Sons, 1952), 116.

16 Zeiger, 44, 65–6.

17 Edmund White, *The Burning Library: Writing on Art, Politics, and Sexuality, 1969–1993* (London: Picador, 1995), 138–9.

18 *The Complete Poetical Works of Percy Bysshe Shelley* (London: OUP, 1943), 432.

19 *Macbeth*, William Shakespeare, *The Complete Works*, ed. Peter Alexander (London and Glasgow: Collins, 1951), 1024.

20 Gray, 'Elegy written in a Country Churchyard', *Poems*, 29.

21 Herbert W. Starr, *Twentieth Century Interpretations of Gray's Elegy* (Englewood Cliffs, NJ: Prentice-Hall Inc., 1968), 7.

22 T. S. Eliot, *The Complete Poems and Plays* (London: Faber, 1969), 180; Carol Ann Duffy, *Selected Poems* (Harmondsworth: Penguin, 1994), 28.

23 Sigmund Freud, 'Thoughts for the Times on War and Death', trans. E. C. Mayne, *Civilization, Society and Religion* (Harmondsworth: Penguin Freud Library 12, 1999), 77.

24 Ludwig Wittgenstein, *Tractatus Logico-Philosophicus*, trans. D. F. Pears and B. F. McGuinness (London: Routledge and Kegan Paul, 1971), 6.4311.

25 Samuel Johnson, 'Milton', *Lives of the English Poets* (London: Dent and Sons, 1968), I. 96.

26 Edmund Goldsmid, *A Collection of Epitaphs and Inscriptions, interesting either from historical associations or quaintness of wording* (Edinburgh, 1885; Collectanea Adamantæa XII), II, 36.

27 *Lovers, Rakes and Rogues*, ed. John Wardroper (London: Shelfmark Books, 1995), 192. Surprisingly, Peter Sacks does not cite this poem in his book *The English Elegy*, in which he argues in Freudian and Lacanian terms, that elegy is founded on a symbolic self-castration in propitiation of the father figure of Death.

28 A. E. Housman, *Collected Poems and Selected Prose*, ed. Christopher Ricks (Harmondsworth: Penguin, 1989), 41.

29 Edward Fitzgerald, *Rubáiyát of Omar Khayyám* (Harmondsworth: Penguin, 1989), 50.

30 Thomas Gray, 'Elegy', *Poems* (London: J. M. Dent and Sons), 30.

31 *The Poems of George Herbert* (London: OUP, 1961), 78–9.

32 Shelley, *Poetical Works*, 550

33 *Poems of Gerard Manley Hopkins*, ed. W. H. Gardner (London: OUP, third edn, 1948), 94.

34 Rosalind Fergusson, *Penguin Rhyming Dictionary* (London: Penguin, 1985), 278.

35 *Poems of Ben Jonson* (London: Routledge and Kegan Paul, 1954), 84–5.

36 James Fenton, 'Philip Larkin: Wounded by Unshrapnel', *The Strength of Poetry* (Oxford: OUP, 2001), 63.

37 'Nothing Gold Can Stay', *Complete Poems of Robert Frost* (London: Jonathan Cape, 1951), 248.

38 Leonardo da Vinci, *The Literary Works*, ed. Jean Paul Richter (London: Phaidon, 1970), II, 242.

39 'Philip Larkin reads and comments on The Whitsun Weddings', Listen Records (Hull: Marvell Press, 1965).

40 See for example paintings by Hans Baldung Grien (1484/85–1545) in the Kunstmuseum, Basel, Switzerland.

41 'Der Tod und das Mädchen', by Matthias Claudius, set by Franz Schubert, D.531 (1817); www.recmusic.org/lieder/c/claudius/d531.html (accessed 14.vii.2004).

42 Georges Bataille, *Death and Sensuality: A Study of Eroticism and the Taboo* (New York: Ballantine Books Inc. 1969), 12.

43 Camille Paglia: *Sexual Personae: Art and Decadence from Nefertiti to Emily Dickinson* (Yale: Yale University Press, 2001), 15.

44 In Paglia, 43.

45 Paglia, 12, 16.

46 A. T. Tolley, *Larkin at Work* (Hull: Hull University Press, 1997), 127.

47 R. J. C. Watt (ed.), *A Concordance to the Poetry of Philip Larkin* (Hildesheim: Olms-Weidmann, 1995), 223–4. The singular noun 'human' never occurs. The plural occurs again only in the very late, light poem 'Dear Charles, my muse'; 'human' occurs as an adjective in 'Sympathy in White Major'.

48 Letter to James Sutton, 24.v.1944, Brynmor Jones Library, Hull, MS DP/174/2.

49 In Jacques Derrida, *The Gift of Death*, trans. David Wills (Chicago and London: University of Chicago Press, 1995), 46.

50 Martin Heidegger, *Being and Time*, trans. John Macquarrie and Edward Robinson (Oxford: Blackwell, 1973), 284.

51 Jahan Ramazani simply conflates self-elegy with reflective elegy in what he calls 'the ancient tradition of the self-elegy or death poem … the genre of the self-standing meditation on the author's mortality'. Ramazani, 120.

52 Freud, 'Thoughts for the Times on War and Death', 77.

53 *Richard II*, Shakespeare, *Complete Works*, 478.

54 Tennyson, *Poems*, 1458.

55 Edward Thomas, *Collected Poems* (London: Faber, 1949), 92.

56 Jonathan Dollimore, *Death, Desire and Loss in Western Culture* (Harmondsworth, Penguin, 1999), xxvi.

57 Sylvia Plath, 'Edge', *Collected Poems* (London: Faber, 1981), 272.

58 Philip Larkin, 'The days of thy youth', written before 1939. *About Larkin* 13, April 2002, 27.

59 Gray, 'Elegy', 31.

60 Oliver Marshall, 'A Letter from Loughborough', *About Larkin* 15, April 2003, 18.

61 Edna St Vincent Millay, *Collected Poems* (New York: Harper and Brothers, 1956), 123.

62 'The Ship of Death', *The Complete Poems of D. H. Lawrence*, ed. Vivian de Sola Pinto and Warren Roberts (London: Heinemann, 1972), II, 979.

63 Housman, 56.

64 Tolley, 127.

65 Epicurus, *The Extant Remains*, trans. Cyril Bailey (Oxford: OUP, 1926), 85.

66 Richard Rorty, *Contingency, Irony, and Solidarity* (Cambridge: CUP, 1989), 23.

67 Auden, 'As I walked out one evening', *Another Time*, 73.

68 'Senecas Troas Act 2d Chor', *The Poems of John Wilmot Earl of Rochester*, ed. Keith Walker (Oxford: Blackwell, 1988), 51.

69 Auden, 'As I walked out one evening', 73.

70 Margaret Drabble, 'Philip Larkin', *Independent Magazine*, 16.iii.1991, 62.

71 Seamus Heaney, 'Joy or Night: Last Things in the Poetry of W. B. Yeats and Philip Larkin', *The Redress of Poetry: Oxford Lectures* (London: Faber, 1995), 146–63. See also James Booth, 'The Turf Cutter and the Nine-to-Five Man: Heaney, Larkin, and "the Spiritual Intellect's Great Work"', *Twentieth-Century Literature* 43.4, Winter 1997, 369–93.

72 Edna Longley, '"Any-angled Light": Philip Larkin and Edward Thomas', *Poetry in the Wars* (Newcastle upon Tyne: Bloodaxe Books, 1986), 128.

73 John Bayley, 'Larkin, Pym and Romantic Sympathy', *About Larkin* 14, October 2002, 13. In a poll of several thousand readers conducted by the Poetry Book Society and the Poetry Library in 2003 'Aubade' was voted the

seventh most popular poem of the last fifty years. The most popular poem
was 'The Whitsun Weddings'; 'Poets' poll crowns Larkin king of verse',
Guardian, 15.x.2003, 8.

74   W. B. Yeats, 'Lapis Lazuli', *The Poems* (London: J. M. Dent and Sons, 1992),
     341.
75   John Gay, *Poetry and Prose* (Oxford; OUP, 1974), I, 253.
76   In James Boswell, *The Life of Samuel Johnson* (London: OUP, 1952), 1358.
77   Richard Monckton Milnes (ed.), *Life, Letters and Literary Remains of John Keats*
     (London: Edward Moxon, 1848), II, 91.
78   'Revenge of the living dead', *Observer*, 3.iii.2002.

Bibliography

Alvarez A., 'The New Poetry, or Beyond the Gentility Principle', *The New Poetry* (Harmondsworth: Penguin, 1962), 17–28.

Aristotle, *Poetics*, trans. Ingram Bywater (New York: Random House, Inc., 1954).

Auden, W. H., *About the House* (London: Faber, 1966).

Auden, W. H., *Another Time* (London: Faber Library edn, 1996).

Auden, W. H., *The English Auden*, ed. Edward Mendelson (London: Faber, 1986).

Avis, Patricia, *Playing the Harlot: or Mostly Coffee* (London: Virago, 1996).

Barnes, Julian, *A History of the World in $10\frac{1}{2}$ Chapters* (Harmondsworth: Penguin, 1989).

Barthes, Roland, 'The Death of the Author', *Image-Music-Text*, trans. Stephen Heath (London: Fontana, 1977), 142–8.

Barthes, Roland, *Mythologies*, trans. Annette Lavers (London: Paladin, 1973).

Bataille, Georges, *Death and Sensuality: A Study of Eroticism and the Taboo* (New York: Ballantine Books Inc., 1969).

Bayley, John, 'Larkin, Pym and Romantic Sympathy', *About Larkin* 14, October 2002, 11–13.

Bennett, Alan, 'Alas! Deceived', *Critical Perspectives on Philip Larkin*, ed. Stephen Regan (Basingstoke: Macmillan Press, 1997), 226–49.

Berkeley, George, *Berkeley's Philosophical Writings*, ed. David M. Armstrong (London: Collier-Macmillan Ltd, 1965).

Betjeman, John, *Collected Poems* (London: John Murray, enlarged edn, 1973).

Bishop, Elizabeth, *Complete Poems* (London: Chatto and Windus, 1991).

Bloom, Harold, *The Anxiety of Influence* (New York: OUP, 1973).

Booth, James, 'From Here to Bogland: Larkin, Heaney and the Poetry of Place', in *New Larkins for Old*, ed. James Booth (Basingstoke: Palgrave Macmillan, 2000), 190–212.

Booth, James, *Philip Larkin: Writer* (Hemel Hempstead: Harvester Wheatsheaf, 1992).

Booth, James, 'The Turf-cutter and the Nine-to-Five Man: Heaney, Larkin, and "the Spiritual Intellect's Great Work"', *Twentieth-Century Literature* 43.4 (Winter 1997), 369–93.

Boswell, James, *The Life of Samuel Johnson* (London: OUP, 1952).

Brennan, Maeve, *The Philip Larkin I Knew* (Manchester: MUP, 2002).

Brighton, Trevor, 'An Arundel Tomb: The Monument', in Paul Foster, Trevor Brighton and Patrick Garland, *An Arundel Tomb*, Otter Memorial Paper 1, 14–22.

Bristow, Joseph, 'The Obscenity of Philip Larkin', *Critical Inquiry* 21 (Autumn 1994), 156–81.

Carey, John, *The Intellectuals and the Masses* (London: Faber, 1992).

Corcoran, Neil, *English Poetry Since 1940* (Harlow: Longman, 1993).

Crawford, Robert, *The Modern Poet: Poetry, Academia, and Knowledge since the 1750s* (Oxford: OUP, 2001).

Crawford, Robert, *The Savage and the City in the Work of T. S. Eliot* (Oxford: OUP, 1987).

Cunningham, Valentine, *In the Reading Gaol* (Oxford: Blackwell, 1994).

Davie, Donald, *Collected Poems*, ed. Neil Powell (Manchester: Carcanet, 2002).

Derrida, Jacques, *The Gift of Death*, trans. David Wills (Chicago and London: University of Chicago Press, 1995).

Derrida, Jacques, 'The Law of *Genre*', trans. Avital Ronell, *Critical Inquiry* 7 (1980), 55–81.

Dollimore, Jonathan, *Death, Desire and Loss in Western Culture* (Harmondsworth, Penguin, 1999).

Drabble, Margaret, 'Philip Larkin', *Independent Magazine* 16.iii.1991, 62.

Draper, Ronald, 'The Positive Larkin', *Critical Essays on Philip Larkin: The Poems*, ed. Linda Cookson and Bryan Loughrey (London: Longman, 1989), 94–105.

Duffy, Carol Ann, *Selected Poems* (Harmondsworth: Penguin, 1994).

Duncan, Andrew, *The Failure of Conservatism in Modern British Poetry* (Cambridge: Salt, 2003).

Dyson, Brian (ed.), *The Modern Academic Library: Essays in Memory of Philip Larkin* (London: Library Association, 1988).

Eagleton, Terry, *The Ideology of the Aesthetic* (Cambridge, MA., Blackwell, 1990)

Eagleton, Terry, 'Larkin: A Left View', *About Larkin* 9, April 2000, 4–8.

Eliot, T. S., *The Complete Poems and Plays* (London: Faber, 1969).

Eliot, T. S., *The Rock* (London: Faber, 1934).

Eliot, T. S., 'Tradition and the Individual Talent', *Selected Essays 1917–1932* (London: Faber, 1932), 13–22.

Epicurus, *The Extant Remains*, trans. Cyril Bailey (Oxford, Clarendon Press, 1926).

Fenton, James, 'Chapter and Verse on Reputation', *Guardian*, 26.vii.2003, 20.

Fenton, James, 'Philip Larkin: Wounded by Unshrapnel', *The Strength of Poetry* (Oxford: OUP, 2001), 45–64.

Fergusson, Rosalind, *Penguin Rhyming Dictionary* (London: Penguin, 1985).

FitzGerald, Edward (trans.), *Rubáiyát of Omar Khayyám* (Harmondsworth: Penguin, 1989).

Freud, Sigmund, 'Thoughts for the Times on War and Death' [1915], trans. E. C. Mayne, *Civilization, Society and Religion* (Harmondsworth: Penguin Freud Library 12, 1991), 57–89.

Freud, Sigmund, 'Mourning and Melancholia' [1917], trans. Joan Riviere, *On Metapsychology* (Harmondsworth, Penguin Freud Library 11, 1991), 245–68.

Frost, Robert, *Complete Poems* (London: Jonathan Cape, 1951).

Gardner, Anthony, 'What will survive of us is love', *Sunday Times Magazine*, 21.xi.2004, 30–8.

Garland, Patrick, 'Down Cemetery Road', BBC 'Monitor' programme, 15.xii.1964.

Garrod, H. W., *The Profession of Poetry and Other Lectures* (Oxford: OUP, 1929).

Gay, John, *Poetry and Prose* (Oxford: OUP, 1974).

Gilpin, George, 'Patricia Avis and Philip Larkin', *New Larkins for Old*, ed. James Booth (Basingstoke: Palgrave Macmillan, 2000), 66–78.

Goldsmid, Edmund, *A Collection of Epitaphs and Inscriptions, interesting either from historical associations or quaintness of wording* (Edinburgh: privately printed, 1885; *Collectanea Adamantæa* XII, 2 vols.).

Graves, Robert, *Mammon and the Black Goddess* (London: Cassell, 1965).

Gray, Thomas, *Poems, with a Selection of Letters and Essays*, ed. John Drinkwater (London: J. M. Dent and Sons, 1963).

Hamburger, Michael, *Philip Larkin: A Retrospect* (London: Enitharmon Press, 2002).

Hamilton, Ian, *Against Oblivion* (London: Viking, 2002).

Hardy, Thomas, *The Complete Poems of Thomas Hardy*, ed. James Gibson (London: Macmillan, 1979).

Hartley, Jean, *Philip Larkin, the Marvell Press, and Me* (Manchester: Carcanet, 1989).

Heaney, Seamus, 'Englands of the Mind', *Preoccupations. Selected Prose 1968–1978* (London: Faber, 1980), 150–69.

Heaney, Seamus, 'Joy or Night: Last Things in the Poetry of W. B. Yeats and Philip Larkin', *The Redress of Poetry: Oxford Lectures* (London: Faber, 1995), 146–63.

Heaney, Seamus, 'The Main of Light', *The Government of the Tongue* (London: Faber, 1988), 15–22.

Heaney, Seamus, *New Selected Poems 1966–1987* (London: Faber, 1990).

Heaney, Seamus, *Seeing Things* (London: Faber, 1991).

Heidegger, Martin, *Being and Time*, trans. John Macquarrie and Edward Robinson (Oxford: Blackwell, 1973).

Herbert, George, *The Poems* (London: OUP, 1961).

Herbert, W. N. and Matthew Hollis (eds), *Strong Words: Modern Poets on Modern Poetry* (Tarset, Northumberland: Bloodaxe, 2000).

Herrick, Robert, *Poems from Hesperides and Noble Numbers* (Harmondsworth: Penguin, 1961).

Hopkins, Gerard Manley, *Poems*, ed. W. H. Gardner (London: OUP, third edn, 1948).

Housman, A. E., *Collected Poems and Selected Prose*, ed. Christopher Ricks (Harmondsworth: Penguin, 1989).

Ingelbien, Raphaël, *Misreading England: Poetry and Nationhood since the Second Word War* (Amsterdam and New York: Rodopi, 2002).

Ingelbien, Raphaël, 'The Uses of Symbolism: Larkin and Eliot', in *New Larkins for Old*, ed. James Booth (Basingstoke: Palgrave Macmillan, 2000), 130–43.

Johnson, Samuel, *Lives of the English Poets* (London: J. M. Dent and Sons, 1968).

Johnson, Samuel, *Rasselas, Poems and Selected Prose*, ed. Bertrand H. Bronson (New York: Holt, Rinehart and Winston, 1958).

Jones, Peter (ed.), *Imagist Poetry* (Harmondsworth: Penguin, 1972).

Jonson, Ben, *Poems* (London: Routledge and Kegan Paul, 1954).

Joyce, James, *The Essential James Joyce*, ed. Harry Levin (Harmondsworth: Penguin, 1963).

Kamitani, Suzuyo, 'Jane Exall – "A Bosomy English Rose"', *About Larkin* 16, October 2003, 19.

Kavanagh, Patrick, *The Complete Poems* (New York: Peter Kavanagh Hand Press, 1972).

Kirsch, Adam, 'A Poet in Full', www.walrusmagazine.com/article.pl?sid= 04/03/10/ 2221215&... (accessed 22 March 2004).

Larkin, Philip, *Collected Poems*, ed. Anthony Thwaite (London: Marvell Press and Faber, 1988; revised edition 2003).

220   *Bibliography*

Larkin, Philip, *Further Requirements: Interviews, Broadcasts, Statements and Book Reviews 1952–1985*, ed. Anthony Thwaite (London: Faber, pbk edn with two additional chapters, 2002).

Larkin, Philip, 'Philip Larkin reads *The Less Deceived*', Listen Records. 'The Poets Voice' (*sic*) ed. George Hartley (Hull: Marvell Press, 1958).

Larkin, Philip, 'Philip Larkin reads and comments on *The Whitsun Weddings*', Listen Records. 'The Poets Voice' (*sic*) ed. George Hartley (Hull: Marvell Press, 1965).

Larkin, Philip, *Required Writing: Miscellaneous Pieces 1955–1982* (London: Faber, 1983).

Larkin, Philip, *Selected Letters*, ed. Anthony Thwaite (London: Faber, 1992).

Larkin, Philip, *Trouble at Willow Gables and Other Fictions*, ed. James Booth (London: Faber, 2002).

Larkin, Philip, 'Worksheets of "At Grass"', *Phoenix* 11/12 (1973/4), 91–103.

Lawrence, D. H., *The Collected Letters of D. H. Lawrence*, ed. Harry T. Moore (London: Heinemann, 1962).

Lawrence, D. H., *The Complete Poems of D. H. Lawrence*, ed. Vivian de Sola Pinto and Warren Roberts (London: Heinemann, 1972).

Lawrence, D. H., *Studies in Classic American Literature* (New York: Doubleday, 1951).

Leonardo da Vinci, *Literary Works*, ed. Jean Paul Richter (London, Phaidon, 1970).

Lodge, David, 'Philip Larkin: The Metonymic Muse', *Philip Larkin: Contemporary Critical Essays*, ed. Stephen Regan (Basingstoke: Macmillan New Casebook, 1997), 71–82.

Longley, Edna, '"Any-angled Light": Philip Larkin and Edward Thomas', *Poetry in the Wars* (Newcastle upon Tyne: Bloodaxe, 1986), 113–39.

Marshall, Oliver, 'A Letter from Loughborough', *About Larkin* 15, April 2003, 18.

Marshall, Oliver, 'Stories from the Doldrums', *Irish Times*, 18.v.2002, 8.

Marvell, Andrew, *The Poems* (London: Routledge and Kegan Paul, 1963).

Marx, Karl, *Vorwärts* 64, 10 August 1844. www.marxists.org/archive/marx/works/1844/08/07.htm (accessed 28 June 2004).

Millay, Edna St Vincent, *Collected Poems* (New York: Harper and Brothers, 1956).

Milnes, Richard Monckton, *Life, Letters and Literary Remains of John Keats* (London: Edward Moxon, 1848).

Milton, John, *Milton's Poems* (London: J. M. Dent and Sons, 1959).

Moon, Brenda, 'Working with Philip Larkin', *About Larkin* 8 (October 1999), 5–11.

Morrison, Blake, *The Movement: English Poetry and Fiction of the 1950s* (London: Methuen, 1980).

Morse, Samuel French, *Wallace Stevens: Poetry as Life* (New York: Pegasus, 1970).

Motion, Andrew, *Philip Larkin: A Writer's Life* (London: Faber, 1993).

Orwell, George, 'Boys' Weeklies', *The Complete Works of George Orwell, Vol. 12, 1940–1*, ed. Peter Davison (London: Secker and Warburg, 1998), 57–79.

Orwell, George, 'T. S. Eliot', *The Complete Works of George Orwell, Vol. 14, 1941–2*, ed. Peter Davison (London: Secker and Warburg, 1998), 63–8.

Osborne, Charles, *W. H. Auden: The Life of a Poet* (London: Michael O'Mara, 1980).

Owen, Wilfred, *The Poems of Wilfred Owen*, ed. Jon Stallworthy (London: Chatto and Windus, 1990).

Paglia, Camille, *Sexual Personae: Art and Decadence from Nefertiti to Emily Dickinson* (Yale: Yale University Press, 2001).

Parkinson, R. N., 'To Keep Our Metaphysics Warm: A Study of "Church Going" by Philip Larkin', *Critical Survey*, 5 (Winter 1971), 224–33.

Paulin, Tom, 'She Did Not Change: Philip Larkin', *Minotaur: Poetry and the Nation State* (London: Faber, 1992), 233–51.

Plath, Sylvia, *Collected Poems*, ed. Ted Hughes (London: Faber, 1981).

Potts, Abbie Findlay, *The Elegiac Mode: Poetic Form in Wordsworth and Other Elegists* (Ithaca, NY: Cornell University Press, 1967).

Powell, Neil, 'A Postcard from Pearson Park', *PN Review* 157 (2004), 6–7.

Ramazani, Jahan, *Poetry of Mourning: The Modern Elegy from Hardy to Heaney* (Chicago: University of Chicago Press, 1994).

Regan, Stephen, *Philip Larkin: The Critics Debate* (Basingstoke: Macmillan Press, 1992).

Ricks, Christopher, 'The Pursuit of Metaphor', *Allusion to the Poets* (Oxford: OUP, 2002), 241–60.

Ricks, Christopher, *T. S. Eliot and Prejudice* (Berkeley and Los Angeles: University of California Press, 1988).

Riding, Laura, and Robert Graves, *A Survey of Modernist Poetry* (London: Heinemann, 1929).

Rochester, John Wilmot, Earl of, *The Poems of John Wilmot Earl of Rochester*, ed. Keith Walker (Oxford: Blackwell, 1988).

Rorty, Richard, *Contingency, Irony, and Solidarity* (Cambridge: CUP, 1989).

Rossen, Janice, *Philip Larkin: His Life's Work* (Hemel Hempstead: Harvester, 1989).

Sacks, Peter M., *The English Elegy: Studies in the Genre from Spenser to Yeats* (Baltimore and London: Johns Hopkins University Press, 1985).

Saville, John, *Memoirs from the Left* (London: Merlin Press, 2003).

Schopenhauer, Arthur, *Essays and Aphorisms*, sel. and trans. R. J. Hollingdale (Harmondsworth: Penguin, 1970).

Schubert, Franz, 'Der Tod und das Mädchen', D.531, words by Matthias Claudius, at www.recmusic.org/lieder/c/claudius/d531.html (accessed 14 July 2004).

Shakespeare, William, *The Complete Works*, ed. Peter Alexander (London and Glasgow: Collins, 1951).

Shelley, Percy Bysshe, *The Complete Poetical Works* (London: OUP, 1943).

Smith, Eric, *By Mourning Tongues: Studies in English Elegy* (Ipswich: Boydell Press, 1977).

Starr, Herbert W., *Twentieth Century Interpretations of Gray's Elegy* (Englewood Cliffs, NJ: Prentice-Hall, 1968).

Stevens, Wallace, *Letters of Wallace Stevens*, ed. Holly Stevens (London: Faber, 1967).

Stevens, Wallace, 'Adagia', *Opus Posthumous*, ed. Samuel French Morse (London: Faber, 1959).

Strang, Patricia, see Patricia Avis.

Stroud, Graham, 'Philip Larkin: "A Sense of Duty"', *About Larkin* 9, April, 2000, 9–13.

Swarbrick, Andrew, *Out of Reach: The Poetry of Philip Larkin* (Basingstoke: Macmillan Press, 1995).

Tennyson, Alfred, *The Poems*, ed. Christopher Ricks (London: Longmans, 1969).

Thomas, Dylan, *Collected Poems 1934–1952* (London: J. M. Dent and Sons, 1952).

Thomas, Edward, *Collected Poems* (London: Faber, 1949).

Timms, David, *Philip Larkin* (Edinburgh: Oliver and Boyd, 1973).

Tolley, A. T., *Larkin at Work: A Study of Larkin's Mode of Composition as seen in his Workbooks* (Hull: Hull University Press, 1997).

Tolley, A. T., *My Proper Ground: A Study of the Work of Philip Larkin and Its Development* (Ottawa: Carleton University Press Inc., 1991).

Walcott, Derek, 'The Master of the Ordinary', *New York Review of Books*, 1 June 1989, 37–40.

Wardroper, John (ed.), *Lovers, Rakes and Rogues* (London: Shelfmark Books, 1995).

Watson, J. R., 'The Other Larkin', *Critical Quarterly* 17.4 (Winter 1975), 347–60.

Watt, R. J. C., *A Concordance to the Poetry of Philip Larkin* (Hildesheim: Olms-Weidmann, 1995).

Whalen, Terry, *Philip Larkin and English Poetry* (Basingstoke: Macmillan Press, 1990).

White, Edmund, *The Burning Library: Writing on Art, Politics, and Sexuality 1969–1993* (London: Picador, 1995).

Wittgenstein, Ludwig, *Tractatus Logico-Philosophicus*, trans. D. F. Pears and B. F. McGuinness (London, Routledge and Kegan Paul, 1966).

Woolf, Virginia, *The Essays of Virginia Woolf, Vol. III, 1919–1924*, ed. Andrew McNeillie (London: Hogarth Press, 1988).

Woolf, Virginia, *A Room of One's Own* (London: Hogarth Press, 1931).

Yeats, W. B., *The Poems* (London: J. M. Dent and Sons, 1990).

Zeiger, Melissa F. *Beyond Consolation: Death, Sexuality, and the Changing Shapes of Elegy* (Ithaca, NY: Cornell University Press, 1997)

Index